Y0-ABD-185

TO BRIAN:

Merry Christmas!
I hope this will help
you though your first
year of what I'm sure will
be a long + successful legal career.

Peter

X-mas 1981

ANGELO BRANCA

VINCENT MOORE

DOUGLAS & MⁱNTYRE
VANCOUVER

ANGELO BRANCA

«GLADIATOR OF THE COURTS»

Copyright © 1981 by Vincent Moore

All rights reserved. No part of this book may be reproduced or
transmitted in any form by any means without permission in writing
from the publisher, except by a reviewer, who may quote brief
passages in a review.

Douglas & McIntyre Ltd.
1615 Venables Street
Vancouver, British Columbia

Canadian Cataloguing in Publication Data

   Moore, Vincent, 1910-
      Angelo Branca, gladiator of the Courts

   ISBN 0-88894-323-7

   1. Branca, Angelo.   2. Lawyers - British
Columbia - Biography.   3. Judges - British
Columbia - Biography.   1. Title.
KE416.B72M6   345.711'0092'4   C81-091267-8

Jacket design by Nancy Legue
Cover photograph by Jim LaBounty
Printed and bound in Canada by John Deyell Company

Angelo Branca, a great and famous virtuoso of and gladiator in the Courts. . . .

> —Hon. J.O. Wilson, chief justice of the Supreme Court of British Columbia, 1963-1973

Much of what is here I learned while working as reporter and chief of official court reporter services, a branch of the Attorney General's Department of the Province of British Columbia. For the rest I have gone to many people, but mainly to the Honourable Angelo E. Branca, Q.C., retired from the Court of Appeal and back at the practice of law in Vancouver.

Judge Branca has neither censored nor approved any part of this book. No responsibility for anything in it rests on him. Opinions and errors, and all statements unless otherwise attributed, are mine.

In converting volumes of notes, reels of tape and a flood of memories into manuscript I had the good fortune to have a son who is a professional historian and author. He confirmed my opinion that I had a significant subject, then advised me how to turn the mass of material into a book.

To Judge and Mrs. Branca, to Christopher Moore and to all who helped, I am deeply grateful.

PROLOGUE

The dinner guests would not go home. They stood in a line the length of the Bayshore Inn ballroom on a warm Vancouver evening in 1978 waiting to have their menu cards autographed by the guest of honour. Women were kissing him. Men embraced him with Latin warmth. Guests from diverse backgrounds and many professions were discussing what Angelo Branca meant to them, and each remembered something different. There had been so much.

Lawyers were telling stories of Branca the defender at the bar, veteran of sixty-three murder defences, judge of the Supreme Court of British Columbia and the great dissenter in the Court of Appeal. Laymen were able to join in because they had all grown up with the legends of the accessible advocate who had the gift of persuading judges and spellbinding juries, available to rich and poor, innocent and guilty—and not much caring to which category his client belonged.

Prosperous retired businessmen who had their humble start in Vancouver's East End recalled that Branca's first clients were bootleggers. Younger people remembered his defence of cabinet ministers in two provincial government scandals. Phil Gaglardi, the former minister of highways whom he vindicated, was at the dinner. Older politicians countered with recollections of the days when Vancouver Centre riding was "the tail that wagged the Liberal dog" in British Columbia affairs and Branca moved among the power brokers.

Former Lieutenant Governor Jack Nicholson was there, doubtless remembering how, five years before, he had read news reports that Branca would succeed him as the Queen's representative, and how wrong they had proved.

For sportsman Herb Capozzi, the white-haired chief guest was also the one-time amateur middleweight boxing champion of Canada. For merchant Ben Wosk, his friend Branca was the friend of the Jewish community, the only Canadian other than John Diefenbaker to have been honoured with the President's Medal of the State of Israel.

Roman Catholic Archbishop James Carney, pleased at the honouring of this leading Catholic layman, was laughing at the story of David Freeman promising Branca that if ever he were in trouble with his own church there would always be a place for him in the synagogue.

Mayor Jack Volrich, son of an immigrant Croatian miner, brought civic good wishes to this son of an immigrant Italian miner. Columnist Denny Boyd, son of an immigrant Scottish miner, paid his respects on behalf of a long line of newspaper celebrities, all of whom had found Branca a provider of lively material for their pages: from cartoonist Jack Boothe and columnists Bob Bouchette and Jim Butterfield down the years to Jack Wasserman.

Member of Parliament Art Lee skipped one of his Cantonese lessons to attend. Asked why he needed language lessons, he explained that his family had been a long time away from China. His great-grandfather arrived in British Columbia to help build the Canadian Pacific Railway in 1883, a dozen years before the Brancas' arrival.

Cabaret as well as cabinet was represented. Philliponis and Filippones were there, hoping their problems with the Penthouse nightclub and the law were over now that Branca was back in practice. They said that in the thirty years before he went to the bench he had never lost a case for them.

Of the good and bad times in East Vancouver through the first half of this century there was much reminiscing, especially after Dr. Maurice Fox told scandalous stories of a time when a young doctor and a younger lawyer had next-door offices over a bank on the corner of Hastings and Main streets. The doctor did *not* mention a certain night in 1934 when he took a bullet out of the hip of Joe Celona. While that racketeer explained to the doctor how he had been cleaning his gun and did not know the gun was loaded, along the corridor other people were looking for Angelo Branca to defend Joe's wife, who said she had used an axe to break into a bedroom, there found her husband with a woman, and shot him. Not fatally, she thought—she had last seen Joe escaping through the window. As it turned out she did not need Branca's services because her husband lent her his own lawyer for her defence, Jack Nicholson. From defending Josie Celona to representing Her Majesty the Queen: what lives of infinite variety these topflight lawyers lead.

Since the gathering was Italian sponsored, most people were talking about the Angelo who for most of his adult life had been the father figure of the Italian community.

The occasion was a testimonial dinner on Judge Branca's mandatory retirement from the Court of Appeal upon his reaching seventy-five. The Italians made it a love feast. A non-Italian could only wonder: a distinguished career in law and public life commands respect, but what qualities in this career inspire such a display of affection? There were tears in the eyes of many of the women who went up to the head table to say "Best Wishes" in Italian to Angelo and his wife Viola.

Branca stirs Mediterranean emotions. He caused one guest who arrived at the dinner as an English-born Canadian named Charles Lee to leave as a proclaimed Italian named Carlo de Messina. This Vancouver businessman had known that his ancestors emigrated from Sicily to England in the early nineteenth century and later anglicized the name. Friendship with Branca encouraged his interest in things Italian; he had sought out his ancestry and found relatives still occupying the family land near Messina. He told the assembly, "Angelo Branca led me back to my roots, and for that I love him. From this night on I will always use my Italian name in everything I do in the Italian community."

It is not only from Italians that Branca draws a *simpatico* response. During dinner Jack Diamond, born in Poland, learned that the Confratellanza Italo-Canadese, the sponsors, were giving $10 000 for a Branca memorial scholarship at Simon Fraser University. He had worked with Branca and others in founding the university before becoming its chancellor. "If it's in Angelo's name, add my $5000 now," he said.

I retain a vivid memory of first meeting Angelo Branca. Being made an official court reporter required that I be sworn in. In those days the registrar of the courts in Vancouver was not empowered to administer the oath. Because a court was being delayed for lack of record, Chief Reporter Theo Horrobin, with documents in hand and me in tow, hurried to the barristers' room of the old Vancouver Court House. From a dozen lawyers he singled out one in the act of changing from street clothes to court garb. "There's Angelo," he said. "He's our man."

Branca needed only a few seconds' explanation, greeted me like a fraternity brother and performed the ceremony on the spot. That surely makes him the only commissioner for oaths ever to swear in an order-in-council appointee while himself stripped to the waist—broad of chest and resembling those sporting prints of famous old-time bare-knuckle prizefighters.

After court, when I was being introduced to my new colleagues, veteran court reporter Alec Donaghy heard that Angelo Branca had sworn me in. Alec said with fervour, "Now there's a great guy. We *love* him." The same word that de Messina had used. For me, nothing has occurred to change Donaghy's appraisal in all the intervening years, during which I reported many of Branca's greatest cases, travelled hundreds of kilometres with him, and was cross-examined by him in a murder case.

Those people at the testimonial dinner were not really celebrating a retirement. They were there to show affection. Nor were they paying honour in the traditional way to a poor Italian immigrant boy who had made good.

Branca was never a poor boy. He is not wholly Italian. He was never an immigrant except to the mainland of British Columbia from Vancouver Island. Like another and mightier man of law, he came down from a mountain.

CHAPTER ONE

Mount Sicker was a town high on the western slope of the 1050-m mountain of the same name on Vancouver Island about eighty kilometres north of Victoria. In 1903, it had 2000 inhabitants. The 1909 edition of the *British Columbia Gazetteer* describes it as practically deserted. Today it is not only deserted but, except on foot, is also inaccessible.

Angelo Branca was born there on 21 March 1903. As George Cumming, Q.C., put it, "The only explanation for his choice of birthplace is his understandable concern that he should be close to his mother." There was also the desire of his mother to be near her husband.

Filippo Branca arrived in the west ahead of the early twentieth-century inflow of Italians. He came from northern Italy, from Turbigo, a community about thirty-five kilometres west of Milan, where the family had a small lumber business. Filippo had three older and three younger brothers, all of whom stayed in their home province; a sister and her husband settled in Buenos Aires.

Early in the nineties, as a single man, he emigrated to Michigan. He worked in the mines there, then moved west to Utah to work in a newly opened coal mine at Castlegate. As soon as he established himself, he sent for his fiancée Teresa and they were married.

For a self-respecting girl from the northern valleys who was following her betrothed across the Atlantic, it was a matter of pride to take her *dote di sposa,* which was much more than her trousseau; it included table linen and bed linen of the best quality within her family's means, all packed in a stout wooden case. Teresa last saw her treasure chest on the New York docks. One can visualize the tears as she sat in their first home in that alien mining town and learned that it had vanished without trace. She was eighteen. To add insult to injury the railroad gave her only $100 for her loss. She never forgave that insult.

At that time the far west was the Promised Land, and the Brancas, with a newborn son, moved to California. Italians of that period, only a quarter of a century after the unification of their country, were still very much people of the old kingdoms that formed it. The pattern of immigration reflected this. Immigrants went where their kinsmen already lived. Vancouver's Italians were then predominantly from northeast Italy and the south. Many had arrived via the railroad labour crews that opened up Saskatchewan and Alberta. On Vancouver Island, the Dunsmuir mines recruited labour from northwest Italy— Lombards and Piedmontese who came mostly by way of the United States. So Filippo Branca followed his fellow Lombards and brought his wife and child to Vancouver Island, to a nameless settlement near Nanaimo, a company town for the new Extension Mine.

Then came the great gold rush to the Yukon. Filippo used his savings to equip himself for the Klondike. While there he carefully hoarded his earnings from the rich gravel of the creeks and came home with $10 000. Legendary figures made more, but by any measure of gold rush winners and losers Filippo was a winner: in 1900, its best year, the Klondike yield averaged only $670 per head.

Home by this time had a name, a by-product of the South African war. When news came of the relief of Ladysmith after a 118-day siege by the Boers, the rejoicing inspired mine owner James Dunsmuir to call his new settlement Ladysmith. Dunsmuir, himself the son, grandson and great-grandson of coal miners, was at this time energetically increasing and lavishly spending the fortune amassed by his immigrant Scottish father, and was meantime running the province as its premier.

Filippo Branca, a methodical man, went back to work

in the mine at Ladysmith while he prepared for the future. There a second child was born, a girl.

While Filippo was seeking his fortune in the Yukon gold fields, a rich mineral discovery was made barely fifteen kilometres from his home. High up on Big Sicker Mountain a prospector named Harry Smith went into an area where a recent fire had devastated hundreds of acres of timber. He stumbled around among the charred stumps for a week until he came upon a spot where the fire had exposed a lode of copper. The Lenora Claim, named after his daughter, entered into mining history.

The Dunsmuirs, dominating mining on Vancouver Island, were always quick to move into a promising development. As soon as test results on the new-found lode were known, a Dunsmuir son-in-law, Henry Croft, bought control. Undeterred by the forbidding terrain, Croft built a wagon road, drilled a tunnel, erected a tramway and started work on a townsite with homes, hotel, school, post office, livery stables and a store. The concession to run the store went to an employee at the Ladysmith mines who had money to stock it—Filippo Branca.

The efforts of promoters, engineers, contractors and miners to make a mine and town 420 m above the valley floor stagger the imagination of anyone looking at the rugged ravines today. They succeeded, and quickly started other mines higher still, and built another hotel and another school and another subdivision of homes.

The yield of ore was so great that the wagon road and the tramway could not carry it. There followed a railroading marvel, the Mount Sicker Railway, a 14-km stretch of switchbacks and trestles which connected the mine first with the recently finished Esquimalt and Nanaimo Railway and then with the smelter that Croft built at tidewater. Hence today's Crofton.

Teresa Branca went to the mountain town with two infants, and there gave birth to another son. Now there were Joseph, born in 1897, Anne, in 1901, and the newborn Angelo. John would come in 1906. When their last child was born in 1910, they named him Joseph after their first-born who had died the previous year.

Mount Sicker's fortunes fell as quickly as they had

risen, for two reasons. The lodes ran into faults, and the promoters quarrelled. The litigation-prone Dunsmuirs went to court. Miners began drifting away to Ladysmith and Nanaimo. In Victoria, the lawsuits became ever more bitter, and the sheriff seized the Lenora Mine. Miners disgruntled about pay and wanting to leave commandeered a locomotive but lost control of it on the steepest grade. It plunged into the bush where it lay for years. Valley farmers ambushed an ore train, felling trees ahead of it, then behind it, to press demands for payment of right-of-way rent arrears. Soon Mount Sicker joined the list of British Columbia ghost towns.

Today only four of the town's buildings have their roofs. The frame of the gazebo that graced the gardens of the Mount Sicker Hotel and the gatepost of its driveway still stand, but of the hotel itself only the foundation remains. The mine shafts await a time when a mining company once again thinks Mount Sicker is a viable property, as one did briefly in the thirties. Some of the miners' home sites are easily discernible, but it is hard to locate where Mount Sicker's Chinatown once stood. The snows of seventy winters and gales from the Pacific have flattened most of man's handiwork.

Before Mount Sicker's bubble burst, Filippo Branca saw warning signs and decided to follow his fortunes on the mainland. As soon as the infant Angelo was old enough for the journey, Filippo closed the store, and the family left the island to move to a bigger pioneering town, Vancouver—seventeen years after its great fire.

Filippo's first venture in Vancouver was to join in partnership with Giovanni Crossetti, who had also been a miner on Vancouver Island, in a grocery store on Main Street. Then the opposite shore of Burrard Inlet beckoned. Soldiers taking their discharge from the Royal Engineers at New Westminster, and given grants of land, had started the settlement of North Vancouver in about 1870, but only now was it offering opportunity for retail business. Filippo ended his partnership and opened a grocery store on First Street, close to Lonsdale Avenue.

The Brancas found a raw town. The streets then were unpaved, and in wet weather and after frost the city council stationed a couple of horses at that main intersection to pull out wagons that became mired. About the time Filippo Branca opened his store, the municipality was obliged to send a councillor to Ladner to buy a heavier team.

Today Angelo Branca's earliest childhood memory is of North Vancouver. He described to me his recollection of a large building near the water, standing in its own grounds and having wide balconies, with people sitting at tables and others leaning over the railing and looking down on those below. When I showed him the photograph of the North Vancouver Hotel reproduced in this book he said, delightedly, "That's it. That's exactly what I've always remembered."

The hotel was built and owned by a most colourful citizen, Pete Larsen. As a young Swedish sailor on a ship bringing materials to complete the CPR, Larsen had deserted at Port Moody and walked to within sight of New Westminster. Fearing he might be apprehended in town, he built a raft of logs and drifted down the Fraser River past the Royal City until, from the North Arm of the Fraser, he saw a field of uncut hay at the McCleery farm in South Vancouver. He offered to cut the hay, was hired and in time saved enough money to open a bar. Next he became a hotel keeper on Cordova Street. Prospering, he crossed the inlet and built the handsome hotel that has stayed in Angelo Branca's memory. It stood on the Esplanade two blocks from his home.

North Vancouver was not big enough for Filippo Branca. In 1909, word came of the death of his favourite uncle, a bachelor who was once minister of finance in a regional government in Italy, and Filippo was an heir. He went to Italy to deal with the estate; while there he checked the possibilities of a project that excited his interest—to start an Italian import business in British Columbia.

Vancouver was the place for that, and the time was right. Then and in the previous years, immigration from Italy was at a level not known again until the fifties. The CPR had an agent hiring labour in Chiasso, not far from Filippo's birthplace, and another in Udine to attract men of the Friuli region, and yet another in Reggio to recruit the Calabrese.

Filippo sold the North Vancouver store and returned to Vancouver's Main Street to start the wholesale and retail food importing business that was to exercise his merchandising talents for thirty years.

Growing up in multiracial East Vancouver helped to make Angelo Branca the man who in 1970 would be nationally honoured for his "outstanding contribution to promoting understanding and co-operation among the peoples of Canada regardless of race." In the area between Powell Street (which was mainly Japanese down to Burrard Inlet) and False Creek, and east-west between Clark Drive and Cambie Street, there were communities of Italians and Scandinavians, an extensive Chinatown and a well-defined Jewish quarter. Scattered among them were groups of Poles and Ukrainians; there were not many East Indians then, though a feature of the landscape was the mountain of cut wood on False Creek Flats piled high by Sohan Singh to keep Vancouver's home fires burning.

Branca senior, of sturdy frame and with flowing moustaches under a broad-brimmed felt hat, was a personality in that lively neighbourhood. A journalist described him as "a genial Italian merchant who never refused credit to a needy countryman." He was one of a group of Italian businessmen who acted as an unofficial consulate to help newcomers. The store became a drop-in centre. People knowing little English came for advice, and Italians having a working knowledge of English made themselves available to help, or came just for old country talk over a glass of wine in the back.

One of the regular callers was a longshoreman who loved to recite stanzas of *The Divine Comedy* in the pure Tuscan tongue, which gave Angelo a lasting interest in the poetry of Dante. Although his parents became English-speaking, the language at home was Italian, and Angelo never lost his interest in it or his fluency. Often in later years court interpreters agreed to stand corrected when he challenged a translation of an Italian witness's evidence.

By the time the family moved to a home on Prior Street

in 1909, the railway companies were filling in much of the False Creek shallows opposite, later to be turned into yards. On the big open space thus created, all the great circuses—Barnum and Bailey, Ringling Brothers—pitched their tents and would send their elephants to be watered outside the Branca home.

Angelo often accompanied his father, who seemed to know everybody, on his calls around the district. He took the boys with him when he lunched at neighbourhood eating places. One was the London Bar, where a man buying a five-cent schooner of beer was entitled to help himself to all sorts of tasty dishes arranged along the counter. At the Klondike Bar, young Angelo saw the respect that the immigrants gave to anyone with some learning. John Carrelli was the bar proprietor and—more impressive—a court interpreter.

Old country characteristics influenced growing up in that part-European, part-Oriental environment. One was the traditional Italian home discipline, all the more accepted here because the Jewish, Chinese and Japanese of the neighbourhood were also strict parents. In those days parental authority was not questioned in Italian households. The cockiest kid on the street accepted father as master of the home.

Pushing a handcart around East Vancouver delivering store orders familiarized young Angelo with the different national groups. He knew Chinatown well when the name really did mean a Chinese community having its own life and manners and mores, from opium manufacturing (legal during his boyhood) to Chinese opera. He still has a mental picture of two leaders of that community who seemed to him to typify the dignified, cultured Oriental gentleman—Won Cumyow, head of the Cumyow family, and Mor Whaun, father of a boy who later was at university with him.

Won Cumyow was the first Chinese child born in British Columbia, son of pioneers who sailed up the Fraser before Vancouver had been named—and before regulations keeping out Chinese women had been passed. Won was born at Port Douglas, where his father had opened a store when the Cariboo gold rush brought that settlement into being. Port Douglas, at the north end of Harrison Lake, was the start of the sixty-kilometre portage to Lillooet Lake. Sir Matthew Begbie held his first trial as judge of the Colony of British Columbia at Port Douglas in 1859. Royal Engineers were then laying out the townsite, and Begbie bought land there—a bad investment, because in a few years Port Douglas was by-passed and doomed by the construction miracle of the Cariboo Trail.

Angelo Branca often saw Won Cumyow using his special talent. Growing up mostly among Indians at Port Douglas, he was fluent in the Chinook that was the trading language used by Indians and settlers from Oregon to Alaska. When he moved to Vancouver and became a court interpreter, cases involving Indians were conducted in Chinook through the intermediary of this dignified Chinese. His son Gordon succeeded him and often took part in Branca's cases during his twenty-seven years as a Vancouver Police Court interpreter.

Going to school at Strathcona, then said to be the largest elementary school in Canada, reinforced the cosmopolitan experience. Although pupils of British stock for a time formed the largest group, the minorities in total outnumbered them, and when the children acted out the prejudices of their parents, the Anglo-Saxon assumption of superiority provoked violent rivalries. "If they called us Dagoes, we Wops would fight," says Angelo Branca today with a grin of pure mischievous joy. "Some of us fought more than others. I believe that's when the kids started to make me the Italians' leader."

Meantime, perhaps as a defensive reaction, most of the non-British children—though not the Japanese—mixed freely and tolerated each other's old country ways and religious differences. Those who grew up in homes where Friday was ritually a meatless day found nothing peculiar about others under an obligation not to eat pork.

Some of Angelo Branca's longest-lasting friendships date back to those Jewish high holidays which required the orthodox to do no work on the day of observance. All preparations for the business of living were made in advance. The fires in the homes would be laid but lighting them on the holy day was one of the prohibited chores. So the good-looking Branca boy was in special demand at those times, and Jewish housewives, matchboxes in hand, would say, "Be a good boy, Angie, and just come in and put a match to the fire."

World War I, which changed Vancouver forever in so many ways, changed life for Angelo Branca. In 1911, his father bought 160 acres of land in Burnaby. The outbreak of war convinced him that he should venture into food producing in addition to food importing. The farm was virgin land. The clearing was slow and back-breaking work, but once it was ready for planting this rich black soil needed no fertilizer. The hard work, after that, was harvesting the bumper crops.

Of this period Angelo says: "That farm was one of the small miracles of my life. The way things grew! It was alluvial land, covered by the leaves of centuries, with Still Creek running through it. For years it never needed manure. We grew cabbages that weighed forty pounds. The beans were enormous. We'd get three crops of hay a year. We had forty acres under hay, and five men with scythes would cut it. When I was thirteen I was scything with them. When the hay was in before the end of June, we'd dam the creek to flood the land, and no sooner had the water drained than the new shoots were springing up for the second crop.

"The climate was different then. Spring would come early, and it would be good. Summer would be hot, sometimes torrid. Lots of thunderstorms, lightning. The Indian summers would take you almost to November. Winter was cold, cold. Hundreds of people would be skating on Burnaby Lake and Deer Lake. Sometimes we'd get three feet of snow.

"We had fifty or sixty head of dairy cattle. I developed muscles manhandling five- and ten-gallon milk cans."

When Angelo was thirteen, his father became one of the first men on Main Street to own—though he would never drive—an automobile. The demands of war made motor vehicles scarce, but Filippo's expanding wholesale business created a need, and somehow he acquired a big old Russell-Knight with a canvas top. To the boy it looked a monster. Someone showed Angelo how to drive it, and he set out delivering supplies to places as far as eight kilometres away—to the construction camp of a contractor building roads in West Point Grey. When things went wrong, he found that garagemen knew little more about the car than he did, so, helped by his brother, he learned how to work on the motor and keep it running. It was not until after the war that a Hudson Super Six, which cost all of $2000, replaced it.

Tinkering with the old Russell-Knight opened up a new interest for Angelo. He decided he wanted to be an engineer. Then he learned that the best engineers were educated, and he certainly had never distinguished himself as a student. "Poor to mediocre" is his own description. For an energetic East End boy life was too full to spend time studying, and his days were crowded with working at the store, playing street games, soccer and rugby—and fighting. He began working to improve his low grades, but he had not yet developed the intensive reading discipline that was to be one of the keys to his professional success, and he never did achieve high marks. When he was senior visiting law lecturer at the University of British Columbia, he told Dr. A.J. McClean, dean of law, with characteristic immodesty, "If they had set examinations like this in my youth Canada would have lost one of her greatest lawyers."

Branca's formative years, spent with parents like his in cosmopolitan Vancouver, are clearly reflected in the man he became. Parallels between father and son are many. In 1911, Filippo Branca founded the Societa Veneta as a community and benevolent association for northern Italians. Members later showed their appreciation by making him honorary president for life. In 1966, his son would found the Confratellanza Italo-Canadese, with similar aims, formed from a merging of several groups.

Father and son were alike in loving Italian culture but putting Canadian loyalty first, and alike in having a penchant for private and personal charities. After Filippo

Branca died in 1939, his executors found accounts total-
ling $59 000 owing to him by customers. Teresa Branca
forgave every penny. Many hundreds of the people whom
their son defended on serious charges were legal aid cases,
in those days another term for charity.

For some years the family divided its time between the
store and the farm. Angelo moved on from Strathcona
School to Britannia High School but spent summers in
the country. Local boys and girls were always with the
Brancas around the farm. One was a bright and smiling
American girl who attended the one-room Nikolai Schou
School nearby (named after the man who proposed the
name of the new community of Burnaby, and became its
first reeve). She so captivated the boy from Britannia
High that when she was only fourteen he told her and
everyone who would listen that he was going to marry her
when they grew up.

Viola's parents were living in Canada because her
father had come to help build the second Hotel Vancouver (demolished in 1949). When they returned to Olympia,
Washington, their daughter went with them, but distance
never cooled the romance.

Many factors conspired to make Angelo Branca a pro-
ponent of interracial relations. The man Vancouver
regards as the archetypal Italian is not wholly Italian at
all. His mother was born of Italian and Austrian parents
near the Brenner Pass in the South Tirol, in what was
then Italia Irredenta ("Unredeemed"), part of the old
Austro-Hungarian empire.

In 1928 Angelo Branca married the girl who had been
his teen-age sweetheart, and the mosaic was extended.
Viola Miller was born an American, of German and
French parents. The name was originally Mueller. So
when Angelo and Viola had two daughters, Dolores Rose
and Patricia, they endowed them with Italian, Austrian,
German and French heredity. One daughter married an
Englishman, the other an Irishman. Angelo's brothers
married sisters, two Canadian girls of Ukrainian parentage. As though to show there was no prejudice, his sister
Anne married an Italian. Tragically, she died giving birth

to their first child. The ethnic pattern is still further blended in the Brancas' seven grandchildren.

An indication of the Brancas' universalism is that when Angelo and Viola celebrated fifty years of marriage in 1978, congratulations came from friends belonging to more than a dozen races and from dignitaries as different as Pope Paul VI, Prime Minister Trudeau and the head of the Bar-Ilan University of Israel.

Before Angelo and Viola married he had an education to finish and a career to launch. By working harder he graduated from Britannia with better but not distinguished marks and, still planning a career as an engineer, enrolled at the University of British Columbia, then housed in what were disparagingly but not inaccurately called the Fairview Shacks, on the grounds of Vancouver General Hospital.

His attendance at the predominantly Anglo-Saxon-Scottish university did not lessen his enjoyment of Italian activities in the East End, and his father noticed how he handled himself in discussions at the Societa Veneta. He had completed a year at UBC when, during one of the arguments that enlivened the Branca supper table, his father said, "Angelo, you ought to be a lawyer." The next morning, there then being no law school at the university, Angelo was at Fairview withdrawing from second-year engineering and claiming the return of his fees. That afternoon he was inquiring how to qualify for law.

CHAPTER TWO

Like many another before him and since, Angelo Branca decided to study law with only a vague notion of what being a lawyer meant.

In the early twenties, would-be lawyers in British Columbia—unless their parents could send them to Osgoode Hall in Toronto or Dalhousie in Halifax or even, as some did, to Yale or Harvard—would serve articles in a law office for five years and attend lectures given several times a week by men recognized as specialists in their field. Branca articled first with Arthur H. Sutton, but after a year he decided that the learning opportunities were limited, since Sutton's main practice was as solicitor to the Municipality of North Vancouver. He looked for a more varied practice, and found exactly what he wanted. For four years he articled to Arthur Fleishman, who had a busy court and general practice. Arthur's son Neil would later become Vancouver's best-known divorce lawyer and would tell of the heartbreaks and the hatreds of husband-and-wife litigation in his book, *Counsel for the Damned.*

Neil recalls, "We loved it when my father took my brother and me to the Branca home to watch Angelo's father make wine. Such a welcome! And grape juice splashing all over the place. That gave Father the idea that he could make wine, so he did. He asked Angelo to taste it. 'What you have there, Arthur,' said Angelo, 'is the best damn vinegar in all Vancouver.' "

Arthur Fleishman solemnly impressed on his student, as his father had on him, that "in this Anglo-Saxon world of Vancouver, the son of alien immigrants has not only to try harder; he has to be better."

Arthur Fleishman's offices were in the Standard Building on Hastings Street, which also provided offices for two men with whom Branca would work closely in years to come: Gordon Wismer, later a formidable attorney general of the province, and Harold McInnes, then Wismer's law student and, forty years later, Branca's companion on the Supreme Court bench.

Law studies opened up a new world to Angelo Branca. Fleishman, with his office midway between the city's Police Court and the province's Vancouver Court House, quickly introduced his student to both.

The justice structure in British Columbia then was similar to what it is today: Police Court (now called Provincial Court) tried the lesser offences; County Court handled more serious criminal cases and civil disputes involving limited sums; Supreme Court dealt with the most serious crimes and with civil suits where the claim exceeded the County Court limit; and Court of Appeal confirmed or quashed such decisions of the lower courts as were disputed.

Police Court tried perhaps nine out of every ten people accused of breaking the law, minor offences making up the great part of the courts' case load. Supreme Court attracted more newspaper attention, and it was there that citizens might find themselves part of the decision-making process as jurors in all criminal and some civil trials. (Today the County Court also has some criminal jury trials.)

All criminal cases in Supreme Court came within the Assize calendar, direct descendant of the medieval English system by which, twice a year, all unconvicted persons held in jail must appear before a jury, thus ensuring that no person could languish in jail without trial for more than a few months. Hence the Spring and Fall Assizes, still scheduled in most county towns in British Columbia but not in Vancouver, where the number of cases now necessitates more frequent Assize calendars.

In Branca's law student days, the Assize was much

more of an occasion than now, especially in the smaller centres. Western Canada never had the ceremonial that opened the Assizes in England up to the late 1930s—the procession of judge and civic dignitaries to the cathedral to seek divine guidance, accompanied by heralds and trumpeters and white-gloved tipstaffs—but the sheriff (descendant of the old English shire reeve), while having less power than his American namesake, was and still functions as the link between Court and people. Young student Branca, his interest newly stirred in the roots of Canadian law, was fascinated to hear the sheriff opening each Assize with the command: "Oyez! Oyez! Oyez! All persons having business at this Court of Oyer and Terminer and General Gaol Delivery, holden here this day, in and for the County of Vancouver, draw near and give your attention and answer to your names when called. God save the King."

The law lectures which were an important part of the student curriculum brought Branca in contact with trained legal minds, and with one man who influenced his career profoundly. If public life in the west ever had a paragon, that man was Mr. Justice Denis Murphy. Branca, as an impressionable student, had him as his lecturer in constitutional law.

Murphy's father, like Branca's, was an immigrant who won his stake in his new country in the gold fields. He left Ireland for the United States and was working in the east when gold was discovered in California. Leaving his fiancée working as a farm girl in New York State, he followed the forty-niners, then headed north when news came of a new "strike" somewhere beyond the Oregon Territory. His group came overland, building their own rowboats when the terrain demanded, and on a sandbar in the Fraser River, near Boston Bar, Murphy found gold.

He returned to the east only long enough to claim his bride and brought her to British Columbia. Like Branca's father, he used his savings to start a business. He built 141 Mile House on the Cariboo Road, which he operated as an overnight hotel for the stagecoach trade, and meantime bought cattle and developed his property into the Enterprise Ranch.

The son who was to become a judge had his early education among the Indian children of Lac La Hache, which is why he could speak Chinook to the Indians in his court, and he had his formal education at the University of Ottawa, of which his oldest brother became rector. There Denis Murphy was gold medallist in every subject he studied, and took a doctorate in philosophy. He spoke French well, and to doctoral examiners he discoursed in Latin for nearly two hours without notes.

Having qualified in law as well he was soon elected to the legislature in Victoria. Contemporary reports say his Reply to the Speech from the Throne was one of the greatest displays of oratory ever heard in the House. Before he had been a member two years, his political future was so much taken for granted that he was appointed to the cabinet without his even being consulted, but within hours he resigned his seat, having decided to devote himself to law. In 1909, he became the youngest Canadian judge, and the first native of the province to be appointed to the Supreme Court of British Columbia, where he sat for thirty-two years.

In 1941, when he seemed clearly destined to be the next chief justice of British Columbia, his sight became diminished, and sadly he announced, "A judge must have mental poise, infinite patience and a capacity for infinite study. Whatever be the personal sacrifice it is, I think, his bounden duty to retire if a judge finds he is failing in any of these qualifications." He thereupon retired. An operation astonishingly improved his sight and brightened his few remaining years until his death in 1947.

Listening to the lectures of outstanding men like Murphy and Reginald Tupper, and spending hours in courtrooms, Branca found to his delight that the law was the life for him. Combative by nature and by conditioning, he relished the challenges of an adversary system. More than that, he discovered within himself a fascination for pure law. He read compulsively about it. His intensive reading developed the capacity for making fine distinctions that marked his career both as advocate and as judge. His ambition to have at hand all the law available led to his building up what was described by a specialist publisher as the largest law library of any one-principal office in Canada.

Police Court was where aspiring young counsel sharpened their legal teeth. Senator J.W. deB. Farris, for years the leader of the B.C. bar, started in Police Court. On his being appointed privy counsellor, the Toronto *Globe and Mail* gave the news a front-page headline reading, "From Police Court to Privy Council." A relative sent the senator the front page but the address sticker was so positioned that it blanked out the headline's last word.

The rewards of success in Police Court were not to be despised. Branca remembers Frank Lyons as "pure magic in Police Court." When mining speculations brought about Lyons's financial downfall, the resulting proceedings revealed that he had amassed between half and three-quarters of a million dollars based on his successful Police Court advocacy.

Yet while doing remarkable things for his clients in Police Court, Lyons could achieve little whenever he appeared in Supreme Court. Looking for lessons in everything, Branca learned from watching Lyons that persuasiveness and courtroom slickness might do wonders in the lower court but they availed little in the higher courts without sound law. He went to the law books. Buying law reports, statutes and legal publications became one of his chief expenses.

Some exceptional lawyers practised in Vancouver in those days. Branca's favourite was the top criminal lawyer J.A. Russell. He was a tall, white-haired man having superb presence in the courtroom, an actor whose knowledge of the law was as impeccable as his deportment. Branca studied the methods that made Russell so successful, particularly his style with juries, and tried to blend them with his own.

Branca said of him, "Joe Russell was my idol when I was a young lawyer. Such style! He lived in a mansion overlooking Lost Lagoon—there's an apartment tower there now. He was like a lot of lawyers; he lost his money in mining speculations. Many of B.C.'s best lawyers then were men from Ontario who came west bringing their law degrees but really hoping to make their fortunes in mining. Some did. Some made mining law. Archer Martin was a great chief justice of appeal but I'll bet more lawyers know him through 'Martin on Mining.' "

More and more Branca found that although Police Court exercised his competitive instincts he was happier in the high courts. He liked the practice of law as he observed it in the Supreme Court, the abrasive quality of the argument that was essential to it and the precision of the language. He developed a knack for using earthy man-in-the-beer-parlour expressions in terms acceptable in court.

One suspects, from the relish with which he recalls certain expressions today, that he was led along that line by Mr. Justice D.A. McDonald. Claud McAlpine, a distinguished member of the Farris firm, was arguing a case and, for his own good reasons, was avoiding committing himself on some issue on which the judge thought he should. A contest of wits ensued, until finally Judge McDonald said, "Please, Mr. McAlpine, either play a tune or get off the piano stool."

One resolution Branca made during his law student days and never forgot was to be respectful to judges who gave him the respect due an advocate, but to stand up boldly to any who did not. That is the nature of the man, but probably his conscious decision stemmed from things he resented in the conduct of some of the idiosyncratic judges of his impressionable years.

The most notorious of these was Chief Justice Morrison, a complex man who had an impact on the courtroom behaviour of many besides the young Branca. On the bench he displayed what his friends excused as a puckish sense of humour but what his victims saw as a streak of cruelty. Whether fun or spite, it was usually aimed at those who could not retaliate.

Aulay MacAulay Morrison was a Nova Scotian and Gaelic speaking. When an enumerator in the 1931 census asked him his racial origin the judge replied, "Pictish." The official thought that unacceptable so he asked, "Where did your ancestors come from?" "The Highlands of Scotland," replied the judge, so the official wrote "Scottish." "Not so," said the judge. "The Scots are just a horde of immigrants who came to my homeland a couple of thousand years ago. I come from the original stock, the Picts."

Lawyers, reporters, registrars, police officers and court clerks all over British Columbia have told how Morrison humiliated them. They dreaded to hear his high-pitched voice announcing their names as a prelude to some rebuke, as in this instance:

THE JUDGE: Mr. Registrar. *Mister* Registrar. Are you a sufferer from piles?

THE REGISTRAR: Why, no, my lord.

THE JUDGE: I'm *so* glad. Would you, then, *Mister* Registrar, kindly refrain from writhing and squirming about as if you were.

The registrar did not deign to explain that towards the end of a long court day he had to move around in his chair to ease discomfort from an old wound suffered in World War I.

With lawyers, Judge Morrison had a petty technique for provoking them by repeatedly mispronouncing their names. One day he consistently referred to H.A. Swencisky, later head of the Vancouver County Court, as "Mr. Svensky." Finally, with dignity, Swencisky said, "May it please your lordship, my name is Swencisky."

"Of course. *Of course*," replied the judge. "How could I make such a mistake. *Do* forgive me. From now on I will refer to you correctly, Mr. *Svensky*."

George Housser, a member of one of Vancouver's best-known firms, reacted strongly to similar treatment. Judge Morrison had set the trap by repeatedly referring to him as "Mr. Bowser." Eventually the lawyer explained to him that his name was Housser, not Bowser. "How stupid of me," said the judge. "How could I possibly confuse you with Mr. Bowser. Mr. Bowser was a *good* lawyer, wasn't he?"

Later, as the judge rose to leave the bench, Housser said

loudly, as though to the other lawyers, "I can practise law without having to appear before this judge again." And, as far as is known, he never did.

If he could not find a victim among the participants, the chief justice would look for one among the spectators. He once sent an usher into the public part of the courtroom to tell a spectator that if he did not sit up straight he would be ejected.

Lawyers particularly had to be on their guard. One so far forgot himself while making a submission that he placed his right foot on an empty chair next to him, rested his right elbow on his knee and supported his chin with thumb and forefinger. The judge, in his most urbane manner, stopped him. "It occurs to me," said Morrison, "that you may not be quite comfortable. Please make yourself at home. Why not sit down? Or, if you prefer, *lie* down."

Angelo Branca once saw Arthur Fleishman undergo the Morrison treatment in a courtroom crowded with lawyers awaiting their turn to make Chambers applications. As he explained his case, Fleishman held his brief in his left hand and was unconsciously jiggling a bunch of keys in his pants pocket with his right hand. "Mr. Fly-shman. *Mister* Fly-shman," came the mispronouncing high voice. "What have you in your hand?"

"In my hand, my lord? Why, my brief," said the lawyer.

"No. No, Mr. Fly-shman. Not that hand. The other hand. The *other* hand."

Four years of articling with Arthur Fleishman had nurtured in Branca a good deal of affection for the older man and he loathed—and remembered—this treatment. But he would find that the most careful study of Morrison's foibles could not guarantee immunity from stricture.

Henry Castillou, later one of Branca's mentors in the local Liberal back rooms, was presenting his case in an uncontested divorce suit. Young Branca carefully noted how he drew from the private detective a progressive narrative describing how he kept the woman under observation and saw her leave home, how he followed her downtown and along Dunsmuir Street and how she turned into the alley behind the Invermay Hotel. Judge Morrison interrupted. "Mr. Castillou. *Mister* Castillou. In the experience of this Court, parties to undefended divorce cases do not commit their adulteries in back alleys. *Get them up to the bedroom!*"

So when Branca had his first divorce case before Judge Morrison, he briskly asked his detective whether on a given date he did or saw anything in connection with a certain hotel room. Immediately came the voice of sweet reason from the bench: "Mr. Branca. *Mister* Branca. You seem in a great hurry. Well, the Court is not in a great hurry, and if you really want a decree for your client you will kindly put in your evidence in the proper detail and order."

The lesson? With Morrison, timing was important. Branca began his case in the early afternoon whereas Castillou's was called towards the end of the morning session, when the lunch hour was looming up. Judge Morrison never allowed anything to interfere with his punctual attendance at lunch with his friends in the Vancouver Club.

Branca the law student was also learning that in the routine business of living there was not equal justice for all. In Vancouver when he was a student, wealth meant privilege. The authorities were habitual respecters of those who had position or possessions.

Two notorious perversions of justice, one international, the other local, contributed to Branca's legal education. Almost throughout his law studies, one of the great controversies of American legal history, the *Sacco and Vanzetti* case, flared intermittently in the world's press. Gunmen killed two men in a Massachusetts payroll robbery. Two Italian immigrants, known to be extreme radicals, were convicted and sentenced to death. Protesters demonstrated in cities around the world, contending that innocent men were being executed not for murder but for their political beliefs.

Angelo Branca followed with interest the much-publicized campaign of distinguished members of the American legal community to upset the conviction. The revered

Felix Frankfurter of Harvard Law School (later of the U.S. Supreme Court) fought with intellect and passion to save the men. He never argued that they were necessarily innocent. His theme was that the State had not proven guilt, and that the sacred instrument of the law should never be used perversely—in this instance to rid the State of individuals whom the authorities considered dangerous. It was a concept of law that Branca took to heart.

Almost seven years after conviction, both men died in the electric chair.

Branca was well advanced in the study of law when the Janet Smith case was exciting Vancouver in 1924 and 1925, and thus was able to recognize how outrageous was the malfunctioning of the machinery of law.

The celebrated case revealed a police force, the Point Grey Municipal Police, whose automatic reaction to a scandal involving influential people was to hush it up. It also exposed an Attorney General's Department that was prepared to connive at the cover-up and to use racial prejudice for political considerations.

A Scottish immigrant girl employed as a nursemaid in the fashionable Shaughnessy district was found dead in her employers' home from a bullet wound that could not have been self-inflicted. A police sergeant testified at the inquest that there was no evidence of foul play, and the jury, at the direction of the coroner, returned a verdict of accidental death.

The Attorney General's Department at first discounted rumours that there had been a cover-up, but did an about-face when politicians realized that a new voice was demanding action—that of the Scottish societies formed from the thousands of immigrants who had poured into Vancouver in the immediate prewar years and who now represented considerable voting power. They heard rumours, never proven, of a wild party at the house the night before the girl's body was found, a party said to have been attended by prominent people who left almost immediately for travels abroad.

The Scottish community's protests at the stifling of an

investigation forced another inquest to be held. This time the verdict was "murder by a person or persons unknown."

The police took extraordinary steps to block or sidetrack the investigation. A Chinese houseboy employed in the same home as Janet Smith disappeared in the night, and seven weeks later was found wandering at 3:00 A.M. Wong said he had been abducted from his bed by men wearing white sheets who held him prisoner and tried to make him confess. He was arrested and charged with the murder.

Then private detectives who felt cheated in a share-out confessed that the agency employing them had received $3500 to extort a false confession from Wong. They testified that the Attorney General's Department and the municipality had each put up half the fee and that the reeve, the police commissioner and the police chief of Point Grey were parties to the plot.

The idea that policemen carrying out a criminal abduction would try to divert suspicion by wearing white sheets is less ludicrous than it now sounds. The Ku Klux Klan was having one of its occasional revivals in Canada. It claimed 8000 members in British Columbia, including adherents who sponsored an unsuccessful motion in the legislature to ban the employment of Oriental male servants in homes where white girls were employed. The Klan headquarters for Canada were in a rented eighteen-room mansion a few blocks from the murder location, and area residents were accustomed to seeing men in white robes and hoods on the grounds, sometimes parading with imitation fiery crosses made of electric lights. (The house, Glen Brae, built by lumberman W.L. Tait, had its seventieth birthday in 1980—as a nursing home.)

Three private detectives were arrested as a result of the confessions, and criminal proceedings were started against the municipal leaders implicated. Wong was freed when a grand jury, which under the law of that time was asked to return "a true bill of indictment," threw the case out.

The Janet Smith case entered the list of unsolved murders, but not before the attorney general perpetrated one more piece of effrontery. He announced in the legislature that, two detectives having been jailed for the abduction, he had dropped the charges against their coaccused citizens of Point Grey. The attorney general was Alec Manson.

Branca was writing his final bar examinations when the affair reached its climax. Thus he came to the practice of law when the walls of privilege were coming under fire. He was thirsting to join in the attack.

CHAPTER THREE

Angelo Branca entered a Damon Runyonesque world when he opened his practice as barrister and solicitor in Vancouver in 1926. He was just twenty-three.

His first clients were bootleggers. Soon they included madams of some of the dozens of brothels operating with the connivance of corrupt police and city politicians. He knew a judge whose first drink of the day, taken on his way to court, was at the establishment of Shue Moy, who was described in Canada's parliament as the king of West Coast gambling. Some of his clients would certainly have known where the biggest floating crap game in town could be found. One, Buddy White, claimed to be the best crapshooter west of Chicago. His specialty was to invite odds on whether he could throw a pair of dice consecutively from double-one to double-six in twenty-one throws. When the stake was high enough, he could.

Branca was never the struggling young lawyer forced to accept any client in order to establish himself. From the start, business was good. The year he began practising was described by historian Dr. Margaret Ormsby as the most prosperous year in the history of British Columbia up to that time. Moreover, he already had the foundations for a practice. A true son of Main Street, he liked to be with people, and he was an enthusiastic "joiner." The Eagles, the Knights of Pythias, the Knights of Columbus, the sports clubs, the Italian groups, Catholic groups and the Liberal Party—he was in them all, and clients came to him from all.

The brisk economy of the late twenties enabled many

immigrants, by working heroic hours, to save money and realize their ambitions of owning a home or starting a business. For people buying homes, Branca did the conveyancing. For those launching out in business, he incorporated companies.

Many of his clients, by the nature of their activities, were prone to conflict with the law, which tended to make Branca's busy office practice into an even busier court practice. Thus was born the legend that would cling to Branca throughout his career at the bar, that of the archdefender, "the man who gets people off, guilty or not."

Today Branca says, "I never gave a damn whether my client was innocent or guilty. I didn't care if he was guilty as hell. I gave him the best defence I could within the law." Asked, "What if he told you he did it?" he replies, "If he came to me during the trial and said, 'I did it, but I still want you to get me off,' I would do my damnedest to do exactly that."

In this he is not making his own rules, merely saying what his profession states is the bounden duty of every lawyer—to protect his client as far as possible from being convicted. From his law tutors he learned that the matter of guilt or innocence is for the judge or jury to decide, not the lawyer, and that an accused is not competent to understand, nor is his lawyer entitled to determine for him, what is guilt under the law. They taught him, too, that everyone has the right to hire the services of a lawyer of his own choosing. With these principles in mind, Branca was always unconcerned that people remembered his defence of vice exploiter Joe Celona and gambling syndicate boss Bruce Snider and forgot his courtroom victories for the Sisters of Charity and St. Paul's Hospital.

Sometimes in his public speaking he tried to correct misunderstanding of the lawyer's responsibilities. He told 300 University of British Columbia students who attended his lecture on man's responsibility to man, "It is difficult for the layman to understand why a lawyer will defend a man in spite of overwhelming evidence of guilt, but everyone is presumed by law to be innocent until proven guilty."

The misconceptions remain. None of his courtroom successes gave Angelo Branca more satisfaction than the *Hughes* case in 1942. With Canada and Japan at war, emotions were stirred by the death sentences on four young men convicted of murdering a Japanese Canadian in a store holdup. Branca's plea for Robert Hughes, the one with the gun, made legal history and saved all four from execution. Yet forty years later a well-informed citizen could say, "Angelo Branca has done a lot for the people of East Vancouver. But I'll never, never forgive him for getting Hughes off."

Because of his prominence in public affairs in his middle years, Branca more than most lawyers provoked the layman's question, "How does it come about that a man who stands for civic betterment makes his living out of defending crime?" Had Branca depended on criminal defending for a living he would have had to close his office. He earned less from criminal defending than from prosecuting. He made a reputation as a criminal lawyer and his living—a good one—out of his competence as an all-round counsel with a large civil practice. Lawyers said, though there is no way of checking it, that his was the biggest general practice of any one-principal law office in Canada. Years before he left the practice for a judgeship, his office was the registered address for more than 400 companies.

So much criminal defending yielded him little financially because Branca broadened the principle, "Everyone is entitled to a defence until found guilty," by adding, "whether he has the means to pay or not." He practised legal aid as far back as 1926, and was still preaching it fifty years later as a dissenting Court of Appeal judge.

Free legal aid as understood today barely existed in the twenties. If a lawyer offered to defend a person without means who faced a serious charge, the Provincial Treasury would pay an honorarium of seventy-five dollars regardless of how long the case took for preparation, preliminary hearing and trial. A more enlightened approach was advocated by Thomas Francis Hurley, an Irish barrister who came to Vancouver in 1911. By example and precept he encouraged the formation of a loose grouping of lawyers who alternated in donating their services to this cause, and Branca joined them. "Donated" is the appropriate word. Hurley and Branca and doubtless others refused to take the seventy-five dollars on the ground that the principle was unjust and the amount was an insult to the profession.

The service was not without its compensations because by winning such cases lawyers often gained a bonus in the form of publicity. A series of successes, especially if the cases warranted high interest in the newspapers, was priceless advertising. This consideration was not likely to have influenced Tom Hurley. To that free spirit, practising law was more a way of enjoying life than of earning a living. There were several men like Hurley around who loved the law, enjoyed the courtroom combat, counted their wins more than their fees and could always sacrifice a few days in a good cause. Some drank too much, or did not keep businesslike books, or overplayed the role, but as a group they helped a lot of people, and they contributed to the gaiety of life in their city.

One St. Patrick's Day, Branca and Hurley were in Police Court waiting for their cases to be called. First the overnight "drunk list" must be disposed of. This process was underway when Hurley rose and addressed Magistrate Billy McInnes: "Your worship, I have not been retained by any of these men but I would like to speak for number one on the list. He speaks very little English. His name, your worship will note, is Oshenko. I respectfully submit that on this Glorious Seventeenth of Ireland it would be a miscarriage of justice to punish anyone with such a fine old Irish name for celebrating too well. I move for dismissal."

Magistrate McInnes, a kindred spirit, set the man free. This magistrate was proof of Branca's theory that the law had many colourful characters in those days because so many of them had colourful backgrounds. His father was a Canadian antislavery agitator who fought in the American Civil War. Billy was born at Dresden, Ontario, the Canadian terminus of the celebrated "underground railroad" by which escaped slaves from the South reached freedom. As a child he listened to stories at the knee of the Reverend Josiah Hanson, the original Tom of *Uncle Tom's Cabin*. Billy's father was lieutenant governor of

British Columbia when Government House burned down.
Father and son both had stormy political careers.

While Billy McInnes was still an inexperienced magistrate, he convicted a burglar and asked legal aid counsel Tom Hurley if he had anything to say before sentence was passed. Inquiries had not produced a single fact that might help his client, who had thirty convictions, but Tom did his best. "Your worship," he began. "It is just a year ago today that we were first blessed by your presence on this bench," and he went on to extol the virtues that had so distinguished his first year, especially that of compassion.

Magistrate McInnes heard him out, then said, "From the bottom of my heart I thank you, Mr. Hurley. I shall always cherish your compliments. But the sentence on your client will still be two years."

"In that event, your worship," said Tom, "may the Court please permit me to withdraw my remarks in toto."

Branca learned a number of things from Hurley. He learned some useful techniques of courtroom acting, for Hurley could have won fame on the stage. But the best lesson he learned from him was that laughter and gaiety had a place in the Court House and even, as he showed years later, in the austere corridors of the Court of Appeal.

The flashiest characters in town, typical Damon Runyon people, were passing through Branca's chambers. At different times, on different charges, he defended two members of Vancouver's small black community, crap champion Buddy White and racehorse owner Roy Alexander.

White was a club operator and gambler, a suave, smiling white-haired man, always showily dressed. People knew whether Lady Luck was smiling on Buddy by his tiepin. If he was wearing the pin with the enormous emerald, all was well. If not, that valuable jewel was lodged once more with "Uncle Evans" as security for a loan to enable him to live in the style he favoured.

Roy Alexander belonged to the large family of descendants of Charles and Nancy Alexander, who were among the black immigrants who settled on Vancouver Island in 1858. Governor Douglas, alarmed at the way his colony was being stripped of its work force by the rush to the Fraser River gold fields, heard that the blacks in San Francisco, most of them fugitives from slavery, were looking for a new homeland during a time of violent antiblack demonstrations. Douglas invited them to settle in his colony, and their descendants live today on Vancouver Island, on Saltspring Island and around Vancouver.

Sometimes White and Alexander were friends, as when Alexander lent his expensive car to White to impress a lady friend. At other times they were not, as when Alexander unexpectedly repossessed the car, to the embarrassment of the lady's escort. As a result, Branca found himself defending White on a charge of attempting to murder Alexander.

The evidence was that White, leaving his club in the early hours to find the car gone, and knowing that at dawn Alexander would be putting his horses through their paces, announced that he was going to Hastings Park to settle with Alexander for humiliating him before a lady. The news travelled faster than White, and Alexander armed himself with a length of two-by-four lumber. This he brought down so hard on White's head that the stick snapped in two, whereupon White, with a knife, put more than a hundred cuts in the unfortunate Alexander.

Somehow Branca managed to persuade the Assize jury to dismiss the charge of attempted murder, but Mr. Justice Murphy, after saying, "I believe you are not a criminal," sent White to prison for two years for doing grievous bodily harm.

Whatever the merits of modern law school training over the old articling procedure, the latter made it possible for ambitious would-be lawyers to acquaint themselves quickly with the arena of advocacy. Unless they were articled to lawyers having mainly office practices, students were exposed almost at once to battle in and around the courtroom.

Angelo Branca spent so much time in court before and in the months following his call to the bar that within six months of opening his office he felt ready to conduct his first case in the Court of Assize. He offered to defend a woman accused of attempting to murder her common-law husband. In lieu of a fee, the case provided him with a lesson he would remember all his years at the bar.

It looked like a hopeless cause. Branca advised the woman to plead guilty, believing he had material on which he could make a touching plea for leniency. She resolutely refused to so plead.

The case came on at the Vancouver Fall Assize of 1926, before Mr. Justice Frank Gregory and a jury of eleven men and one woman. Judge Gregory, who had been Colonel Gregory before he became a judge, was a military-looking man, erect of bearing and firm of stride. After the jury had retired to consider its verdict, Branca, feeling he had done rather well, was in the tiled third floor corridor when he heard the sound of Judge Gregory's boots, with steel tips and heels, resounding from the judges' hall. As the judge turned the corner and came face to face with the twenty-three-year-old defender, he took his short curved pipe from his mouth and said, "Can't think why that damned jury is taking so long. Your client's guilty as hell." They had been out scarcely half an hour. Fifty-eight minutes after retiring, the jury came back with the verdict: not guilty. Branca resolved that never as long as he was at the bar would he try to change the mind of a client who wanted to plead not guilty.

Several Police Court successes of sufficient interest to earn headlines followed. As a result, a reporter of some eminence was sent to cover one of his cases in order to write a feature article. It was a case Branca lost, but he did so with such style that the reporter wrote of "a ripple of applause from the spectators in the courtroom as he sat down after holding the large throng spellbound." The article was headed "The Boy Barrister." Branca was making his mark.

By the time he had been three years at the bar, ambitious students who wanted early experience of trial work were applying to serve articles with him. The first of a long line of articled students was a young man of great promise and self-confidence. Duncan Crux completed his articles with Branca and was a leading all-round barrister and solicitor before turning to high finance and becoming, in the sixties, the central figure in the rise and fall of the Commonwealth Trust empire.

Branca, mindful of all he had gained from early exposure to the higher courts, often had his students gowned and at his side when he was defending in Supreme Court, and sometimes sitting in as spectators when he was not. Having told them to be sensitive—as he always was—to every remark made by the judge, to see if it could be turned to advantage, he was delighted when one student came back to the office with a characteristic story of Senator Farris in action. Using the chance remarks of judges, the senator could win cases.

The hardware and appliance firm of Mac and Mac were suing the CPR, claiming that a fire which damaged their warehouse was caused through track workers leaving burning material undoused at quitting time. It seemed that an assortment of people had passed between tracks and warehouse that night, all happening to be carrying cameras.

A young man saw a small fire and took pictures. Then a maiden lady whose hobby was photography happened to pass and she photographed the fire, which by now was larger and nearer the warehouse. Next a courting couple came by; the young man was a keen photographer, and the fire was still larger. They all tendered enlargements of their pictures to the court in support of the *Mac and Mac* case.

The senator, defending the CPR, sat watching the evidence against him literally piling up. He pulled a single photograph out of his file, studied it intently and replaced it. He repeated this half a dozen times. Finally Chief Justice Morrison could restrain his curiosity no longer. "Is it possible," he asked, "that you, too, Senator, are going to spend half a day putting in photographs?"

This was the opening the maestro was seeking. With a smile, and a bow to the jury to make sure they felt included in the joke, he replied, "Oh, no, my lord. *We* were not so fortunate as to have *all* our photographers patrolling the back lane of Cordova Street on that historic night." The jurors all laughed, as he intended they should.

Then, when their time came, they threw the case out.

Within the East End community, people of any prominence were expected to accept certain responsibilities. An old-style ward alderman like Harry DeGraves, if he came across a hard luck story, would consider it his function to round up some more fortunate person who could lend a hand. More than once he called Branca to tell him about a family with sickness in the house and no fuel, and the lawyer would telephone his client George Kirk, of the Kirk Coal Company, and that good citizen would donate a load of coal and deliver it free of charge. It was not the best way for a lawyer to keep his clients, but it was part of coexisting.

DeGraves woke Branca late one night in 1929 to say there had been a shooting and someone would be required to defend a young Italian on a hanging charge if they ever caught him. He added that there would be no money in it. This was the *Nasso* case, later luridly described, in a book long out of print, as "A Black Flash of Passion in Vancouver."

In the Italian community on Keefer Street, twenty-six-year-old Domenico Nasso loved nineteen-year-old Concettina Agostino. They became engaged. Papa Tony Agostino said that before he could marry his daughter the young man must save $300. Domenico was a carpenter, but to earn money faster he went as a miner to the little Rocky Mountain settlement of Nordegg, near Banff.

Nasso took longer than promised. Finally he arrived to claim his bride, saying he had $310. Tony doubted his word about the money and went on to say that, anyway, he had promised Concettina to Sardario, son of his best friend Di Facio, still in Sicily. As he rose from his chair, waving his pipe, Nasso shot him through the heart.

The fourteen-year-old brother of the girl hit the gunman over the head with a broom, then dived under a table when the gun was pointed at him. A click, then another, indicated that the gun was misfiring, and brother and sister fled. Nasso followed and fired two shots, both missing. The girl ran into the corner store, and a bullet smashed through the window.

Bullets and perhaps all passion spent, Nasso disappeared. After midnight, he gave himself up and admitted the shooting. He had $155 in his pockets. Angelo Branca, a month after his twenty-sixth birthday, had his first murder defence.

The case, at the Vancouver Spring Assize of 1929, was marked by high drama. The widow demanded a life for a life. Pointing to Nasso she said, "I want justice. My husband die. I want him die."

Nasso denied nothing except the intent to kill, saying he pulled the trigger intending only to scare his victim. But he, too, made his contribution to drama. He testified that Agostino's condition for consent to marry his daughter was that he "put his hand in the Black Hand." In the twenties that was a term for joining the Mafia.

The jury was out only forty minutes, and found Nasso guilty. There was no recommendation for mercy. He was sentenced to be hanged. The sentencing was described by a newspaper thus: "Nasso stood up bravely under the ordeal. He did not change colour when he learned of his fate, and he retained the same stoical demeanour in the Provincial Police cell."

Nasso was hanged on 23 July 1929 at Oakalla Jail. Before he went to the place of execution he gave his jailer a letter addressed to Branca thanking him for trying so hard and saying he was ready to meet his Maker.

In 1928, with the law practice flourishing, Angelo Branca and his schooldays sweetheart Viola Miller set their wedding date. They were married on 18 June at the Catholic Church of St. Michael's in Olympia, Washington, the home town of the bride's parents. They set up their first home on Triumph Street near Exhibition Park.

Expansion was in the air. Vancouver absorbed the municipalities of Point Grey and South Vancouver. The first quarter of 1929 brought the greatest boom Vancouver had known. It had eighty-three millionaires. And there was only one lawyer to every 933 people. (By 1981, the ratio would be one to 208, a comparison which, if it is not to be misleading, must take account of the increase in institutional lawyers through the advent of public prosecutors and defenders and the growth of government and business law departments.)

Demonstrating the upsurge in public confidence, people turned out in thousands to cheer any civic event, whether it was the laying of the foundation stone for the new Hotel Vancouver or the triumphal homecoming of native son Percy Williams after sprinting for two gold medals at the Amsterdam Olympic Games.

The populace, conscious of prosperity, rushed to profit from it. Record numbers of speculators invested record amounts of money in a record number of new issues on the Vancouver Stock Exchange. Angelo Branca, participating in most things in the community, was not going to be left out of this. Friends were riding with the market to ever higher profits. As the market prospered, his own investments increased. Soon his resources, like those of most of the young professional men he knew, were in junior stocks, mainly mining and oil. Angelo and Viola bought a new home in the 2500-block of Cambridge Street. "Everyone was going along as though there would be no tomorrow," he says ruefully now.

The crash of October 1929 devastated his assets. He did not have any Advance Oil, which went from $18 to $0.69, or George Copper, which dropped from $12.25 to $1.10, but the seemingly sounder stocks he had bought fared almost as badly. Even the conservative investors met disaster when Home Oil went from $26.50 to $3.15, and the shares of The Asbestos Company, listed as one of Canada's top fifty companies, dropped from $27 to $1.

For many it meant ruin. For Branca it was the first real setback of his life. The need for discipline, which years later he would teach law students was a requirement for success in that profession, was already instinctive to him. As he and Viola contemplated the ruins of their investments he said, "We've been running the biggest charity practice this side of Ross Mountain. This has to stop."

They retrenched, at the office and at home. They decided that until they were on their feet again she would have $2 a day to run the home and he would walk to and from the office to save the streetcar fare. In 1930, the rising young lawyer was walking four miles a day to save fourteen cents.

CHAPTER FOUR

"Old Fighter Branca," the *Vancouver Sun* called him in 1978 in type half an inch high. The term was apt. "Fighter" describes both his temperament and his courtroom and public image. It also recalls that he was once amateur middleweight boxing champion of Canada.

Two factors having much to do with Branca's professional success have been his energy and his physical fitness. Many marvelled at the long hours he worked and the fast pace at which he did everything. An average of fourteen hours a day, six days a week, for thirty years, is his estimate. Not many knew how intense was the fitness regime that helped him to keep it up. For fifteen years he ran ten miles most days. (How did a busy lawyer spare time for all that running? By starting about 6:00 A.M.—often 5:30, says his wife—and using the measured track at McLean or Hastings parks. This was running, not jogging, geared to ten miles in sixty minutes.)

At Britannia High School he played rugby. With his natural energy he was in his element in a sport aptly described as "elegant violence." His position was hooker, at the centre of the violence. After graduation he played most of the sports available, and when he was a lawyer he still took part in athletics. He ran, and was beaten, in the first six-mile race promoted by the Sons of Italy in 1927.

One sport in which he had no interest was swimming, though his brothers could swim across the inlet. Contact sport, conflict with a personal adversary, is more to his taste.

One of the oddest stories in the province's sporting history is of Angelo Branca taking up boxing at an age when most boxers hang up their gloves, and winning a championship.

With his expanding law practice demanding longer hours, Branca was hard pressed to find time for long-distance running. Half a block from his office was the police gymnasium. The courtroom animosity of prosecution witnesses and defence counsel never interfered with his relationship with the police. He squeezed many a half-hour of exercise between his law office interviews. He worked out on the punching bag and with a skipping rope. If a policeman lacked a sparring partner in the ring, Branca obliged.

The police at that time had a noted boxing instructor, a well-liked old Negro named George Paris. He told Branca he had more natural talent than he had ever seen in a novice, and said he could make him a champion. Branca had a different ambition. The Depression was beginning to bite, and he wanted to start an athletic club for the jobless boys of East Vancouver. Boxing was having a boom. Jimmy McLarnin, born and raised in the East End, was well on his way in the career that brought the welterweight championship of the world to Vancouver in 1934. The boys whose interest Angelo Branca wanted to capture were more likely to be impressed by a successful boxer than a successful lawyer.

He started the Queensberry Athletic Club, named after the celebrated Englishman whose Marquess of Queensberry Rules governed the sport of boxing worldwide until recent times. During his visit to Vancouver in 1888, the marquess had "graciously consented" to referee a boxing contest at Hart's Opera House (a former skating rink) on Carrall Street, but ruined the gesture by not arriving until the bout was over.

In 1934, the Meraloma Club, which still flourishes, was a power in Vancouver sporting circles. That was the year in which its football team lost to Sarnia in the Grey Cup final. To the East End, the Meralomas represented all the arrogance of the Kitsilano-Kerrisdale-Point Grey elite.

Having a strong boxing section, the club sponsored a tournament to select the province's amateur champions. Branca was thirty-one, had been a practising lawyer for eight years and had never boxed in a contest in public. He was persuaded to enter to boost his boys' club and to strike a blow for East Vancouver. One Saturday night, in the old Vancouver Auditorium, Branca was in the final, fighting before 7000 people. His opponent was Jim Stevens of the Meralomas. The gong sounded, and for half a minute Stevens almost overwhelmed Branca with a flurry of punches. Then Branca counterpunched, and inside a minute he had won by a technical knockout.

This win qualified him for the Pacific Coast "Golden Gloves" championships, to be held that year in Portland. Poor Paris thought he had a thirty-one-year-old worldbeater, and he was deeply disappointed when lawyer Branca felt he must keep an appointment to meet Attorney General Gordon Sloan on the day of the tournament. He had a family to support, and it was the middle of the Depression.

He had another reason to welcome the clash of dates that excused him from boxing in Portland. On the night he fought Jim Stevens at the Auditorium, he had sat with his young wife watching the preliminary bouts. She had never told him that she worried about his boxing, but as the time for his contest approached he found she was trembling. He stopped entering tournaments.

Only once was he persuaded to box in public again, and that was for a good cause—to help the pioneering Hastings Community Association raise money to build a community centre. Jack Henderson, of Vancouver, was rated as one of the best boxers in Canada. After he had beaten the top middleweights in eastern Canada, someone put forward the idea of matching him with Angelo Branca for the Canadian championship, with all proceeds going towards the community centre.

The organizers added 1500 chairs to the 5000 seats already in the Forum and sold every one, and the contest took place before the largest audience seen in the building up to that time. Branca knocked out Henderson in the second round. Throughout Branca's career the handsome bronze statuette of a boxer, the trophy he won for his Canadian amateur championship, has decorated his desk whether in law office or judge's chambers.

Keeping physically fit, which he relates directly to mental alertness, has been a passion all his working life. He weighed 160 pounds and stood five feet nine inches at fifteen years of age when playing rugby for Britannia. He was inside the middleweight limit of 160 pounds when he boxed in the thirties. He weighed 180 pounds when he retired from the bench.

Not many would adopt his work and eating regime: for breakfast, a cup of black coffee; midday court recess devoted to working, though he could be persuaded to spare a few minutes for coffee if someone wanted to talk; another cup of coffee at the end-of-day adjournment; followed by another session with papers or witnesses or law books, and a substantial dinner. That was his normal routine when he was fighting cases in the courts.

When out of town, he would work in his hotel room, first on the current case. Preparation for the upcoming session complete, out would come files of cases due to be heard in weeks to come. The case at bar must have been a difficult one if the day and evening went by without his dictating a few tapes for mailing to his office for transcription.

On upcountry Assize tours his work habits amazed local lawyers. Alan Graham, Q.C., prosecuting at a Cranbrook Assize, came into court one day shaking his head in puzzlement. He knew his adversary Branca's program the previous day: a long day in court defending a man charged with murder; from 5:00 to 7:00 in the evening interviewing witnesses; then off to a spaghetti dinner given in his honour by the local Italian community at which, of course, he made the main speech. After that he would be back in his hotel room reviewing his case notes and preparing his cross-examination for the morrow.

What caused Graham's wonderment was that on the way into court he had been stopped by the building manager who wanted to know whether this lawyer from Van-

couver had the right to demand a janitor be at the courthouse at 7:00 every morning just to let him into the law
library.

Long hours at his practice plus his gymnasium and road
work did not exhaust his energies. He had inherited the
Italian love of the soil and the Lombardese way with
flowers, and in every spare hour he tackled gardening with
vigour. Gardening has been a hobby and a relief from the
pressures of law all his working life.

Next to the Brancas' Cambridge Street home were two
vacant lots owned by the City and on offer at $200 each,
but no one would pay that price in the thirties. They were
overrun with hard to clear Himalaya berries. Hating to
see good land wasted, Branca attacked those berry canes,
turned the soil over twice, manured it, then made it a
vegetable garden. "By the time I had it like I wanted it,"
he says, "I was able to give everyone up and down the
street an open invitation to help themselves—beans, cabbages, lettuce. The peppers—I've never been able to grow
peppers like those since."

Reminded of times years later when the flowers in the
garden of their West 24th Avenue home made it a show-
place, he exclaimed, "Do you remember the daffodils? We
had a carpet of yellow daffodils—it would be, I suppose,
fifteen feet by twenty-five feet—and the daffs were those
huge King Alfreds, every one tight against the next. It
was a glorious sight."

A routine of constant pressure usually calls for some
form of indulgence. Branca smoked heavily. When he was
in his fifties, X-rays revealed a condition requiring major
surgery. He lost a lung but there was no malignancy.
Before long he was smoking again, increasingly.

Before Branca became a judge, Joe Cohen bet him
$1000 that he could not give up smoking for a year, with
the stake going to an Italian charity. The cheque, framed,
hangs in his den. "I realize now Joe did it for my own
good," he says.

Later Joe Segal bet him $2000 that Branca could not
give up alcohol for a year. After eleven abstemious
months, Segal called him to say, "I hear you and Vi are

going on a European holiday. I wouldn't want you to arrrive in Italy and not be able to try all those beautiful wines. So you win. The cheque's in the mail and all you have to do is fill in the payee." (Branca's friends run the gamut. Cohen of Sony Canada and Segal of Fields and Hudson's Bay stores, as well as Jack Diamond, are named in *The Canadian Establishment,* Peter C. Newman's book "About the 1,000 Men Who Run Canada.")

Branca drank wine at home from boyhood and still does, and he has made wine with some expertise as a hobby for years, but he has seen too many drink-ruined lawyers to be more than a convivial social drinker. Sadness comes into his voice when, speaking of some legal acquaintance who fell short of his potential, he says, "Too bad. He didn't take care of himself."

Branca struck blows for the East End in the courtroom as well as in the ring, though the connection was incidental. He never used the courtroom as a forum for campaigns. He always represented a client, never a cause. The East End involvement arose from the way the drinking and gambling laws were applied. The Police Commission and city hall acted as though those laws applied only to Vancouver's east side. The police dry squad and gambling detail were the busiest sections of the force. In September 1936, thirty-three cabarets, restaurants and clubs lost their licences, and not one of them was west of Granville Street.

Branca was in demand to defend the raided operators. Once when defending the Venice Cafe he cried, "Why always pick on the East End?" and complained that restaurants in the West End were allowed to serve liquor without interference. "Whisky cached under the tables flowed like water at a recent police banquet in a West End restaurant," he told the court. A rebuttal by the police only confirmed his charge. A police spokesman told a newspaper, "It is grossly unfair to single out the Police Department for such criticism when organizations like the Board of Trade and the Association of Professional Engineers hold similar functions almost every night in the West End."

Many of Branca's courtroom successes of that kind were won when fighting against partiality in the enforcement of gambling laws. Among the clubs he defended on gaming charges was the Broadway Social Club, which had a registered membership of more than 2500. He argued that the club was doing nothing that was not being done with impunity for higher stakes at the Vancouver Club, the pinnacle of prestige. In that case he secured a decision which altered the operation of the law. Up to that time, despite a ruling of the Supreme Court of Canada making bona fide clubs legitimate places for certain forms of gaming, British Columbia had continued to ban such clubs. The *News Herald* reported, "One of the most interesting cases ever heard in Police Court was won by a splendid piece of pleading by A.E. Branca. This was his defence of the Broadway Club on a gaming charge. In it he showed beyond cavil that it was a bona fide club." The ruling was used to legitimize similar clubs in communities all over British Columbia, including several in Vancouver with memberships running into thousands.

Street fighter as a schoolboy. Champion boxer as a man. Courtroom fighter as a lawyer. The pattern is consistent. "Gladiator" was one of Chief Justice J.O. Wilson's words for him in welcoming him to his Supreme Court bench in 1963. Once Branca agreed to defend someone, that person had a champion who would not stop fighting until there was a decision.

A squalid statutory rape trial, *Rex* v. *Moody and Lawson,* illustrates Branca's tenacity in defence. The trial in 1951 was scheduled to last under three days but became the longest alleged rape case in British Columbia legal history because Branca fought and fought.

Two longshoremen driving from Seattle for a weekend in Vancouver picked up two runaway girls aged fourteen and thirteen and took them to a motel on Kingsway. In the early hours of the next morning the younger girl left the cabin by a window and walked for several kilometres along Kingsway. When a policeman stopped and questioned her, she told of going to the motel and said the two men had had sexual intercourse with her.

The men were put on trial. The simple issue was

whether the story that the younger girl told the police officer was true. Branca (appearing for Moody) and Hugh McGivern (for Lawson) based their defence on the men's assertions that there had been heavy drinking but no sexual intercourse. What turned a two-day trial into an eleven-day wrangle was Branca's step-by-step opposition to Mr. Justice Manson's conduct of the trial.

At the preliminary hearing the older girl at first said she had seen the sexual acts her friend complained about. Under Branca's cross-examination she admitted she had passed out from liquor and all she knew was what the younger girl had told her.

Branca assumed that that admission closed the door to her saying anything incriminating at the jury trial, and the prosecutors, Tom Hurley and George (later Mr. Justice) Murray, did not try to introduce her original statement. To Branca's horror, after the girl said she remembered nothing, Mr. Justice Manson leaned over and said, "Little girl, now tell the story you first told." Immediately Branca jumped up and objected. The judge told him to sit down or he would be removed from the court. Branca replied that he would remain on his feet until his objection was recognized. "Arrest him," cried the judge. "Contempt of court."

Two court orderlies took up position on either side of the lawyer, and the three headed for the lockup downstairs. In the lockup Branca had time only to take off his gown when he was asked to return to the courtroom, where the judge, having changed his mind, ordered the Crown to proceed.

Murray continued with the girl's evidence, making no mention of the retracted statement. But before long Judge Manson and Branca were in conflict again. The Assize Book, in which the clerk notes procedural incidents, records the proceedings thus:

Mr. Branca objects. Court adjourns to consider objection. . . . Mr. Branca objects to evidence of witness. Court objects to Mr. Branca interfering. . . . Mr. Branca asks for retirement of jury regarding his motion. Court refuses. . . . Motion to Court of

Appeal. Court upholds Mr. Branca's motion. . . . Court adjourns to study authority for objections. . . . Mr. Branca objects to re-examination. Court disallows objection. . . . Motion by Mr. Branca. Court overrules motion. . . . Motion for directed verdict refused. . . . Mr. Branca asks Court to allow objections to charge to the jury. Court refuses. Mr. Branca objects and argues. . . .

No series of entries more suggestive of dogged defence can be found in any Assize Book since the Supreme Court came to Vancouver in 1902.

George Murray managed to guide the Crown's case through most of the turbulence between trial judge and defence lawyer, but Tom Hurley, an advocate of the old school with a well-grounded respect for judges, was scandalized at Branca's constant clashes with his lordship. When the two old friends differed on one objection, Branca told Hurley he had always admired him for his concern for the rights of the individual, "but not any more." At this Hurley naturally took offence, and it was a long time before their mutual regard restored the friendship.

As the door closed on the jurors going out to consider their verdict, Branca jumped to his feet to object that the judge, in his charge to the jury, had spent two and a half hours explaining the prosecution's case and only six and a half minutes for the defence.

Manson, unmoved, retorted, "Throughout this trial your attitude has been one of defiance."

The strain of waiting hour after hour for the jury's return drove the whimsical McGivern to poetry. The idea of arch-defender Hurley acting as prosecutor struck him as hilarious. To create a diversion, McGivern had a sheriff's deputy deliver to Crown counsel's room a note headed "Prognostication," on which he had scribbled:

> Tom Hurley was a lawyer bold.
>   He acted for the poor.
> He pleaded with a voice of gold,
>   And his defence was sure.

Until Misfortune, gaunt and grim,
   On Hurley cast its frown
And Tom found, through its fickle whim,
   He acted for the Crown.

And now he roars with righteous heat,
   "Give me their blood!" He wails,
"Take honest men from off the street
   And fill up all our jails."

The jury sat with puzzled look.
   "We think it strange," they mused.
"We'll scrap each section of the book.
   Discharge the two accused."

One brave woman wrecked McGivern's prognostication. Word leaked out that from the moment the jurors started their deliberations, the eleven men favoured acquittal and the solitary woman wanted the two accused jailed. They pleaded with her to make it unanimous; she said she would hold out forever. After ten hours, they sent a message to the judge that agreement was impossible. He discharged them and ordered a new trial.

Sometime after 3:00 A.M., Branca went home and told his wife that defending a fellow you despised, and losing a couple of weeks to do it, and antagonizing both the judge and your old friend Hurley, then finding yourself with a hung jury and a new trial, was a hell of a way to practise law but there was no other once you had accepted a defence.

Branca and McGivern won in the end. Mr. Justice Wood and a different jury tried the men on the rehearing. The charges were the same; the same counsel fought the case. They completed it in three days, and the jury said not guilty.

CHAPTER FIVE

Winning cases that attracted newspaper attention helped the Branca practice survive the Depression and extended his reputation over a wider area. The thirties were a lean time for lawyers as for others, and would have been lean indeed for Branca had he depended for his fees on the hard-hit east side.

During the Depression, Branca, looking out of his second-floor office windows, would have seen a charge by mounted police along Hastings Street when the longshoremen were on strike; or police carrying rifles on each corner of the intersection during the invasion of men from the relief camps; or women taking food through the police cordon to demonstrators occupying the upper floors of the Carnegie Library opposite. He might even have heard the boos of protesters drowning the voice of Mayor Gerry McGeer when he tried to make a speech at the church nearby.

Branca's growing reputation was bringing clients from farther afield, but to neighbourhood people he could still be generous with his time. The *De Bortoli* case showed that, and says something about the people who lived and worked in the East End. All who knew the relationship between teachers, parents and pupils at Strathcona School recall the respect that immigrant parents gave the teachers, and the affection of the teachers for the students.

Pete De Bortoli was a poor student but a likable boy. When he landed in jail at nineteen, convicted of intent to

murder two policemen, his former teachers were incredu-
lous. Pete told a teacher who visited him in jail that he
had not been near the crime, and a witness swore Pete
was elsewhere, but the court believed he had manufac-
tured the alibi. "You know me," said Pete. "I'm too dumb
to be that smart."

Other teachers found that the neighbourhood was convinced Pete had been railroaded. "Better see Branca,"
people told them. Three teachers who went to Branca's
office learned that he had not been on the case, knew
nothing about it and was not going to pay out of his own
pocket for a transcript of the trial. He told them that if
they could raise the cost of the transcript, and if it contained any grounds at all, he would appeal without fee.

Two women teachers went collecting around the community. If people could not afford to give, they were help-
ful with advice. "Go see Mrs. So-and-So on Alexander
Street. She always gives," they were told. There they were
warmly invited in, marvelled at the ornate furnishings,
collected a donation and decided when they saw how
many nubile "daughters" the lady seemed to have that
this was no place for respectable young teachers.

The money for the transcript was soon collected,
though they suspected much of it came from bootleggers,
because not many other people in the area had money to
spare.

Branca read the transcript. Four men in a car and two
police officers in another had fought a bloodless gun duel
while careering through Vancouver streets after a robbery
attempt. The question was whether Pete had been one of
the four. Branca lodged an appeal.

On a June night in 1935 he caught the midnight boat to
Victoria. In Court of Appeal he ignored Pete's alibi. He
challenged the evidence of identification, submitting that
it was not enough for the Crown to prove that paint from
the gunmen's car had been found on Pete's *brother's* coat,
which Pete sometimes wore, or that shells similar to those
fired at the police were found in his *brother's* room, which
Pete sometimes used. Branca was back that evening to
tell the teachers the outcome: conviction quashed. The
boy was free.

When I asked Branca about the case almost forty-five years later, he had forgotten all about it. Under prompting, some details came to mind and he asked, "Was that the fellow who got twenty years for a bank robbery on Broadway and I got him off, and he rose to become one of our better bootleggers?" In fact, the sentence was twelve years and the robbery was of a drugstore. He had total recall of his first high court success in 1926, but a success ten years later was routine and thus unmemorable.

One fine Sunday morning in the unusually hot summer of 1938, Angelo and Viola Branca were driving to Holy Rosary Cathedral for early Mass. They had planned a round of golf after church, and the first service there was earlier than in their own parish. On Hastings Street they saw men running and police giving chase, and heard shouting and the smashing of glass. The big windows of Woodward's and Spencer's stores were in shards. On the sidewalk lay the prone figures of women, stylishly dressed, motionless and one headless. They proved to be manikins wrenched from window displays. It was Bloody Sunday, 19 June: the post office riot.

Fortunately for Branca, there were many other witnesses. He had already been named as prosecutor for the next Assize, and a lawyer is barred from prosecuting if needed as a witness. (On one occasion in the Interior, a lawyer received a long-awaited appointment to prosecute at the Assize and had to surrender it and become a witness because he happened to see a murder.)

This was Branca's first assignment to prosecute at an Assize, and it was to become the most politically charged Assize in the history of the province. How did he relish prosecuting unemployed men—Branca, who in the public mind had been cast in the role of champion of the underdog? His reply illustrates his idea of a lawyer's responsibilities: "It didn't bother me one bit. I knew there was a lot of sympathy for the post office rioters but that was no concern of mine. My job was to present the facts, all the facts."

The post office riot was unusual in that many decent, law-abiding citizens openly sympathized with the demonstrators. It created, for the time being at least, two folk heroes: the leader of the demonstrators, orange-sweatered Steve Brodie, and CCF politician Harold Winch, whose appeals to angry crowds averted worse violence.

After the closing of the relief camps, the thousands of unemployed in Vancouver had tried to live by tag days and "tincanning"—collecting in the streets—until the city council banned that activity as begging. An estimated 150 unemployed men marched into the post office, the art gallery and the Georgia Hotel, their object being to force the authorities to provide relief. The tactic was to be non-violent, and Brodie told the men they should demand to be arrested and tried by law. The authorities had a different tactic. They refused to arrest the demonstrators and ordered them to vacate the premises.

The men in the Georgia accepted the hotel manager's offer of $600 for relief funds, and left. A month later the others were still holding the two public buildings when strong forces of RCMP and city police assembled outside. They gave the demonstrators twenty minutes to get out, and after half an hour they fired tear gas. At the art gallery, the men came out choking and coughing, but heeded Harold Winch's appeal to remain peaceable.

At the post office, police in gas masks went in and, as the *Sun* report says, "clubbed the men into the streets where they were attacked by other police. The sight of the police swinging into the fleeing men with their clubs and billies infuriated the crowd." Demonstrators and spectators began smashing windows. They damaged thirty-four stores, a government office and a bank.

The situation worsened as the day wore on. A crowd estimated at 2000 gathered in front of the police station demanding the release of the 23 who had been arrested. Police faced them with loaded rifles. A woman spat at an officer, causing him to throw up a hand, which enraged people nearby who thought he had struck her. Harold Winch, standing on a car roof, defused an ugly situation by hauling the woman up beside him and making her say she had not been hit.

Ten thousand people packed the Powell Street Grounds

after word had gone round that a protest meeting would be addressed by Brodie. They were further inflamed by what they learned there. The orange sweater intended to make their leader easily recognized by the demonstrators had also made him obvious to the police, who had beaten him so thoroughly that he was in hospital.

More demonstrations took place at the police station, more store windows were smashed and crowds milled around downtown until midnight. Thousands assembled at Pier D in support of a delegation that was leaving for Victoria on the night ferry. When it became known that the delegation's meeting with government was postponed, there were calls to throw the police out of the post office and reoccupy it. This time Harold Winch climbed a lamp standard to plead with them, and again more bloodshed was avoided.

Mayor George Miller broadcast to the public on radio and blamed the disorders on Communists. The voters were not impressed, for soon afterwards, in a municipal election in which the Non-Partisan Association achieved almost a complete sweep, they ousted its leader the mayor.

Steve Brodie, put out of action before the property wrecking began, was not among those whom Branca prosecuted. Forty years later, when Brodie was retired in Victoria, his memories of those times were not of Bolshevist plotting but of the faith of Vancouver's East End people in the British monarchy. Interviewed by Howie Smith for the radio documentary "Bloody Sunday," Brodie said, "You could walk into a hundred houses in the East End of Vancouver and on the kitchen wall you would see a picture, cut out of a newspaper, of His Royal Highness the Prince of Wales where he had been to visit unemployed miners. The caption, quoting him, was 'Something must be done.' But most of the people who had his picture on the wall interpreted that as 'Something will be done.' You'd be surprised how much the Prince had to do with keeping the people in hope in spite of all their despair."

Branca was working on the Crown's case against the Bloody Sunday rioters when labour conflict flared into violence at Blubber Bay on Texada Island, and his Assize calendar swelled as a consequence.

Bitterness during a four-month strike against the Pacific Lime Company intensified when the owners tried to keep the mine and plant operating with imported labour, and the Provincial Police sent a strong force to the island. Violence erupted as the Union Steamship Company *Chelohsin* docked at the settlement and a further contingent of imported workers came ashore.

Police ordered the strikers crowding the dock, mostly white men, to disperse. They refused. At this point about a hundred Chinese who were also on strike moved out of their bunkhouses and towards the dock. They may or may not have been going to reinforce the hostile mob. The police thought they were and fired tear gas, then charged. Twelve strikers were taken to hospital. A policeman who became separated from the others was kicked unconscious.

The political recriminations were almost as bitter as the strike. Heeding allegations of police provocation and collusion with strikebreakers, Attorney General Gordon Wismer recommended a judicial inquiry. Premier Duff Pattullo overruled his recommendation. The Crown charged more than fifty strikers with rioting or unlawful assembly. Union officials in turn caused charges to be laid against a police constable for doing grievous bodily harm and against twenty strikebreakers for lesser offences.

The Assizes, followed with intense interest by a partisan public, were peaceful compared with the turmoil that had produced the charges. In the event, by normal operation of the law, the number of those who stood trial in Assize Court was much reduced. Of the twenty-three arrested in the post office riot, seven had their cases dismissed at their preliminary hearings. Branca, after interviewing scores of witnesses, secured the attorney general's authority to stay proceedings against others. Juries were sympathetic, especially after hearing witnesses like the one who said, "The tear gas was worse than the gas attack that nearly killed me in the war." Juries convicted only two rioters, and Mr. Justice Murphy let both off with a fine, which sympathizers paid.

In the Blubber Bay cases, those whom the union charged were all acquitted in County Court. Of the strikers and their coaccused supporters, many were acquitted in Police Court and County Court. Twelve were sent for trial at the Assize and there convicted, some of rioting and some of unlawful assembly; they were given prison sentences ranging from three to six months.

Knowing that the company paid the expenses of all who gave evidence on its behalf, Branca undertook to press the attorney general to pay the expenses of those who gave evidence for the strikers.

The Assize ran from 12 September to 21 December, and by the time it was over the labour climate was improving. The exceptional length of the session gave Branca some sly amusement. In those days the attorney general, not having any staff prosecutors, appointed the Crown prosecutor, for the duration of the Assize, from lawyers in private practice. For two or three years Branca had thought his achievements at the criminal bar had earned him a turn as prosecutor, but in those lean times many other good Liberal lawyers wanted the perquisite. Those who controlled such patronage thought Branca was a young man in too much of a hurry and told him his turn would come. In fact, when it did come he was at thirty-five the youngest ever to be so appointed.

Of more significance for the Branca family was that payment was by the day, and in those years no other Assize had exceeded four weeks. When his eighteen weeks' Assize was over, Branca's bill to the attorney general was $11 280—derisory by today's standards but wealth in the Depression. For the first time since Black Thursday the Brancas were financially on their feet again.

The drawn out contests of that Assize strengthened Branca's acquaintance with the remarkable Murphys. Facing Judge Murphy daily, he had at his side Paul Murphy, who had been appointed assistant Crown counsel for the Assize before it was known his father would be presiding. Branca found he had an associate as dedicated to preparation as himself.

"There was never a more thorough trial lawyer than Paul Murphy," he says. "When he took medical malpractice suits he would study every known textbook and take coaching from a medical consultant on the matter in dispute, and he would go into court able to talk about that operation like a top surgeon. Doctors dreaded his cross-examination.

"All three Murphy boys were brilliant lawyers. All died young. Paul and Denis, the identical twins, were the unconventional ones. Bill was the perfect corporation lawyer, company director, wartime brigadier, D.S.O. winner. He was one of the wittiest men in town. When Harry Sullivan became a Supreme Court judge, some of us gave him a dinner and asked Bill Murphy to make a speech. He said it was fitting that the Murphys should be looking up to a Sullivan on the bench because the Murphys had always looked up to the Sullivans, even back in the old country. At the dawn of Irish history, when the Murphys were inventing the potato, even then they looked up to the Sullivans. They had to, he said, because the Sullivans were still up in the trees."

CHAPTER SIX

By 1939 Angelo Branca's awareness of the link between politics and professional advancement was forcing him to one of the major decisions of his career. His life ambition had been formed by the time he finished articling—to be a judge of the highest court of his province. Should he pursue the ambition by concentrating on the practice of law? Or by running for political office?

From the days of the first appointment to the British Columbia Supreme Court after Confederation, which Dr. Ormsby's classic *British Columbia: A History* calls "a blatant political circumstance," the main stairway to the bench in this as in other provinces was by way of politics. Many of the best judges this province ever had, and certainly all the worst, went to the bench from the political arena.

Already a lawyer for a dozen years and busy in politics for longer, Branca knew how many judges were former cabinet ministers, M.P.s or M.L.A.s. It was their ultimate reward. Unless a person loved the excitement of governing, a judgeship or other patronage appointment was about all that politics offered a good lawyer. When Senator Farris unexpectedly resigned as provincial attorney general while at the top of his power, he explained that he simply could not afford the financial sacrifice that the post entailed. His ambition never was to be a judge. Years later, when the post of chief justice of the B.C. Supreme Court could have been his, he let it go to his brother Wendell. Such were the prerogatives of Liberal power.

Branca was born a Liberal at a time when almost every Italian in Canada was a Liberal. He laughed when I told him of Chief Justice J.O. Wilson's experience while conducting citizenship ceremonies as County Court judge of the Cariboo. Among the candidates was a little man who, beaming with anticipation, clearly knew what he was supposed to say when questioned. So Judge Wilson called him first and asked, "Well, Giuseppe, do you know what it means to be a Canadian?"

"Sure, Judge," said Giuseppe. "Sure. Vote Liberal."

The Liberal Party welcomed the articulate and energetic young Branca from the Italian community. They needed all the friends they could find to combat the challenge of the small but growing CCF in East Vancouver, and quickly introduced him to the techniques of electioneering perfected by the Liberals in Vancouver Centre riding, techniques that were giving the city a reputation for the worst politics west of Montreal.

As late as 1950, when delivering the vote had become more straitlaced, Bruce Hutchison could write in his book *The Fraser* of "the famous machine that . . . for almost thirty years has appointed its princelings to senate and bench, has won elections with more money than prayers and always found that investment profitable."

The new recruit observed how the notary Di Paoli, when planning the Italians' big celebration of Columbus Day, or the Sons of Italy and the Veneta picnics, would call Centre Liberal Party, and on the day hundreds of gallons of beer would arrive, as well as party bagmen who would join in the fun to make sure everyone understood who had sent it.

The "princelings" who went to senate and bench were often lawyers from the Farris office. At a lower level were those who owed their government jobs to party influence, especially in the Attorney General's Department. This was the system that kept the wheels of politics turning, but Branca recognized its seamy underside when he saw how the sheriff's office, if it needed extra talesmen for jury duty, short-cut regular channels and called Centre Liberal Party's Division Two office, which always had individuals of irregular work habits ready to go to the court-house and pick up a fee, meagre though it was. Not being in Division Two himself, he wondered whether those jurors felt any partiality towards some highly political lawyers who were.

It was characteristic that the naked competitiveness of politics should so strongly appeal to him. The rewards are there. You go all out to gain them. If you don't, the others will. Branca became a zealous party activist. He even cut short his honeymoon for the Liberal Party.

He and Viola had set their wedding date when a provincial election was called. The party had a special mission for him. They were anxious to retain the Rossland-Trail seat and they believed Trail was the key.

West Kootenay lore says that from its earliest days the great Cominco company, in its hiring of smelter labour, had worked on the theory that Italians, with a higher dietary intake of olive oil, were less susceptible than most to the leadworkers' scourge, silicosis. It hired Italians in hundreds. (Coincidentally, Branca's father then had probably the largest olive and olive oil importing business in the west.)

By 1928, the Italian vote counted in the Rossland-Trail riding, and for the election the Liberals begged Branca to team up with a cabinet minister and, along with the party's chief organizer, Maj. Stan Moodie, to mount a high-pressure campaign there. Three days after Angelo and Viola were married, the bride was back with her parents while the bridegroom and the politicians barn-stormed for "Long Jim" MacDonald in one of the last of the old-style elections. Both sides played tricks that were long remembered in the Kootenays.

Knowing that Branca was corralling all the Italian voters for the Liberal candidate, the Conservatives countered by hiring a big Swedish straw boss to make Conservatives out of all the Scandinavians who abounded in the mining and logging camps. All morning on polling day, this man delivered carload after carload of his compatriots to the Conservative campaign rooms.

The local Liberals, worried by his success, looked to the

graduate of Vancouver Centre school of electioneering to do something. Branca said that if the Swede did not recognize him he would cope. As the vote boss deposited another carload of newly converted Conservatives in town, Branca congratulated him on his fine work and invited him to share a bottle of rye in appreciation. After more than a few drinks he was happy to accept Branca's suggestion that someone should drive him to pick up the next consignment.

The car that pulled to the curb was driven by a Liberal who, when they were halfway up a mountain road leading to a mine thirty-five kilometres from town, found a pretext to lure the man out of the car and left him there in the warm sunshine. He delivered no more votes.

"We had to do it," says Branca. "The other side were pulling more stunts than we were."

Perhaps that was why the other side won. That was the year the Conservatives returned thirty-seven members and ousted the Liberals. Branca's man lost by 467 votes. The cabinet minister, whose Omineca riding had been thought a safe seat, also lost. He had to wait five years to regain it. He was Attorney General Alec Manson.

The abuse heaped on the Centre "machine" ignores the fact that men of exceptional ability ran it. It delivered the vote, but it elected men who contributed much to good government. Because of his part in its politics as the top man of its Division Three, Branca sat in the higher councils of Liberal power when, following in the footsteps of the Farris brothers, a quartet of outstanding Liberals from Vancouver enlivened provincial and national politics. Three of them belonged to families having historic links with the country.

Gordon Sloan was that rarity, a fourth-generation British Columbian, descendant of great-grandparents who settled on Vancouver Island in 1849. His grandmother was the first white child born in Nanaimo. His father was a federal M.P. and a provincial minister of mines.

As a young man fresh from the Farris firm he became a brilliant attorney general. He believed the attorney general should himself fight the cases affecting his province that went to the Supreme Court of Canada, and he did so with success. He graced politics until made a judge, eventually becoming chief justice of British Columbia. His Royal Commissions and Sloan Reports on forestry influenced the industrial development of the province.

A dominant figure during Branca's political heyday in Centre was a man of giant frame and strong personality, Henry Castillou. His grandfather was a cavalryman in the French army that went to establish the Emperor Maximilian on the throne of Mexico. When that dream of empire ended with Maximilian's execution by firing squad, Joe Castillou sought refuge north of the Rio Grande.

He distinguished himself by driving a herd of longhorn cattle all the way from Texas to the Cariboo, where he became a rancher. Henry Castillou was born there, and was raised to ride the range and mend fences better than the best ranch hand. His fame among the Indians of the central Interior came with him when he moved to Vancouver to practise law, and he represented Indians in many trials. His activities in Vancouver Liberal politics ended only when he went back home to be County Court judge of Cariboo County.

Another lawyer-politician then busy stimulating or enraging his fellow Liberals was Gerry McGeer, variously M.P., M.L.A., senator and mayor of Vancouver, bubbling with ideas and an errant genius in his own way. Every time he came up with an original project his enemies would call it "McGeer's Folly." They said that of the present city hall, and it was years before people appreciated how farseeing McGeer had been by building it on a site then considered out of town.

Branca and McGeer were both sons of immigrant fathers of unusual talents. Both boys delivered milk to their fathers' customers. The senior McGeer, an Irish immigrant, built up a dairy business in South Vancouver. He also wrote poetry that won publication in London literary journals.

Both individualists, Angelo Branca and Gerry McGeer rarely saw eye to eye as lawyers or as Liberals. In his vote-catching campaigns to clean up civic corruption, McGeer cast a wide net, and Branca went to the defence of lower-ranking police officers whose tricky role as plainclothes investigators brought them within McGeer's blanket allegations. Branca fought him in the Police Commission, in court and in the press, and won a long battle for reinstatement to service or of pension rights for seventeen officers fired by McGeer. Branca and McGeer were usually on opposite sides in the Liberal councils.

For years they were hostile, but as they matured the mutual dislike slowly turned to friendship. Visitors to the mayor's chambers during McGeer's reign always remarked on the busts of his two heroes, Abraham Lincoln and Mackenzie King, which decorated his desk. On McGeer's early death in 1946, his brother Manfred presented the King statue to Branca as a memento of Gerry's friendship.

Of all the lawyer-politicians of Vancouver Centre, Gordon Sylvester Wismer was the one whose sheer ability impressed Branca, to the extent of holding his loyalty through times when Wismer had more critics than friends. He admired Wismer as a superb courtroom lawyer, equally successful as prosecutor or defender, and as a crowd-pleasing politician. He came to see him also as a reforming attorney general even when he was being accused of manipulating the issuance of liquor licences to strengthen his political position.

Wismer was a magnificent specimen of the political animal. One commentator wrote, "Gordon Wismer has not a mean bone in his big body." The *Toronto Telegram* civic affairs specialist Ron Haggart, a Vancouver native, wrote in that paper: "In spite of his good works the stale air of the old-time boss seemed always around. In his campaign rooms a young reporter could pass the time of day with hulking goons whose certain faith was that when the election was over they could get jobs as beer parlour waiters in the hotels of Wismer's downtown constituency."

The "good works" that helped Wismer retain Branca's support were the measures he either bulldozed or slyly eased through a contentious legislature. His amendments to the liquor laws changed forever the social habits of British Columbians. He probably altered drinking habits across Canada, for six provinces borrowed from his beer parlour legislation. He gave B.C. its first approach to an enlightened juvenile offender program, and he countered anti-Semitism by an ingenious use of the seditious libel laws.

When Premier John Hart resigned, Wismer seemed certain to succeed him, but in the weeks before the leadership convention resistance surfaced. The Farris interests supported him but his power broking had alienated B.C.'s representatives in the federal government and many of the Young Liberals, while the Interior constituencies reported growing resentment against Vancouver's domination.

Jimmy Sinclair and Art Laing sponsored a challenger, "Boss" Johnson, a backbencher, a self-made industrialist from New Westminster. The nickname did not denote his masterful qualities but came to him because his Icelandic parents, having christened him Bjorn, familiarized it in their idiom to "Bjosse" and his schoolmates distorted this to "Boss." He preferred Byron.

Branca always went into an election as he did a court case. His rule was: prepare, prepare; leave no possibility uncovered; work at it. Supporting Wismer, and hearing that Johnson's backers were drumming up delegate support in the interior of the province, he took it upon himself, through a few calls to men like his friend Pisapio in Trail, and Wismer's former law student Harold McInnes in Penticton, to trade on some old loyalties.

In the closing week, worried despite Wismer's supreme confidence, and knowing that man's talent for persuasion, Branca urged him to take another trip to the Interior. His suggestion unheeded, Branca then offered to fly with another campaigner to Prince Rupert and from there to drive to Vancouver, canvassing support in all the constituencies on the route south. Wismer laughed the idea off.

An exceptionally large assembly at the convention chose Johnson by 475 votes to 467. "A swing of five votes and we'd have had a different premier," says Branca. "I could have locked those up without any trouble in a swing through the central Interior."

Published reports said Johnson won because a delegate with eleven Wismer votes arrived too late to cast them. "I never knew whether the report of a delegate losing himself in the hall was true," says Branca. "By then, I think, Wismer's ambition was not the leadership. He dearly wanted to be a judge, especially after the Liberals lost power in Victoria, but he had enemies in Ottawa, and the Blair Fraser article didn't help him."

Fraser, writing scathingly of Vancouver politics in *Maclean's Magazine,* repeated stories about liquor licences. Wismer sued for libel, and won. He took the action, he explained, because the family had had a good name in Upper Canada for 200 years and he did not want those Wismers in Ontario to think he had sullied it in the west.

Long before these events, Branca had made his own political decision. In the late thirties he realized he now had to choose a route towards fulfilling his ambition to be a judge: via Victoria's legislative buildings or via the courtroom? He and his wife discussed which it would be.

The choice was hard. No one could look at the roster of judges without remarking how many had held political office. Against that, Branca loved practising law. He wanted to keep his technique sharp with frequent examining, cross-examining, arguing and addressing juries. He was dismayed to see how courtroom adversaries whom he had once admired no longer had their forensic skills when they returned to the courts after several years in politics. Royal ("Pat") Maitland was one. Remembering his formidable talents before he gave his full time to politics as Conservative leader, Branca expected a hard fight when he opposed him some years later in the Supreme Court of Canada. He was saddened to find him so out of touch with advocacy that when the judges began to press him Maitland apologized to the court and handed the case over to his associate counsel, Alfred Bull.

Also, the need to compromise that is so much a part of politics never comes naturally to Branca. In a profession proverbially accused of delays, Branca always pressed for action, and he would be intolerant of the procrastination that is almost inevitable in government.

A once-and-for-all decision was made. Liberal politics as an active side interest, yes; candidacy for elective office, no. Today Branca says, "You can't be a good lawyer and a good politician. I married the law and I stayed married to it."

Did the appointment of a certain controversial politician to the bench shortly before the moment of decision disillusion him? When asked that question the usually frank Branca only smiles. The politician was Alec Manson.

Meantime Branca was enjoying all kinds of community activities without the constraints on his time and his law practice that would have been involved in his being a member of the federal or provincial parliament. He was a force in several civic organizations. As chairman of the Hastings Ratepayers' Association he led a group of citizens who were trying to force city hall to provide more amenities for the East End. The cry then, as now, was, "City council discriminates against East in favour of West." Then, as now, the most visible evidence for that argument was the West's enjoyment of more public parks and recreation facilities.

Branca believed the area where he had spent his boyhood needed a park, and he also thought it was a disgrace to the city that rail passengers arriving at Union Station gained their first impression of Vancouver from the depressing sight of the dump and sewer outlet. He soon whipped up plenty of public support but encountered city hall's objection that these were Depression days and there was no money in the treasury to buy land. (The City had been near bankruptcy. The City of North Vancouver was officially bankrupt.)

Through Alderman DeGraves he learned that the Great Northern Railway owed $20 000 in taxes on its land holdings in the area, which included the dump. The railway company did not have the money to pay, and Branca urged the City to take over the land in lieu of taxes. But the municipality required provincial government legislation to make such a takeover legal and federal financing to pay for park construction.

Branca collected some of his political debts from politicians for whom he had campaigned. He persuaded Premier Duff Pattullo and Attorney General Wismer from Victoria, federal cabinet minister Ian McKenzie and other politicians to meet to view the site. Then he quietly briefed his newspaper friends. After setting the stage with a few words of introduction, Branca seized a stout stick "that just happened to be lying there" and beat the undergrowth. At once a swarm of rats broke cover and scattered the official party.

That was enough. The provincial government passed an enabling act making it legal for the City to forgo the taxes, take over the land and vest ownership of the land in the Parks Board. The federal government undertook to put up $75 000 at $15 000 a year for five years to develop it. Thus East Vancouver acquired False Creek Park.

Branca worked energetically, often sharing leadership with DeGraves, on other local projects. These included the construction of the swimming pool at the foot of Windermere Street and the building of the Hastings Community Centre, providing not only the hall but tennis courts, bowling greens, a box lacrosse field and facilities for other sports.

Vancouver became known for progressiveness in the field of community recreation. The Hastings Community Centre was the subject of a report to Rotary International in Chicago, and a description of how it was achieved was circulated to all Rotary clubs in North America.

Branca used the correspondence columns of newspapers to protest against policies of the Vancouver School Board. This interest in school matters would develop many years later into his efforts to bring university facilities nearer to East Vancouver. When the campaign to establish Simon Fraser University was launched, he enthusiastically joined the founding fathers. They made him a senator and the senate elected him a governor. Only the student confrontations with the law in the sixties, when neutrality made it desirable that judges not be university governors, caused him reluctantly to resign from the board. In 1975, the university conferred on him the degree of honorary doctor of laws, a distinction he also holds from St. Martin's College in the state of Washington.

He was also a governor of the Sacred Heart Convent School in Vancouver, though he points out that it was the easiest job he ever had. "No governor ever tried to tell the Sacred Heart sisters how to govern their school," he says.

Branca made one essay into elective politics when he was invited by the Non-Partisan Association to run under its banner for the Vancouver Parks Board. Twelve aspirants contested four seats. The NPA-backed candidates, including Branca, won all four.

That was 1938. By the time his two-year term of office ended, Italy had come into the war. The association, claiming to be nonpartisan, was not nonracist. It refused to endorse him for re-election. Of course, he fought the election, running as an independent. And, of course, bereft of any endorsation, he lost. Ironically, so did the NPA. The seat he had won for them two years earlier went to the CCF.

The decision to pursue his ambition through his talents as a lawyer rather than through fickle politics began to seem the right one.

CHAPTER SEVEN

All Branca's legal, political and community activities together do not explain why he became the acknowledged leader of British Columbia's Italians before he was forty. Surely it was because he taught them, during the clash of ideologies in the thirties, how they could be good Italians and good Canadians. He emerged as their leader when they were beset by the Depression and wooed by Fascism.

There were other leaders in the community, notably W.G. Ruocco. While the Brancas were identified with the Societa Veneta, the Ruoccos ran the Sons of Italy, an older fraternal group having more members, and Billy Ruocco was a prominent personality in many organizations. But Angelo Branca became the accepted leader when his warnings about the hollowness of Fascism came true and he helped to steer the Italian community through some of the consequences of flirting with it.

With the Depression deepening, Italians across the continent were subjected to a barrage of propaganda about Mussolini's economic miracles. The degree to which interference in Canadian affairs was attempted by Italian officials is documented by Toronto writer A.V. Spada in his book, *The Italians in Canada*. Spada quotes the irritated words of Mussolini when answering criticism from the editor of an Italian-language newspaper in Montreal: "We invite the comrades in Montreal to give him the lesson he deserves, with hot lead and cold iron." In 1934, Mussolini announced, "Fascism has become a world phenomenon," and ordered consulates in every major city in the Western world to subvert existing Italian organizations and start new ones promoting Fascism.

They organized Fascist clubs from Nova Scotia to British Columbia. In eastern Canada they were generally named Fascio Luporini after a Fascist officer killed in Florence in a riot which he helped to provoke. The Vancouver *fascio* was rather less Fascist than the others; it was not named after any modern Fascist martyr but was called the Fascio Giordano Bruno after a sixteenth-century theologian who was burned at the stake but later honoured as a profound philosopher. (This noncommittal title did not save its key men in Vancouver from being rounded up by the police when Mussolini declared war in 1940. One man's only offence was that, being consulted as a man of some learning, he had suggested the name!)

It is not surprising that many Vancouver Italians were seduced by the propaganda of their consulate. They were not alone in admiring the Mussolini creed. Some East Enders today recall an editor of the *Province* addressing their *fascio* and declaring that what Canada needed was a Mussolini.

With Italy's declaration of war against Ethiopia in 1936, the consulates in North America stepped up the propaganda. In the latter half of the thirties, many Canadian Italians believed they could support Fascism without being disloyal to Canada. Prime Minister R.B. Bennett's justice minister refused even to see deputations of Italians who wanted him to restrain the consulates from promoting Fascism. Prime Minister Mackenzie King through his repudiation of sanctions tacitly supported Mussolini.

Branca and others began warning the community of the danger of their groups being taken over by career officials from Italy. He remembers Italian social events at which he and his wife remained seated while most of the audience stood to attention for the singing of the Fascist anthem "Giovinezza." Filippo was more theatrical. He would clamp his wide-brimmed hat firmly on his head, glare around the room and walk out.

That did little good, any more than it helped to scold the women showing off their steel wedding rings, symbols that they had donated their gold bands to buy ambulances for the Ethiopian campaign. (The vice-consul in Montreal announced that the gold had been sent to the mint in Ottawa and exchanged for money for the Italian Red Cross, but A.V. Spada wrote, "Many years later those gold rings were located in California. The far-sighted Fascist officers kept the gold on this side of the Atlantic, just in case.")

Branca's concern was for the Italian community. His parents had long been naturalized Canadians and British citizens. The rest of the family were all born in Canada except American-born Viola, by this time a Canadian citizen. But he had chosen to combine his Canadian way of life with the enjoyment of an ancient culture of which he felt a part. As a lawyer, he knew that a community containing many aliens professing admiration for a foreign ideology would immediately incur the penalties of the War Measures Act if that foreign country became an enemy. Branca, very much a man of action, tried to act before the worst could occur.

In May 1940, when Italy was still neutral, he formed a committee to make plans for a pledge of loyalty to Canada from the Italian community. He hired the Hastings Auditorium, placed advertising and sent 2000 circulars around East Vancouver announcing a mass meeting for the evening of 10 June. That morning North America heard the news that Mussolini had declared war on the Allies.

In the consternation that engulfed the Italian community, Branca and his associates worked to spread the word that the meeting must go on. About 380 people attended. Branca presided, explained the object of the meeting and said, "The world has been shocked by an act of perfidious cowardice. This declaration of war by Mussolini will be recorded by history as one of the most cowardly and traitorous actions since the beginning of time."

The meeting approved the forming of the Vancouver Canadian Italian War Vigilance Association. It cheered a resolution declaring all members unequivocally behind the war effort of the Canadian government. It elected

Branca president by acclamation, and he took advantage of the enthusiasm to collect $425 in cash and much more in pledges towards donating an ambulance to the Canadian Red Cross.

The Italian community in Victoria adopted the Branca model and established a loyalty association. So did Italians in Trail, where 396 aliens born in Italy were working at the Cominco smelter.

Branca's initiative gave British Columbia's Italians a rallying ground where they could demonstrate loyalty to Canada. But some were caught in the implementation of the War Measures Act, including several prominent members of the Fascio, the Sons of Italy and the War Veterans' Club. The veterans' service had been with the Allies in the First World War, but the consulate had made their club a Fascist propaganda vehicle.

Between 150 and 200 Italians in British Columbia were sent to Camp Petawawa in Ontario, and separated families suffered hardship; but their property was not seized and detention conditions were not harsh. A newspaperwoman who visited Camp Petawawa in 1941 told me how the camp food was supplemented by delicious Italian meals cooked in the kitchens of one of Toronto's best restaurants, whose owner was a detainee.

Branca's office became a clearing house for information about those detained and for advice on obtaining their release. He composed appeals in many cases where a family had lost its breadwinner or a business its one-man operator. The Canadian government appointed two judges to hear appeals against detention. Some detentions were mistakes, and these were soon rectified. Gradually the judges worked their way through the calendar of appeals and released most appellants. Practically all those from British Columbia were home before the end of 1942.

The difference in the official treatment of the Italian and Japanese Canadians was brought home poignantly to Branca. Soon after the Pearl Harbour shock, he and his mother were walking near his home when they met a Japanese whom they knew as a neighbour. She and her husband had established a jewellery business in Vancouver and built for themselves a home that was their pride and joy. As they greeted her she broke down and, looking tearfully at Teresa Branca, said, "War come with Italy. You stay here. War come with Japan. We must go away. We must leave our beautiful home. We lose everything. Why?"

Branca's father was spared the anguish of seeing war come between his adopted country and his native land. Filippo Branca retired from business early in 1939, and in April of that year he died at the age of sixty-nine.

Forty years later, Angelo Branca has no complaint about the application of the War Measures Act to the Italians. "A government's first duty in time of war is to defend its people," he says. His anger he directs at Dr. G. Brancucci, then consul in Vancouver, and career officials like him in other Canadian cities who abused their positions to mislead Canadian Italians. It still rankles him that when Italians whose chosen home was Canada were being sent to detention camp, Brancucci was free to leave with his family, by virtue of consular immunity, for wherever he chose.

In the seventies, Branca again warned against allowing Italian government officials to take control of Italian community affairs in Vancouver. He no longer fears ideological corruption, but he believes there is so much demonstrated business and professional talent in the community, people conversant with Canadian ways and methods, that it is an impertinence for itinerant officials from abroad to claim to know better. He says control of the community by consular officials brings dangers, and points to the rift created among Vancouver's Italians by the cultural centre controversy during the seventies.

A move to build a cultural centre began within the community, and some fund raising was done; but progress was slow until a dynamic young consul, Dr. Giovanni Germano, arrived in Vancouver in 1972. Using the authority of the consulate and the co-operation of young professionals among the more recent Italian immigrants, he led a campaign to raise money from the community, borrow money from banks and beg money from government. Now the handsome Leonardo da Vinci Centre stands on an imposing site on Grandview Highway, a $4.5-million building which on opening day received a gift of $333 333 from the provincial government.

It became the pride of one segment of the Italian community, represented by the Folk Society, and the scorn of another segment, led by Branca. His supporters are the organizations comprising the Confratellanza Italo-Canadese, formed by him in the seventies by a merger of several groups. A distinguished visitor from Italy went home thinking Vancouver's Italians were lucky people to own two beautiful centres. He had been entertained by the Folk Society at the da Vinci Centre and by the Confratellanza at the Arbutus Club rented for the occasion. No one told him of the feud.

Of the da Vinci Centre Branca said publicly following its opening, "If the Italian Consul and his hierarchy had only stayed out of the affair, the Italians of Vancouver would not be faced with a $1.4-million debt. They and their children and their grandchildren will be working to pay off the bank. Again the Consul has left the country and left them to carry the burden."

He objected to the method of financing—a government grant conditional upon the sponsors burdening the community with a liability for twice the amount. His condemnation stems from his philosophy, as he explains: "I think the Canadian theory of multiculturism is quite out of place. I believe the traditions, customs and culture of an ethnic group are important to that group, and that its people should be encouraged to keep them. By doing so the cultural life of that group will be enriched and these things in turn will enrich Canadian life. But I am strongly opposed to multiculturism as it is developing in Canada, both on the federal and the provincial scene.

"While ethnic groups should be encouraged to keep their languages and customs, they should be told that the cost of maintaining these things must be borne by the group. If they cannot be so maintained, then they are not worth keeping.

"I learned to speak my parents' language at my

mother's knee. And this I have always believed; that foreigners who make Canada their home have a duty to become Canadians and to conform with the culture of Canada while maintaining their own if it is worthy of survival.

"For all the years of my activities with the Italo-Canadian community we have worked to maintain the culture of the Canadian Italian without the help of the Canadian taxpayer. We have given thousands of dollars to local charities. Then came the multiculture movement, federally and provincially supported—to try, it was said, to counter the melting pot tendency seen in the United States. In the States immigrants have become good American citizens, I think."

Believing the public has little idea of the government largesse distributed to ethnic organizations, and the types of ventures that benefit, Branca asks: "Is it because governments must show favour in order to win the votes of the ethnic groups? I don't know. I hope not. Why don't we spend the money on things that are more important in our national life? Why don't we teach ethnic groups to speak and think Canadian? What about a culture that is distinctively Canadian, the culture that we have been building since long before Confederation?

"I am unequivocally against the Canadian tax dollar going to maintain cultural centres for ethnic groups and against any of my tax dollars going to promote ethnic cultures."

In his undeclared war with Branca the Italian consul won one victory. He compiled a book, *The Italians in Western Canada*. In its 191 pages Dr. Germano includes the names of hundreds of Vancouver Italians, but he nowhere mentions Branca, the first son of an Italian father ever to become a high court judge in Canada.

Yet the *Eco d'Italia* newspaper of Vancouver, the Italian-language journal of British Columbia, called Branca "the finest Italian-Canadian of them all!!"

Angelo Branca's Italian heritage includes his religion. When the second Catholic parish in Vancouver was established in 1905 (after Holy Rosary), Angelo Ernest Branca was one of the first names recorded in the baptismal register. Sacred Heart was by no means a mainly Italian congregation. (It would wait thirty years for its first Italian pastor.) Parishioners came from a dozen countries, and their church coexisted with Protestant, Jewish and Buddhist places of worship nearby. This situation made Branca an ecumenist long before Pope John, and nurtured the interfaith activities that would bring him recognition across and outside Canada.

It also explained why he would have differences with Archbishop Duke about Catholic university education. Archbishop William Duke brought from his native New Brunswick a nineteenth-century sense of Catholic aloofness from other faiths. He decried Catholic participation in non-Catholic religious services when other prelates were beginning to accept it. An unhappy instance was his disapproval of Catholic ex-servicemen joining their old comrades in Armistice Day religious ceremonies.

The same attitude led the archbishop to discourage a trio of Catholic laymen—Dr. David Steele, lawyer Paul Murphy and Branca—who for years worked for Catholic university education in British Columbia. They believed the objective should be a Catholic presence on a secular university campus, with a theological faculty and denominational facilities for Catholic students.

Realizing some government help in funding would be essential, they presented a plan to the provincial government and a case in support. Power broker Gordon Wismer said, "Sure you have a case. Sure you have a Catholic population. But these things have to go through the legislature. Where are your Catholics in the legislature? Have you one?" They had two; two more than on Vancouver city council. The 1951 census showed that 12.5 per cent or one-eighth of the population of Vancouver was Roman Catholic, but in those days few Catholics offered themselves as candidates for public office. Aloofness carried its penalties. Branca went around addressing Catholic groups, promoting and adjudicating public speaking contests and urging his listeners to work for representation reflecting their numbers.

The government gave their plan for a university college what its sponsors considered a fair reception, and eventually a scheme was approved in principle. It proved too secular for "the Iron Duke." He wanted a Catholic university. Provoked by failure at the moment of long-worked-for success, Branca stamped out of a meeting with the archbishop, saying, "Where the hell are you going to get the money?" The project lapsed.

The next prelate was of another generation—Archbishop Martin Johnson, whose broad humanity became known to a wide public through his wise words when serving on a Royal Commission on liquor. The Branca-Murphy-Steele plans were dusted off and a Catholic college was established at the University of British Columbia.

Two popes have sent Branca citations for his work for his church, and in 1977 he was invested by the Papal Pro-Nuncio to Canada as a Knight Commander of the Order of St. Gregory the Great.

Did Branca's religious beliefs ever affect his decisions as a judge? The question was asked because an article in the *Vancouver Sun* said he "sometimes appeared to be influenced by his Catholic religion." "Never in the slightest," he told me. Did anyone in the church try to influence his ideas on law and morality? "No archbishop, bishop or priest ever mentioned anything of the kind," he replied. Divorce? "As a judge I heard and decided as many divorce cases per year as any judge on the bench. Oh, wait a minute. Once when I was a lawyer a priest suggested I should not handle a certain divorce case. I should have referred him to canon law—I've lectured on a Catholic's duty to Church and to State. I was so taken aback I couldn't be civil. I told him to go to hell."

Despite all his activities in the Italian and Catholic communities, Branca still had energy to spare. He raised money for good causes whether sponsored by church or synagogue. With Jewish people Branca's associations have been almost lifelong. As a boy, he knew the largely Jewish areas around East Georgia and Keefer streets as well as he knew any part of the city. As a young man, he had all the news of the Jewish community from his regular chats on the street with the red-bearded Rabbi Nathan Mayer Pastinsky when the one was heading for the office and the other was returning from his dawn kosher ritual at Colman Kolberg's butcher shop.

For many years Branca chaired the finance committee of Habonim Camp Miriam, a Jewish holiday camp entertaining children of all denominations on Gabriola Island in the Strait of Georgia. He helped raise many thousands of dollars for camp buildings and fees for children unable to pay.

Branca enjoys working with Jewish businessmen. This practitioner in written contracts and covenants likes the way some of them, once a basis of trust is established, will do business on a handclasp. "The paperwork can come later," he says. "There's one man—I could call him right now and say, 'I'd like to borrow a million,' and I think he'd say, 'Come right over. I'll have the cheque ready.' Then I'd tell him what it was for."

His work with people of both faiths over many years led to his becoming Pacific Region cochairman of the Canadian Council of Christians and Jews, which in 1970 honoured him with its national Human Relations Award for his "outstanding contribution in promoting understanding and co-operation among people of Canada regardless of race."

The honours heaped upon him by Jewish organizations are a measure of the work he has contributed. The B'nai B'rith society of Vancouver chose him as Man of the Year in 1972 and made him guest of honour at its annual banquet. The Jewish community established the Angelo Branca $3000 annual scholarship for a Canadian student to attend Yeshiva University in New York City, the largest Jewish university in the United States. In 1977, he became the second Canadian (after John Diefenbaker) to receive the President's Medal of the State of Israel. On a visit to that country he and his wife were guests of the Israeli government.

When Branca was in his last year as a judge, his Jewish admirers across Canada made a gesture that touched him deeply. They persuaded the trustees of Bar-Ilan University in Tel Aviv, Israel, to make him an honorary fellow "in recognition of his uncompromising passion for justice, in admiration of his unique personality which embraces deep wisdom, purity of heart, mind and courage, his dedication as a great Christian gentleman, which inspired him to distinguished humanitarianism, championship of freedom, and in appreciation of his warm friendship for the Jewish community of Canada and his steadfast support of the State of Israel, helping further the well-being of its people and the enhancement of its cultural life."

The qualities catalogued in that citation were nurtured in Branca by the lively, crowded, generous multicultured society that made up the old East Vancouver.

CHAPTER EIGHT

The Italian Catholic Branca had a stormy forty-year friendship with Scottish Presbyterian Alec Manson, the attorney general who tried to hush up the Janet Smith affair, the politician who helped to shorten Branca's honeymoon and the judge who twice ousted him from the courtroom.

They struck sparks off each other in court. They differed on practically everything outside court, yet remained friends. Did certain similarities, less obvious than their differences, explain their mutual regard? Their independent minds, perhaps, or their total unconcern with what more conventional people might think of them?

Their differences were striking. After years spent around courts, seeing dozens of judges at work, I rate Mr. Justice Manson the worst judge I ever knew. Many times in his court I have squirmed at his antagonism towards French Canadians and his prejudice against husbands whose plaintiff wives won his sympathy because he heard their stories first. He believed Provincial Police witnesses ("my boys") and distrusted the RCMP (who took "his boys" over). When he thought a man was guilty he would be more prosecutor than judge.

With all that, one could not help liking Judge Manson. His faults were all as a judge. Being so eager to build a better world to his design, he should have stayed in politics. He was one of the most energetic cabinet ministers British Columbia ever had, but he lacked a judicial mind.

Born in St. Louis, Missouri, in 1883 of loyalist parentage, Manson was brought up in Quebec's Eastern Townships by a grandmother—"raised," as he said, "on poverty, Presbyterianism and good Scotch porridge." He opened the first law office in Prince Rupert in 1908, and was elected M.L.A. for Omineca in 1916 when he was thirty-three. In five years he was speaker of the House, then minister of labour, and a mercurial attorney general for six years. He restructured departments, created a new Provincial Police Force, and revised liquor administration and the game laws.

Branca became aware of Manson when, as a young man, he read with wonderment the harangues of this extraordinary politician. In 1922, the year Branca was nineteen, these headlines enlivened the newspapers: "Manson warns against prairie labour influx: no mercy for drifters." "Manson law to make putative fathers pay." "Manson strong advocate of arrest for debt." "Must use attrition on Orientals here, counsels Manson." "Senate must go—Manson." "B.C. Police to be semi-military, says Manson." "Oust Orientals from pulp mills, is Manson plan." "Premier reproved by attorney general." "Attorney general on Asiatic Menace." "Manson urges campaign against Orientals." "Mounties, if guilty, should be jailed and lashed, says Manson."

To the Brancas, happily coexisting with their Chinese and Japanese neighbours in the East End, the voice from Victoria sounded like some ogre's, and Angelo was prepared to loathe him when they met en route to Trail in 1928. By the time they had fought an election campaign together, they had become the best of friends.

Manson was more maverick than party man. Returning from a visit to his sick father in Missouri, he learned that in his absence his party leader Premier John Oliver and cabinet colleague Duff Pattullo had spoken at meetings in Omineca. "I wish to hell they'd keep out of my riding," he shouted to political writer Russell Walker. In his book, *Politicians of a Pioneering Province,* Walker recalls Premier Oliver saying, "Those two young fellows are almost too much for me. In caucus, if Manson isn't on his feet McGeer is."

Manson's constant crusading made things too uncomfortable for his colleagues. First they left him out of the cabinet. Then in 1935 they persuaded Ottawa to make him a Supreme Court judge.

The urge to help humanity remained, and inspired him to untold acts of private charity. Many a convicted man was surprised to learn that the judge who jailed him was keeping track of his progress and privately planning to help him upon his release. He was the only judge in Canada who, when granting divorces, instructed the parties on how to bring up the children, then supplied them all with a transcript of his advice.

Elevation to a judgeship did not dam the stream of public preachments from bench and podium. Invited to address the Ministerial Association, he told them their churches had failed. As guest of a prison reform society he lamented the abolition of the rock pile. From the bench he said he was fed up with the B.C. bar.

He once ignored lawyer Gordon Dowding's protest against the delaying of a case; then when that future speaker of the legislature persisted, he leaned down from the bench and said quietly, "Go jump in the lake." He called police "blundering inefficient dumbbells" and blamed them for the increase in crime. After hearing the evidence of a doctor's wife, he demanded that the Medical Council strike the husband's name from its rolls, saying the man was not fit to look after human life. How a struck-off doctor would pay the substantial family maintenance he ordered he did not explain.

When Manson was chairman of the War Service Mobilization Board during World War II, he heard that a trade union organizer from eastern Canada had come to Vancouver "to study conditions" at Dominion Bridge Company. Before the man realized what was happening, Manson had him drafted into the army. "He had come to stir up trouble," said Manson. "We can't have strikes in wartime." Labour organizations tried to have him removed from the bench. He retorted that he was a labour man himself, born and raised among the poor.

Judge Manson boasted that by the severity of his sentences he stamped out an epidemic of rape. Believing that "it is the judge's duty to protect the rights of society as well as those of the accused," he took no offence at being called "the Hanging Judge." He sentenced fourteen convicted murderers to death, and declared, "I never lost a night's sleep over any of them."

Judge Manson was always chivalrous to women in distress. The mother of a youth whom Branca was defending travelled far to stand by her son at his trial, so the judge directed her to a seat close to the jury box so that she could hear the evidence. She was a handsome woman and she smiled sweetly at the jurors whenever they caught her eye. Soon they were passing the time of day with her as they resumed their seats after each recess and on each new day, but always before the judge came in.

By the time he had heard the evidence, Judge Manson's sympathies were with the girl complainant, and he was disgusted when the jurors refused to convict. He never knew how that woman influenced their verdict.

Branca more than once complained in Appeal Court that Judge Manson, having decided a case in his own mind, weighted his summing up for the jury accordingly. Those parts of the evidence favourable to his view he would recount in measured and emphatic tones. For adverse evidence he would soft-pedal the volume and speed up the tempo. The transcript would prove to the Court of Appeal that the trial judge had reviewed the evidence for both sides, but the cold print could not reveal the difference in emphasis.

Walter Pavlukoff, whom Manson sentenced to death in 1953 for the murder of a banker, alleged exactly this in his appeal. Pavlukoff was highly articulate though his formal education had ended in grade eight at Strathcona, ten years after Branca sat in the same classroom. Psychiatrists rated his intelligence quotient as among the highest they had ever measured. From the prisoner's dock at his trial, he accused the judge of making plain to the jury his opinion that he was guilty. Manson retorted, "Humbug and impertinence." When told that the Court of Appeal had upheld the verdict, Pavlukoff stabbed himself to the heart and died.

An elder of the Presbyterian Church, Manson loved to poke fun at teetotallers and at those Presbyterians who merged into the United Church of Canada. When Premier W.A.C. Bennett, on the coming to power of his first Social Credit government, banned liquor in government buildings, Judge Manson dug back into English law to find an edict proclaiming that "the King's Writ shall not run in the sanctuaries of consecrated churches and the chambers of his majesty's judges." Armed with that finding, and in defiance of the premier's order, Manson served whisky to many a guest in his chambers in the old Vancouver Court House. One guest, Mac Reynolds of the *Sun,* described a typical gathering:

Judge Harry Sullivan, round and Irish and be-robed, arrived in the office. Said Manson, the Shriner and past grand master of the Masonic Lodge, to Sullivan, as he brought forth a bottle of rye from a filing cabinet, "This filing cabinet belongs to the Presbyterian Church. Some United Church bugs come through that window, and I keep this whisky in the cabinet to preserve it from contamination. Harry, would a Dogan like you take a drink of Presbyterian whisky?" Said Harry Sullivan, "And what else would I be coming in here for?"

Who would have believed, seeing these two friends happily cracking jokes at each other's expense, that a few years earlier Manson, as acting chief justice, had been so displeased at Sullivan's appointment that he refused to swear him in?

Like Branca, who always took a briefcase full of Vancouver work with him when he went to engagements in the Interior, Manson hated to run out of work while on circuit. Presiding over a Supreme Court civil sitting at Rossland, he had two trials aborted and faced two empty days in his hotel room at Trail. Within a couple of hours he gleefully told me, "I've got hold of a list of all the senior and middle management at Cominco. There are lots of good Scots names among them, and a friend is coming in to tell me which of them might be a good touch for a donation to St. Andrew's Hall. Then I'll get busy on the telephone." The imposing Manson House on St. Andrew's campus at the University of British Columbia is a memorial to his tireless fund raising.

Branca's familiarity with Manson's preferences and prejudices helped him in many court cases, and once enabled him to win a judgement that made new law in Canada, though not for long. The judgement ruled that peeping Toms were criminals. The case was to be fought over three years through five courts from the lowest to the highest in the land.

A Richmond woman, undressing for bed late one night in 1947, saw a man peering through a six-inch gap in the drapes and screamed, "A man at my window." Her son picked up a carving knife, chased the man for three hundred yards and held him until a police constable arrived. They took him to the police station, where a corporal detained him for two and a half days. In court he was convicted of conduct likely to cause a breach of the peace.

He asked Neil Fleishman to appeal, and Fleishman presented the Court of Appeal with a question of law: Can a man who runs away at the first scream be guilty of breaching the peace? The court narrowly decided he could not, and quashed the conviction.

"Tom" then sued the son and the two officers in Supreme Court for damages for false imprisonment on the ground that being a peeping Tom was not an offence under Canadian law.

Branca entered the case as counsel for the three captors, and at once recognized the strength of Tom's case that peeping into a woman's bedroom at night was not a crime. Nothing in the Criminal Code of Canada prohibited it.

To establish that under long-standing common law such conduct was an offence justifying arrest without warrant, he traced English law back to a statute of Edward III in 1360, then painstakingly showed continuity down the centuries to the Revised Statutes of British Columbia, 1948. Part of his pedigree was an enactment of 1381 stating, "None shall henceforth make any entry into any lands or tenements but where entry is given by the Law."

The case came before Mr. Justice Manson. He loved ancient law, and this part of Branca's case particularly impressed him. He dismissed Tom's action.

Tom appealed to the Court of Appeal of British Columbia, which found the case so intriguing that after days of argument it asked for more submissions in writing, then came down with a thirty-one-page judgement. This upheld the right of the son and the constable to apprehend Tom without a warrant and dismissed the case against them, but against the corporal it awarded $100 for Tom's overlong detention.

Branca had prudently based his case in Court of Appeal on modern as well as ancient law, for that court, while awarding him judgement, rejected the reason adopted by Judge Manson based on the 500-year-old English statute. Mr. Justice O'Halloran, who had a sly sense of humour, accepted the historical lineage of the precedent but pointed out that the law was made at a time when England was less concerned with peeping Toms than with unruly mobs, which "made entry where entry was not given by the Law" in order to seize and hang two chief justices.

The effect of the British Columbia court's decision was that for most of a year the law said a peeping Tom was liable to arrest by citizens or police without a warrant, and to conviction for a criminal offence at common law even though his conduct was not expressly covered by the criminal code.

This particular peeping Tom was persistent, and so was Fleishman. The son of Branca's old principal briefed Harry Bray, K.C., of Vancouver, vastly experienced in the appellate courts, to go to Ottawa to appeal to the Supreme Court of Canada. Branca's clients asked him to economize by retaining Ottawa counsel to represent them there.

The Ottawa court completely reversed the British Columbia decision, ruling that "a Peeping Tom who intrudes on private property at night, looks into a lighted side-window of a house where he can see a woman preparing for bed, and on being discovered runs away, is not guilty of a criminal offence." It further ruled that "an inmate of the house who pursues the Peeping Tom and detains him is liable in damages for false imprisonment." To clinch the matter, the court laid down that "a peace officer who arrests without warrant a Peeping Tom is liable in damages for false arrest since no criminality is involved in merely peeping and running away."

Though the Court of Appeal did not upset a Manson judgement, the Supreme Court of Canada now had. It awarded Tom fifty dollars in damages against the arresting officer and ten dollars against the son.

When Branca was working on one of his most difficult assignments—to try to end Doukhobor burning and bombing—Manson took him aback by an unexpected experiment in leniency. Six Sons of Freedom terrorists had already been convicted by juries, but Manson, the hitherto hard-line judge, shocked law enforcers by imposing sentences of from one day to three months in return for the terrorists' promise to keep the peace. These sentences meant immediate release, the men having been in custody while awaiting trial.

Attorney General Wismer was incensed, calling the sentences wholly inadequate, extraordinary and manifestly wrong. He asked the Court of Appeal to increase all the sentences drastically, urging in one case an unprecedented revision from three months to fifteen years.

The Court of Appeal, in a two to one judgement, declined to interfere. "The leniency we now uphold may not achieve its purpose," said Mr. Justice O'Halloran. "If he [Manson] is right posterity may acclaim him as a great judge, farseeing beyond his generation." Unfortunately for posterity, ten, fifteen and more years later some of the same men were still going through the courts and jails for similar acts.

Manson's ousting of Branca from the courtroom during

the *Moody and Lawson* rape trial was followed by a more dramatic ejection four years later.

Branca was defending a woman on a motor manslaughter charge. She was alleged to have driven a car which ran out of control and struck a taxi, causing the taxi to plunge into Burrard Inlet and an elderly passenger to be drowned.

The woman's defence was that her friend, a Vancouver architect, was driving the car and became unconscious at the wheel, and the car ran away downhill. She reached over to control it but stepped on the gas pedal instead of the brake. Her friend supported her evidence, testifying that he was sober when they left a local club and clearly recalled sitting in the driver's seat. The next thing he remembered was waking up in hospital.

Mr. Justice Manson, a demon for work at seventy-two, had the court sitting on a Saturday. In cross-examination the prosecutor implied that a witness had spoken of seeing the woman driving the car while it was still proceeding normally. Branca jumped to his feet to interject, "That was not the evidence at all." This exchange followed:

THE JUDGE: Mr. Branca, sit down.

BRANCA: With respect, my lord, I will not sit down. I am entitled to a ruling on my objection.

THE JUDGE: You will sit down, or leave this courtroom.

BRANCA: If I leave, my lord, I will not return.

THE JUDGE: Officer, bring the Sheriff.

The court orderly did so, and Branca, escorted by Sheriff Moodie—the same Stan Moodie who had barnstormed West Kootenay with Manson and Branca on behalf of "Long Jim" MacDonald twenty-seven years before—left the courtroom. As they marched past Mr. Justice Harold McInnes's chambers that company-loving judge was at his door. "Angelo, my old friend." he said. "Come in and have a cigarette."

"You'll need a habeas corpus order," said the lawyer. "I'm under arrest."

Branca does not apologize easily. The judge ordered a recess and sent the prosecutor to tell Branca he could resume the trial if he would apologize to the court. Branca refused. The judge adjourned court to Monday, setting Branca at liberty meantime.

A weekend of feverish consultation followed. Calls went to Victoria. Judge Manson asked Gordon Wismer to talk to Branca as an old friend. He did so, to no avail. Branca would not apologize. Finally Chief Justice Wendell Farris called with a blast: "Branca, what the hell are you up to?" Branca explained his stand. The chief justice said, "I don't want to take a strong line unless I have to. I'm telling you as a friend. You cook up some half-assed apology that will satisfy Alec and won't hurt your own damn pride, and let's get the Assize going again. I have a heavy trial list."

When court assembled Branca read from a scrap of paper, "My lord, to the extent that I may have been blameworthy I apologize. I think I can safely say that in my thirty years' practice at the bar I have always endeavoured to maintain the decorum of the court."

Judge Manson turned to the jury and said, "I'm sure Mr. Branca regrets the incident as much as I do. I think the situation arose because Mr. Branca works much too hard. When one overworks he does things he would not otherwise do." To Branca he said, "I rule now that your objection was well taken."

The reconciliation was brief. At the end of the judge's charge Branca said, "With the greatest respect, your lordship has put the case for the Crown as fully as possible but not the case for the defence."

Judge Manson snapped, "Your imputation that I have summed the case up unfairly is not appreciated."

The jury returned a verdict of "guilty with a strong recommendation to the most extreme leniency." Judge Manson fined the woman $750. She was the only accused person at that Assize in 1955 to escape with a fine.

The other six accused received the following sentences: two, to be hanged; one, fifteen years' imprisonment for armed robbery; one, seven years' imprisonment and a whipping for rape; one, two years' imprisonment and a whipping for indecent assault; one, two years' imprisonment for causing bodily harm. Present-day judges might live their whole judicial careers without handing down the heavy retribution represented by that month's work.

Expulsion from the court that Saturday helped Branca. He used the weekend to work on a conspiracy prosecution for the federal government against gasoline dealers accused of price fixing. When the trial date arrived, he found to his dismay that out of a roster of nine Supreme Court judges he had once again drawn Mr. Justice Manson. This time Branca would be prosecuting, not defending.

The fact that Manson and he had just had another courtroom "scene" meant nothing to either of them. Branca's problem, as every lawyer knew, would be to restrain the judge from usurping his role of prosecutor and doing something that would give ground for appeal.

After months of preparation and a twenty-three-day trial, Branca secured a conviction against all the dealers, but the predictable happened. The dealers appealed on the ground of an error by the trial judge, and won. Though the Court of Appeal directed a new trial, the Crown abandoned the prosecution.

The Law Reform Commission of Canada deplores plea bargaining, and the public has a vague idea that it is un-Canadian. Plea bargaining usually means seeking an arrangement whereby an accused person who expects to be convicted agrees to plead guilty, perhaps to a lesser charge, in return for a reduced penalty. The prosecutor, uncertain that he or she has the evidence for a major conviction, believes the public interest is served if the agreement ensures some punishment without a long and possibly abortive trial at public expense. Obviously, the bargain, to be worth anything, requires the co-operation of the judge, and most Canadian judges, unlike their

American counterparts, either treat plea bargaining with the utmost caution or will have no part of it whatsoever. Judge Manson loved plea bargaining.

A Bralorne miner faced certain conviction after $30 000 worth of raw gold was found at his home. A complicating factor was that it would be easy to prove unlawful possession but not easy to prove the gold came from the Bralorne mine. Unless this was admitted, the company would have difficulty establishing ownership.

The company was more worried when it learned that Angelo Branca had been retained to defend the man. It engaged a leading lawyer (and future lieutenant governor), Walter Owen, to go to Quesnel to recover the gold.

The outcome was a plan, approved by Judge Manson, whereby Branca's client pleaded guilty and admitted that the gold belonged to the Bralorne company. In return, he received a lesser sentence than he could have hoped for if tried and convicted. The prosecutor thought the sentence satisfactory, seeing that the man's confession saved the province an expensive trial, and the owners recovered their gold. The man went to jail.

One day Branca received a call: "Alec here. Your thieving gold miner becomes eligible for parole next month. The jail gives him a good report. Make out a parole application and I'll endorse it and we'll lose no time getting him out." Later Branca learned that, unknown to him, part of the plea bargaining had been Judge Manson's private arrangement with the employers to help rehabilitate the man. When he came out of jail, the company gave him a job well away from its gold handling operations, and he was never in trouble again. This involvement was typical of quixotic Judge Manson. It may have helped the thief that his name was MacGregor.

Branca and Manson differed in their views on juries, and, as usual, they aired their differences.

A man, not defended by Branca, was acquitted of a charge of rape, whereupon Judge Manson told the jury, "If this man is not guilty of rape, then I don't know what guilt is. This is a most disgraceful performance." He ordered the sheriff never to call these twelve for service as jurors again.

The *Sun* editorialized that Manson's reprimand of the jury "is full in the B.C. tradition of justice dating from the first judge to bring British justice to the Colony, Sir Matthew Begbie." It cited Begbie's words from the bench in 1863: "Gentlemen of the Jury, you are a pack of Dalles horse thieves. Permit me to say, it would give me great pleasure to see you hanged, each and every one of you, for declaring a murderer guilty only of manslaughter."

Branca took the unusual step for a lawyer of writing to the newspaper to say that Mr. Justice Manson's dismissal of the jury should be condemned rather than commended. His letter disagreeing with both judge and editorial ran to two columns, and the *Sun* made it the main feature on the editorial page, headlined, "Queen's Counsel Assails Jury Dismissal by Judge."

The letter—incidentally, an expression of Branca's love for the Canadian system of justice—ended: "In my book this jury did its duty in accord with the highest traditions. I admire it for its courage. I for one regret its reward. This, of course, is entirely aside from my firm belief, expressed with the greatest of deference to the learned trial judge, the Hon. Mr. Justice Manson, that he had no jurisdiction to so discharge the said jury at all."

The *Victoria Colonist,* siding with Branca, said, "The dismissal of the jury can be held to strike at the roots of the trial-by-jury system. If juries became seized of the idea that they must please a judge rather than decide a case according to their own good sense, then the basic impartiality of the jury system would collapse."

Here are two anecdotes giving additional glimpses of the Manson personality. On one occasion, the judge was delivering his charge to the jury in a courtroom of the old Vancouver Court House overlooking the street. As he talked, carefully choosing his words, a screech of tires was heard from the street below, then the crash and crunch of colliding metal.

The judge walked down from his bench to the window,

94

gazed at the crash scene and walked back to his chair, all without pause in his review of the evidence. He was quite unaware that the jurors were grinning and winking. They had noticed, in the judge's walk to and from the window, that for comfort he had kicked off his shoes and was sitting there—gowned with all the majesty of the law—in his socks.

Once I drove Judge Manson from Nelson to Cranbrook, where he was to open the Assize the following morning. It was a fine October evening when we set out. At Creston we stopped briefly for refreshment. As we left the coffee shop, we met a trucker who said, "It's blowing a blizzard up there. You'll never make Cranbrook tonight."

There were snow tires in the trunk, but every service station was closed. I suggested we spend the night in the Kootenay Hotel, but the judge said, "It'll be worse by morning. I've never kept a jury waiting in my life. Let's go."

With summer tires in a raging snowstorm it was a hair-raising trip, made more so by the sight of vehicles that had gone off the road. But through it all, Judge Manson sang and sang. In his powerful baritone voice he sang everything from hymns to Negro spirituals, from the "Old Hundredth" to "Old Black Joe." Whenever he was momentarily at a loss for his next song he would fall back on "Shenandoah." My fondest memory of him will always be of a mountain road, rock face on one side and Moyie Lake down the bank on the other, headlights illuminating the swirling snow, and Judge Manson happily singing, "'Crawss the wide Missouri" with the fervour of one born not far from that river more than seventy years before.

Branca's last associations with Manson reveal something about both men. The legislation that in 1961 forced retirement of Supreme Court judges on reaching seventy-five became law when Manson was seventy-seven. He was deeply outraged and took every opportunity to protest, contending that no parliamentary amendment could negate his lifetime appointment.

In the last criminal trial of his career—a rape case notable only for the weakness of the evidence—he used his charge to the jury to publicize his grievance. Then he shocked the court by sentencing the accused to twenty-five years in prison.

Branca was retained to argue an appeal, and he severely criticized Judge Manson's handling of the trial. The Court of Appeal quashed the conviction and so pointedly questioned whether any conviction could be sustained on such evidence that all thought of a new trial was abandoned, and the man who had faced a twenty-five-year sentence walked free.

The day on which Manson imposed the twenty-five-year sentence was his last day in Criminal Assize. Another young man brought before him for sentencing that day, for whom the jury had recommended leniency, was inflicted with a fifteen-year term, whereupon the prisoner's mother heaped abuse on the judge, shouting, "You vindictive old bastard. You old bag of shit. You ought to be shot, you . . ."

As court orderlies hustled her away, one of the lawyers whispered, "It's the judge's swan song. Someone's got to say a few words." Crown Counsel George Murray rose and, with easy eloquence, gave the valediction, being able to pay perfectly sincere tributes to "a fearless and forthright judge" and "one with the courage of his convictions."

Nicholas Mussallem, whom Branca had asked to represent him at the sentencing, rose and said he wished to associate himself with the remarks of Mr. Murray. Assistant Prosecutor (later Provincial Court Judge) John Davies also rose and said he wished to associate himself with the remarks of Mr. Murray.

Don Smith, the official court reporter, rose. He said he wished to associate himself with the remarks of the lady who spoke before Mr. Murray.

Judge Manson bowed and left the bench.

Angelo Branca, as the lawyer who so severely and publicly criticized Manson's handling of his last trial, seemed the unlikeliest choice to champion Manson's fight against enforced retirement. That Manson chose him shows the relationship they had. The judge called Branca and said he was fighting the retirement law on all fronts. He had petitioned the Queen. He had enlisted Senator Farris to do what he could politically. Would Branca be his counsel and fight his case in the Supreme Court of Canada?

Branca was skeptical, but when he read the brief that the judge had prepared he was surprised at the ingenious case Manson had built. Here was a deeply researched review of every enactment and precedent, ancient and modern, that helped his argument. Manson was full of ideas, too, about how to attack the legislation. One was to contest the first judgement of the judge appointed in his place, on the ground that an appointee to a judgeship not legally vacant had no jurisdiction. It was incidental that the judge happened to be Mr. Justice Craig Munroe, newly appointed from the ranks of the Conservatives.

The Queen did not accede to the petition. Senator Farris raised the matter in the Senate, but the Liberals were out of power. Branca, fascinated though he was by the novelty of some of Manson's arguments, had in the end to give him his hard legal opinion that his lawsuit could not succeed in the Supreme Court of Canada. In this matter the Parliament of Canada was supreme.

All his career Manson was the kind of man who would fight for a cause until convinced it was hopeless, then look around without recrimination and eagerly espouse some other cause. He was financial adviser to the Presbyterian Church in Vancouver. The church gave him an office and, abandoning his fight to stay on the bench, he worked hard and happily there until illness and death at eighty-one.

To the last, visitors to that office included ex-convicts whom the ex-judge was helping to go straight.

CHAPTER NINE

When war broke out in 1939 Branca was thirty-six, a family man with two school-age daughters and a one-man practice. He joined a Vancouver reserve battalion and spent four nights a week, Sundays and summer holidays as Fusilier Branca of the Royal Irish Fusiliers of Canada.

His secretary was a remarkable young lady, Tosca Trasolini, who achieved local fame as an athlete and was also a licensed air pilot. As spokeswoman for "The Flying Seven," an all-women group of fliers, she volunteered their services as a unit to fly transports, to ferry new planes or to bomb the enemy. Because the authorities remained silent on this offer, Branca retained his capable secretary for several years.

In the war years he spent a disproportionate amount of his time defending servicemen in trouble with the law. Two of his cases involving soldiers as clients went into the law reports. One changed Canadian law by a famous decision. The other he recalls with sadness as a miscarriage of justice.

Rex v. *Hughes,* apart from its importance in legal history, contained elements that made it a public drama, the emotional factor arising from the timing. At the height of the anti-Japanese clamour following Pearl Harbour, when an attack from the sea was still feared, a Canadian soldier killed a Vancouver Japanese in a store holdup; the soldier and three other young men were sentenced to be hanged.

Angelo Branca answered a ring at his door on a night in April 1942 and admitted a woman who asked that he save her son, who had just been sentenced to death. He was the soldier who had carried the gun. Branca heard her out and, though she had no money, said he would launch an appeal.

A layman reading the 900-page transcript today would wonder what Branca could have found to appeal. The four days of evidence amounted to this: Robert Hughes, aged nineteen, single, a private in the Canadian army awaiting posting to Europe, arranged with three companions to steal a car and rob two stores in Kitsilano. At the second store, the Japanese storekeeper raised the alarm, and her son ran from the back premises and grappled with Hughes, who was holding a gun. The son was fatally shot.

The evidence evoked little sympathy for Hughes. A sixteen-year-old girl told of being with the boys when they were planning the robberies and of her part in obtaining a gun and ammunition. (She told the court she had been expecting to marry Hughes.)

Before the raid they went to Lulu Island to practise with the gun, and Hughes shot a wild duck at seventy-five feet which they cooked and ate. Less than half an hour after the shooting at the store, when the stolen getaway car had become stuck in soft sand on English Bay and abandoned, Hughes visited another girl and took her to the Embassy Hall, where they danced for the rest of the night. (This girl also told the court she had been expecting to marry Hughes.)

When Hughes was asked if he had anything to say why sentence of death should not be passed, he turned to the jury and said, "I hope you guys feel good because you want to string up four boys for some lousy Jap. You can string me up. I'm not afraid to die. That's why I joined the army. I would have got it over there anyway."

The depth of public feeling pro and con aroused by the news of the death sentences may be judged from letters to the newspapers. "Why four for one? If we have a Jap invasion here I will get four Japs for these boys," said a letter in the *Province*. Another said, "We are calling for reserves for this coast. These boys' sentences should be handled by giving them a chance to kill many more Japs. Remember Pearl Harbour!"

A letter writer who signed herself, "Englishwoman Thirty Years in Canada" wrote, "Thank God we have in our fair city some fearless judges," clearly meaning the twelve jurors who, knowing their verdict meant death sentences, nevertheless felt bound in conscience to vote "guilty of murder." Set against the black marks that British Columbia and Canada earned over the alien expulsions and confiscations of 1942, the verdict is a heart-warming comment about twelve citizens who at that anxious time considered a Japanese life as sacred as any other. To some others it made no difference that the dead man had been born and spent all his twenty-seven years in the Vancouver area nor that his father had been in Canada forty years, his mother thirty and his grandparents even longer.

On the appeal, Branca represented only Hughes. After minutely sifting the evidence, he had just one particle on which to work, two lines in all those 900 pages. A Crown witness had mentioned Hughes saying, "The man came at me, and the gun went off by accident." That word "accident" was the straw at which Branca clutched.

There was no precedent for using "accident" as a ground of appeal in a murder case of this type, because an English legal principle which had been followed unreservedly in Canada since the *Beard* case in 1920 established that where death occurs during the commission of a felony, though death may not be intended, that is murder.

Branca did not attack the principle. He sought to establish the primacy of Canadian law where defined in the Criminal Code of Canada over English criminal law defined by cases. He developed an argument that for Canadians the law was the criminal code enacted by the Parliament of Canada, and that the criminal code did not say what the *Beard* case said. Maybe it should, but it did not.

Tom Hurley was appealing on behalf of one of the other

youths. Steeped in English criminal law, he could not associate himself with Branca's idea. He pointed out the cases in which Canadian courts had explicitly followed the *Beard* case.

Branca consulted other lawyers whose legal opinion he valued. Most thought the *Beard* case was an insuperable barrier. He finally went to Mr. Justice Murphy, by then retired from the bench. To him Branca enlarged on his argument that the Parliament of Canada had codified the country's law and, in doing so, had said that for murder to be committed there had to be an intent to kill or to do such injury as would be likely to cause death, and a recklessness as to whether it caused death or not. If that was the law of Canada, any evidence of accident obliged the judge to instruct the jury on the possible alternate verdict of manslaughter. The trial judge, in line with the *Beard* case, had not done this, and in that omission, argued Branca, lay ground for a new trial.

Judge Murphy thought the argument novel but tenable. Branca made it his main ground of appeal. The contest in the British Columbia Court of Appeal was close. Five judges of Appeal heard argument for more than four days. Four of the judges wrote lengthy judgements. Chief Justice McDonald and Mr. Justice Fisher decided against Branca, the chief justice saying, "I am satisfied the law of England is the law of British Columbia."

Mr. Justice Sloan and Mr. Justice O'Halloran agreed with Branca, the former saying that if the English cases defined murder in terms different from those of the Criminal Code of Canada, then the code governed.

The fifth judge was Mr. Justice McQuarrie, who rarely wrote a judgement longer than "I agree." On this occasion he wrote four paragraphs, agreeing that the appeals should be allowed. So by a decision of three to two the British Columbia Court of Appeal quashed the death sentences and ordered a new trial.

The decision aroused much interest among all concerned with criminal law. An editor for one of the law reports wrote, "The judgment of Mr. Justice Sloan . . .

may run athwart the view commonly entertained since the decision in the Beard case. The question is undoubtedly ripe for submission to the ultimate tribunal."

The attorney general of British Columbia thought so, too. He appealed to the Supreme Court of Canada to reinstate the death sentences.

On the train journey to Ottawa and in their hotel on the night before the hearing, Angelo Branca went over his argument with Tom Hurley, William Schultz and John Burton, representing the other three appellants. They remained doubtful that the Supreme Court of Canada would throw *Beard* into the discard. Hurley considered the *Beard* proposition sound law and founded on a proper concern for public safety. Branca said the law in Canada was what the Parliament of Canada said it was, and its voice was the criminal code.

They went over it again at breakfast. Some new point in the discussion lodged in Hurley's mind. They were walking down Wellington Street on the way to the Supreme Court when Hurley stopped in his tracks and said, "Angelo, me boy. Bedad, ye have it. Ye have it won."

He was right. The full bench of nine judges of the Supreme Court of Canada upheld Branca's argument, and ordered that the accused have new trials.

One year less a day after their first trial opened, the four accused were again arraigned in Assize Court, this time before a different judge and jury, and with Branca now defending Hughes. Again the case lasted all week, and again the jury returned late Saturday night with their verdict. This time it was: all accused not guilty of murder, all guilty of manslaughter. Three received ten years' imprisonment and one who had been only seventeen at the time of the crime was sentenced to nine years.

The Canadian criminal code had been upheld as the law of the land, but no one argued that the sections on homicide and intent, as newly defined, went far enough in the interests of public safety. The following year the Parliament of Canada amended the criminal code, and culpable homicide committed without intent during the commis-

102

sion of a crime, in certain defined circumstances, was returned to the category of murder, not manslaughter.

Branca, though he had taken advantage of the law as written, welcomed the amendment as warmly as anyone. "Ever since," he says, "anyone who goes out to commit a crime and takes a lethal weapon with him has to realize that the possible consequence may be murder even though he did not intend to kill. Ever since, that has clearly been the law."

When, in 1964, Judge Branca first wore the scarlet and black robes of an Assize judge, those charged before him included two men accused of breaking and entering a store and possessing stolen goods. As the judge took his place on the bench one of the men stared at him open-mouthed. A few minutes later this man interrupted the proceedings to ask that the case be adjourned to the next Assize. That would have meant a different judge. He seemed unable to give a reason, and his companion would not consent to any adjournment. The judge refused.

Something about the man who made the application tugged at Judge Branca's memory. He checked the man's details: Robert Hughes, aged forty-one. It was the same Robert Hughes whom he had saved from being hanged more than twenty years before.

Hughes and the other man, Russell Beaver, having been on bail while awaiting trial, had duly surrendered themselves for the first day's hearing. The Crown saw no reason why they would not return next morning, so their bail was extended for the night. Next morning Beaver returned to the courthouse, but not Hughes. Judge Branca learned that Hughes had spent the night at home with his wife and, in the morning, had left in his car saying he was going to the court. A bench warrant was issued for his arrest. Two days later, Hughes's body was found in a secluded spot, with a bullet wound in the head and a revolver lying nearby.

Two items competed for prominence on the front page of Vancouver newspapers on 2 May 1945. One read, "Huns Surrender Unconditionally." It proved to be premature.

The other was, "Woman Brutally Murdered, Tossed into English Bay." Angelo Branca still thinks that William Hainen should not have been hanged for her murder.

Hainen and Domenico Nasso were the only two who paid the extreme penalty out of the sixty-three people whom Branca defended on murder charges. He had no quarrel with the Nasso verdict. The Hainen verdict he thought was wrong.

Olga Hawryluk, aged twenty-three, single, from the Peace River country, had come to work in Vancouver. At the time of her death she was cashier at the Empire Cafe and had earlier been a waitress at the Good Eats, both all-night cafes on Granville Street.

William Hainen, aged twenty-eight, single, was a Vancouver man, a former hardrock miner, who had come home from Camp Borden on army embarkation leave.

The evidence was that just before dawn a woman and her daughter in an apartment overlooking English Bay were awakened by a woman's screams. They threw on some clothes and went to the beach, and saw a soldier in battle dress rise from behind some logs at the water's edge. He passed the women with face averted as if to avoid scrutiny. They asked him if he had heard the screams but he did not reply. The daughter courageously followed, turned a flashlight on him and asked him a second and third time. He then answered, "No," and hurried away. She stopped a passing car, and the driver called the police. Within an hour, a hatless soldier in blood-stained battle dress was arrested.

Meantime the two women had discovered, at the water's edge, the body of a young woman whose head had been battered by blows from two pieces of driftwood lying nearby. They also found a soldier's cap with Hainen's identification number.

Angelo Branca was appointed by the attorney general to defend Hainen. The circumstantial evidence linking him with the man at the beach was so strong that a defence of unproven identity was hopeless. When Branca gathered evidence on Hainen's drinking in the hours before the killing, a more feasible defence emerged. He needed evidence of expert witnesses to say that a man who had consumed so much alcohol could not form any intent, least of all a murderous intent.

Branca found not one but three psychiatrists prepared to swear just that. One was a Vancouver psychiatrist in private practice and the others were army psychiatrists. In his office, he went over with them again and again the quantities and timing of Hainen's drinking as he had them from his witnesses, and the three specialists remained emphatic. If the opinion they expressed to him in the office were accepted, Branca thought, the verdict would be manslaughter and Hainen would escape hanging.

The Crown showed that Hainen and his sister, with other people, had gone on a drinking spree. They visited beer parlours, a dance hall and cafes from the late afternoon to the early morning, when they separated. Between 3:00 A.M. and 4:00 A.M., Hainen was in the Good Eats cafe when Olga Hawryluk came in to have a cup of coffee on her way home from her night work. Hainen spoke to her and asked her to go out with him, and she refused. When she left he followed her.

Branca established that Hainen's alcohol consumption was as follows: half a thirteen-ounce bottle of rye at noon; twenty-four to thirty beers and a drink of rum between 2:00 P.M. and 8:00 P.M.; fifteen beers between 9:30 P.M. and 11:00 P.M., and more than half a bottle of rye afterwards.

To his first psychiatrist Branca listed these amounts of alcohol and the times when they were said to have been consumed, and this exchange followed:

Q Doctor, bearing in mind the amount of liquor I have outlined, would you say the accused was able to form a conscious intention of killing a person or of inflicting an injury likely to cause death?

A I do not think he would be able to form that intention.

Crown Counsel C.M. Whitehouse, K.C., opened his cross-examination of the psychiatrist thus:

Q Doctor, please note carefully a number of points I am going to put to you, and give me your answer at the end of them. Would beating a person to death with repeated blows show intent? Would placing the body where it would be carried away by waves show intent? Would an attempt to avert his face when approached by the women, one of them carrying a flashlight, show intent?

A One might judge from those points that he was able to form intention.

Branca tried to nullify the effect of that answer by re-examination:

Q Doctor, assuming the truth of the facts I first gave you, does your first opinion still stand?

A Yes.

That should have nailed it down for the defence, but Whitehouse persisted. He obtained the court's permission to further cross-examine:

Q Doctor, assuming the truth of all I said, do you take that position inflexibly?

A No.

Branca sought to retrieve matters by getting the firm answers he wanted from the army psychiatrists. They were as emphatic in their replies to his questions as they had been in his office: that amount of alcohol, consumed in that time, would make it impossible for a man to form murderous intent. Under Whitehouse's cross-examination, the firmness of their assertions oozed away.

So although Branca had secured from seven witnesses, Crown and defence, that Hainen was drunk or under the influence of drink, he had not obtained the positive evidence of incapacity promised by the three experts. The jury of eleven men and one woman brought in a verdict of "murder, with a strong recommendation of mercy." Hainen was sentenced to death.

Branca took the case to the British Columbia Court of Appeal, his principal ground being Hainen's inability to form an intent owing to his drunkenness. On the appeal, the lack of strong support from the defence psychiatrists proved fatal.

Hainen was executed just when other soldiers were arriving home from the war.

Family portrait taken in 1913 when Angelo (*left*) was ten years old. Teresa, little Joseph, Filippo, John and Anne.

Branca's earliest childhood recollection: the North Vancouver Hotel, two blocks from his home. (*Vancouver Public Library*)

Hastings Street, about 1906. For thirty years Branca would practise law from the second floor of the Royal Bank Building (*left*). (The Carnegie Library is on opposite corner.) (*Vancouver Public Library*)

The busy intersection of Hastings and Main, showing Branca's office building on right-hand corner. (*Vancouver Public Library*)

Angelo Branca, a young barrister
and solicitor in the thirties.

The old Vancouver Court House was the scene of Branca's career from law
student days to his judgeship in Court of Appeal. (He met his future wife when
her father came to Canada to help to build the second Hotel Vancouver, *left.*)
(*Vancouver Public Library*)

The much-loved cartoonist Jack Boothe drew this
impression of "The Boxing Barrister" in 1934 for the
Vancouver *Province*.

The Liberal Party's humble Vancouver Centre riding office "ran" B.C. politics and "appointed its princelings to senate and bench." (*Vancouver Public Library*)

The Hastings Street scene that met Angelo and Viola on their way to church 19
1938—the Bloody Sunday post office riot. (*Vancouver Public Library*)

Moments after being photographed by the press, these politicians were
scattered by an onrushing wave of rats, clinching their resolve to finance a park
for the east side. Branca shows his plan to Alderman John Bennett, City
Engineer Charles Brackenbridge, Senator Stan McKeen, Premier Duff Pattullo,
Attorney General Gordon Wismer, Defence Minister Ian MacKenzie, Parks
Chairman Rowe Holland and Alderman Harry DeGraves.

Mr. Justice Denis Murphy, a law student's model. (*Patricia Murphy*)

The notoriously idiosyncratic Chief Justice Aulay MacAulay Morrison. (*Vancouver City Archives*)

Lawyer Tom Hurley, like Branca, contributed gaiety to the courthouse.

Mr. Justice Alec Manson, who sentenced fourteen murderers to death and "never lost a night's sleep over any of them," struck sparks off Branca in the courtroom, ejecting him twice. (*Vancouver City Archives*)

Chief Justice J.O. Wilson, a great judge with an "innate feeling for the law."

Courtroom 309 in the old Vancouver Court House never changed in the fifty years Branca knew it—only the faces. This 1940 Appeal bench (*rear*) comprises (*left to right*) Justices O'Halloran, McQuarrie, M.A. MacDonald (chief), Sloan and D.A. McDonald. (*Vancouver Public Library*)

Viola Branca with daughters
Patricia (Battensby) and
Dolores (Holmes).

Back in Vancouver a paper ran the headline, "Court Annoyed. Postmistress
Trial Delayed. Her Lawyer's Gone Fishing." (*Left to right*) Dr. Reuben
Rabinovich of Montreal, Branca and Hollywood producer Lew Deak.

The nineteenth-century prophecies of Lukeria Kalmykova, a Doukhobor leader in Russia, would complicate Branca's prosecution of several hundred Freedomites in 1950. Seated with her is protégé Peter Verigin I, before he led the Doukhobors to Canada in 1899. (*Vancouver Public Library*)

At the "bookie" trial of 1951-52, trial prosecutor (later Magistrate) Gordon Scott (*left*) faces a massed array of defence lawyers: Albert (later Mr. Justice) Mackoff, Branca, D.L. Fraser, John (later Chief Justice) Farris and Senator Farris; (*behind*) Tom (later Mr. Justice) Dohm and John Wismer.

Robert Sommers and the battery of defenders in the 1958 B.C. forestry licence bribery trial: Nick Mussallem, Branca, D. McK. Brown, Alfred Bull, J.R. Nicholson and H.R. Bowering. (*Photograph by Don McLeod; Vancouver Province*)

The Honourable Angelo Ernest
Branca of the B.C. Court of
Appeal, drawn by Robert Banks.
(The Advocate)

Brethren of the Court of Appeal in Branca's last years on the bench,
including (*left*) Chief Justice John Farris and (*third from left*) Angelo Branca.

Higher and lower courts switch precedence: Branca in the courtroom presided over by his daughter, Provincial Court Judge Dolores Holmes. (*Photograph by Peter Hulbert; Vancouver* Province)

The photograph that prompted one journalist to compare Branca to roles played by Spencer Tracy. (*Photograph by Paul Rockett*)

CHAPTER TEN

Peacetime found Angelo and Viola Branca with a comfortable home and two daughters of high school age. He also had a compulsion to work which kept him at the office most evenings—a condition not thought to be good for marriage or for child raising.

Of his marriage Branca says, "No man was ever luckier." His luck was more than in marrying a woman of warm personality and happy disposition; her strengths were those that provided a secure and stable relationship in a home in which the husband and father was devoting eighty to ninety hours a week to his profession.

Viola accepted that that was his nature. She brought up the girls. She could do it successfully because she had a firm agreement: whatever the demands of his calling, unless he were out of town, Angelo Branca would be at the supper table with his wife and girls every night of the year.

The busy lawyer would drive across the city from office or courthouse, spend at least an hour with the family, then usually be back at 208 East Hastings by 7:30 P.M. while Viola saw that the girls did their homework or domestic duties. They would probably be sleeping when their father came home. When he was out of town, around supper time would come a telephone call from him, unfailingly.

The family followed that custom of all four having supper together through all the years from the girls' childhood until careers or marriage intervened. The fact that supper was the prime institution in the family made special demands on Viola since both she and her husband encouraged their daughters to keep open house for their friends. A generation later both daughters would be conscience-stricken on recalling the catering and entertaining they imposed on their mother. They were day students at Sacred Heart Convent, where they always had boarder friends, often from Latin America, who loved to be invited for a meal out of residence, along with their local friends.

Nor was it only they who kept their mother busy playing hostess. For their father, Sunday supper, after an afternoon of energetic gardening, was a highlight of the week in the home and, gregarious as ever, he habitually pressed sundry young people to "come and have supper with us." Fourteen at the Sunday supper table, twelve of them young people, was a common occurrence.

Some of those guests still remember the host sitting quietly at the head of the table, listening to every word but letting younger ones dominate the conversation. A future son-in-law, Mel Battensby, on first meeting him told Patricia, "After what I'd heard and read about your dad I expected him to have fiery red hair and an angry red face, and here he was, dark and quiet and all smiles, letting his daughters do the talking."

By the time they were entertaining their children's friends, the Brancas were long settled in the Dunbar residence on the west side of Vancouver that was their home for more than twenty-five years. They had moved from Cambridge Street to West 24th Avenue in 1937.

Viola, living four blocks from the Church of the Immaculate Conception, busied herself in parish affairs. She also created for herself an interest that has rewarded her in pleasure ever since. She and friends started a crafts group which for thirty years has met weekly to make gift and decorative articles. Their work won such a reputation that all their creations are bespoke, and sales have produced more than $40 000 for half a dozen charities.

Viola took charge of the family holidays—a few weeks in the summer in a Union Steamship Company cottage on Bowen Island, where Angelo joined them on weekends. He never wanted to be far from his office, but was occasionally tempted by his love of fishing. He fished the streams around Vancouver and creeks in the Bridge River valley, where his brother John kept hotels at Gold Bridge and Bralorne. Later Branca's successes in fighting big fish in salt water spoiled the pleasure he once found in casting the fly.

Their first real family holiday came a year after the war. Branca thought it was a success. The family thought otherwise, because he drove them from Vancouver to Chicago, New York, Washington and back in three weeks. "We stopped at every place of interest," says his younger daughter. "Then he put his foot on the floorboards until we reached the next. I think he photographed every historic site from Custer's Last Stand to the Battle of Bull Run."

What happened when he and Viola took their first overseas holiday was completely in character. Branca, a collector of coins, was friendly with Harold Bradshaw, a lawyer who was the leading western authority on Japanese postage stamps. The Bradshaws and the Brancas planned a six-week holiday together in Japan. Viola and the Bradshaws took a leisurely trip by freighter. Angelo followed later by air and met them with the news that law business compelled him to shorten his trip to four weeks. Thanks to Bradshaw, they saw a great deal in a short time, but calls from the office pursued Branca. Two and a half weeks after arriving in Japan, he was on a plane for Vancouver.

Happy though he is to visit places of historic interest, where he relates scenes to his reading and gives his imagination free rein, Branca is an impatient traveller, easily irked by frustrations in public transportation or public dining rooms. When Viola and he took their first trip to Europe and their plane landed back in Montreal, he did something that was not intended to amuse or impress and had no connection with fear of flying. As he stepped off the gangway, the Honourable A.E. Branca, Supreme Court judge, knelt down on both knees and kissed the ground of Canada.

In Branca's sentiments, Canada takes first place. Since his wife does not speak Italian, he never spoke it in his own home. He never passed it on to his daughters, and they discovered its attractions for themselves when they were long out of high school. Dolores, after graduating from law school, spent half of two successive years in Italy, mostly living with relatives. She achieved some fluency in the language, and has since been sufficiently active in Italian affairs in Vancouver that the Confratellanza Italo-Canadese voted her Italian of the Year in 1976.

In the early fifties, when comparatively few women were lawyers, Dolores delighted her father by being called to the bar and joining him in his practice. She left the practice on her appointment as Provincial Court judge in 1975, and holds court at Burnaby.

The Brancas' friends included many couples whom they had known from the earliest days of their marriage. Among them were Frank and Lillian Braidwood, whose son Tom joined Angelo's firm straight from law school, never to leave it. So did David Nuttall, son of Branca's old RCMP friend Cpl. Ernest Nuttall.

When Branca went to the bench, his former students took over his practice, and on his retirement as a judge he rejoined them in the firm of Braidwood, Nuttall, Mackenzie, Brewer, Greyell and Company, more familiarly known as Braidwood-Nuttall.

Branca in 1945 was still the same "well set up, well muscled" figure described by a reporter in 1926 but "sturdy" now substituted for "slim"; he was still dark-haired. Later came the white hair that caused writer Eve Rockett to seize on his resemblance to film actor Spencer Tracy. To her, at seventy he was "lost Spencer Tracy heroes recaptured." It was not only his resemblance to the actor that prompted the thought. Voice, mannerisms and physical energy made one believe Angelo Branca could have played the Tracy part in *Guess Who's Coming to Dinner* without some of us noticing the substitution, especially when the old liberal played by Tracy exclaims, "Well I'll be a son-of-a-bitch!"

Branca dressed well if a little less conservatively than some lawyers, thanks to his stylish Italian tailor. At the end of a spring day when the lawyers had hung up their gowns and were leaving the courthouse, Branca would be in a lightweight light-coloured suit while most of his contemporaries wore dark business suits.

Friends tell a tongue-in-cheek story which belies his reputation as a "snappy dresser." They say he had an old friend who became wealthy. Branca handled some personal affairs for him but felt he could not accept a fee. The friend wrote out a cheque and insisted that Branca name a charity. His choice was one of those East End agencies that minister to people down on their luck. Branca, knowing the Mother Superior and thinking he might pay his respects to her, walked over from his office with the cheque and, by-passing a line of hungry men, stepped smartly to the front. There the young nun in charge sweetly but firmly explained that there were others ahead of him and there was food enough for all. Branca handed over the $5000 and left—for once reduced to silence.

He was not always the best-gowned lawyer in court. One of his secretaries, knowing he was opposing Senator Farris in a civil jury case and wanting to see her boss in action against the maestro, watched from the public gallery and found it nerve-racking.

Part of the time she wanted to cry out because the senator, it seemed to her, always rustled papers or caused some distraction at the moment Branca was dragging some admission from an adverse witness. Most of the time she felt humiliated at the sight of her boss striding around trailing a large loop of torn hem from his gown which he had stepped on and ripped. At the first recess, with needle and thread borrowed from courthouse secretaries, she insisted on making repairs. He was unimpressed, so she sharply reminded him that he had a reputation to maintain, and what would Mr. Justice Manson say?

Earlier Judge Manson had started a campaign to raise lawyers' standards of courtroom dress, which he called "sloppy." He said that unless they appeared in his court correctly dressed he would not "see" them. This pronouncement tickled the news sense of a *Sun* editor, and he sent a photographer racing to the courthouse. The photographer is supposed to have snapped the first gowned figures he spied in the corridors. The front-page picture was of a pair of grinning lawyers and the caption said that counsel wishing to be "seen" in court "must appear in proper dress, such as worn here by Angelo Branca and Tom Hurley."

Being "not seen" is an old English euphemism used by judges to indicate to a barrister that he is improperly dressed or lacks status to appear. Branca often appeared before British Columbia's most "unseeing" judge, Chief Justice Archer Martin, but never in Admiralty Court.

The formidable chief justice deplored the abolition of wigs from British Columbia courts in 1905 and, being the federal judge in Admiralty in the west, he insisted on their being worn in that court until 1942. Many young lawyers like Branca never went to the expense of buying wigs, and if they found themselves required to appear in Admiralty Court, which hears claims for losses at sea or in other navigable waters, they cast around to borrow one.

Knowing how punctilious Chief Justice Martin was, one young lawyer in borrowed wig made sure that he was properly dressed. This ensued:

THE LAWYER: May it please your lordship, my name . . .

CHIEF JUSTICE: The Court cannot see you.

THE LAWYER: I beg your lordship's pardon?

CHIEF JUSTICE: Call the next case.

The downcast lawyer removed himself to the corridor and checked again. Wig? Collar? Vest? Gown? Oh, my God! He was wearing *brown* shoes.

When bachelor Tom Hurley, in his sixties, married widow Maisie Armytage Moore, his best man was Angelo Branca, and Viola was matron of honour. The church was crowded with judges, lawyers and a fine assortment of criminals, as well as Indian chiefs from all over the province. As the couple walked back from the signing of the register, Tom was claimed by two little girls, newly acquired grandchildren. Fondly putting his arms around their shoulders he remarked in mock horror, "I should have had notice of this," whereupon his best man told him, "I'm surprised you didn't insist on examination for discovery before the ceremony." And groomsman Bill Masterson, who prosecuted when Tom defended in many a courtroom contest, said, "Today's the first time I've seen you cornered when you didn't come up with some fancy application for an adjournment."

Maisie Hurley was as noted a character as Tom and as devoted a champion of the underdog. Her cause was that of the native Indian. She was founder, publisher and editor of *The Indian Voice* and was the only white woman to be an honorary chief of the Native Brotherhood.

Maisie was the daughter of a Scottish mining engineer named Campbell-Johnston whose profession took him to Wales, to India and, in 1890, to British Columbia, so she learned to speak Welsh, Hindustani and Chinook. Teenaged Maisie eloped with a young Anglican minister from the Nicola Valley but the marriage never took place. She said they had "theological differences." Her parents sent her out of harm's way to a private school for young ladies in England. She eloped again, to marry an American boxing promoter. They raised a family in the United States, and after her husband's death she married Tom Hurley.

Because she was a cousin of the Duke of Argyll, as a wedding present Tom obtained for her—by what illegal means only he knew—the embalmed heart of the fifth Earl of Montrose, who was executed for treason in 1650 through the plotting of his archenemy the eighth Earl of Argyll, Maisie's ancestor. There was an outcry over the ancient artifact leaving Britain, and Maisie returned it after Tom's death.

Tom had an able young partner to whom Maisie Hurley imparted some of her interest in Indian land claims. He later won historic legal victories on behalf of the Nishga, and attracted notice in Ottawa. In the eighties, Mr. Justice Tom Berger's *Report on the Mackenzie Valley Pipeline Proposal* is influencing Canada's northern development.

CHAPTER ELEVEN

The end of the war marked the start of the great years for Angelo Branca. Already almost twenty years a lawyer and still in his early forties, he would have another eighteen years of prosecuting, defending and running a practice before leaving the bar for the bench.

In those years he came to the peak of his powers as an advocate. His courtroom style gradually became quieter, so that the purple passages, though fewer, stood out all the more. From time to time headlines would tell of "Branca in clash with" some judge or lawyer, but his basic technique took this form: in civil suits, an orderly presentation with a crisp and never laboured submission on the law, unless a skeptical judge provoked him to argument; in criminal matters, a persuasive pitch to the jury; in both, searching cross-examination without pause between an answer and the next question.

Branca's cross-examination was often unorthodox, sometimes bold. In a trial at New Westminster, he was having no success with his questioning of an attractive woman of twenty-six who, completely self-possessed, stonewalled all his efforts to induce her to admit that she was not averse to socializing with men. Finally he took a risk by asking, "For instance, would you go out with me?"

She looked over to Mr. Justice Verchere, obviously wondering, "Do I have to answer that?" When the Judge remained silent, she gave a long, cool, appraising look at the lawyer, in his late fifties but still the trim, good-looking actor, then said, "Yes." She took another look and added, "Yes. I'd go out with you." Branca looked hard at the jury to make sure they had his point, and changed the subject.

Branca the trial lawyer is best remembered around the courts for his winning ways with juries. From watching Joe Russell twenty years before, he had learned that success in criminal cases comes from mastery of the law coupled with the ability to communicate with lay people who make up juries. So in a style that was peculiarly his own, he would position himself in front of the jury box and address himself to a particular juror as though concerned with him or her individually. When he felt he had convinced the juror he would move on to another, and another, until all had been subjected—almost privately, as it were—to his persuasion.

His voice contributed to that persuasiveness: not deep, no resonant organ tones, but clear and beautifully modulated. David Roberts, editor of *The Advocate,* puts it best: "He has that quality all great counsel must possess, an ability to make his audience listen to his plea. In small part this is due to his beautiful voice, which would do credit to a cardinal, and which he uses like a finely tuned violin to entrance his hearers."

Some thought they detected a hypnotic influence. "I'm not the only one," says retired court reporter Jack Nelson, "who insists that in his heyday there was a mesmeric quality in Angelo Branca's advocacy."

His facility for insinuating himself into the minds of juries was best seen in his defence of motor manslaughter cases—charges of causing death by wantonly negligent driving. These he rarely lost.

His method with juries in those cases was to paint a picture of his client as a driver like themselves, no more criminal than they but caught in a frightening driving situation. Then he would coax them to think of occasions when they had taken chances and escaped the consequences. All jurors in such cases are drivers. They would never pass the "Challenge" stage if defence counsel suspected they were not. It was extraordinary how Branca could win sympathy for accused drivers. Many times, working hard to keep up with Branca's flow of words, I found myself thinking, "There but for the grace of God go I." If jurors thought the same, the case was won.

Hugh McGivern, Q.C., won a reputation for his successes with juries. Lecturing at UBC Law School on how to defend in a jury trial, he used to conclude his course, "I've told you all I know about jury trials. Now take a day off and go down to the courthouse and watch Angelo Branca handle a jury."

Conventional tactics required defence lawyers in rape cases to do all they could to keep women out of the jury box. If a woman's name was drawn out of the tally box, defence counsel would say, "Challenge," and the sheriff would say, "Stand aside"; only after the defence had exhausted all its challenges would the prosecutor be able to say, "Content," and see a woman take a seat in the jury box. Over the years Branca often ignored that convention, and rarely did his cause suffer through his doing so. "I found women as jurors could be very hard on their own sex," he says. "It usually depended on what they thought of the complainant."

"Attack is the best defence" was an instinctive reaction, not a cliché, with Branca. He exploited to the limit any error made by representatives of the Crown in prosecuting, even if it meant attacking fellow lawyers or policemen he knew as friends. His reasoning was that when all the might of the State is arrayed against the individual, it is wrong for the State to exceed its already great powers.

This creed was tested at Kamloops after two men, returning from an abortive moose hunt, saw by moonlight a handsome beast standing in a farm pasture. They shot and butchered it, took the hindquarters and left behind the carcass of Brigadier General Bostock's prize bull.

Police quickly traced the beef to a basement and charged its possessor, who admitted that he was one of the rustlers. They accused another man of being his partner and charged him. When this man appeared in Branca's office with cash to fight the case, Branca advised him that he had a poor defence and might be wise to plead guilty in hopes of a mitigated sentence, but the man would not hear of it.

Branca found himself fighting an uphill battle in Kamloops Assize Court, knowing that the Crown prosecutor had the confessed thief in the lockup below and would probably call him to incriminate his client. To verify his fears, Branca went to the lockup during the lunch adjournment and asked to be allowed to talk to the prisoner. The jailer refused him access and, when pressed, said the Crown prosecutor had ordered that no one was to see the man, "and he particularly mentioned you."

Back in court, Branca moved that the judge dismiss the case because of the prosecutor's action, but Mr. Justice Whittaker refused. The prosecution closed its case, and Branca announced that he would not call any defence evidence.

Addressing the jury, he scarcely mentioned the evidence but spoke for an hour on his being denied access to a witness. He attacked the motives and the competence of the prosecutor, reminded the jury that the Crown had no vested ownership in any witness, not even its own, and pointed out that the Crown's duty was not to obtain a conviction but to bring out all the relevant facts. What had the Crown to hide, that it should deny the defence access to the one man who presumably knew the truth?

The old Kamloops Court House is the worst designed in the province. Even the soundproofing of the jury room was poor. When those awaiting the verdict in the courtroom heard the raised voices of jurors saying "goddamned prosecutor" and "not fair," they knew it was going to be a not guilty verdict. It was. Branca and British justice both operate on the basis that juries are fair.

Branca hated to lose a case, but he hated still more to lose a legal argument. He particularly wanted to win an argument on a matter in which success would have meant a ruling broadening a convicted person's options in launching an appeal. When the judgement went against him, he threw his papers into his briefcase, snapped it shut and, as he headed for the door, called out over his shoulder to opposing counsel, "Bill Craig, you've just set the law of Canada back fifty years."

Later these two friends would sharpen their legal claws on each other in argument when Mr. Justice Branca and Mr. Justice William Alastair Craig were brethren on the Court of Appeal.

His most embarrassing loss—laughable now but mortifying at the time—was in a civil action that he began on behalf of a client to recover a substantial sum. Branca lost no time in filing the papers, but the solicitor on the other side was Nick Mussallem, and he was a notorious procrastinator: a charmer in and out of court, capable of brilliance but hating the routine chores of practice. (Once I heard an outstandingly successful lawyer reprimanding Nick for some oversight: "I wish I had half your talent. But I do read my mail and check my appointments book and send out my bills." Mussallem looked Walter Owen in the eye and asked earnestly, "But don't you find, Walter, that all that stuff interferes with the practice of law?")

Mussallem would not file a statement of defence in response to Branca's statement of claim. Finally Branca called him and said, "Nick, I could move for judgement in default, but I really believe there's an issue for trial here. If you don't file your defence soon I'll be tempted to file one for you."

Mussallem, ingratiating as ever, replied, "Why don't you do that? You'll do it better than I."

Branca drafted a defence in reply to his own claim and, that document duly filed, was able to proceed to trial. Mussallem fought the case on his opponent's statement of defence, and won.

Years later, for what may have been his greatest case Branca chose as his assistant Nick Mussallem.

Despite the reputation he gained for provoking courtroom excitement—"Any fireworks from Branca today?" we used to ask at the end of the day—the drama and the confrontations were all calculated, not temperamental.

"I soon found," Branca told me, "that to be a good man in court, especially with juries, you have to be an actor. You have to know playacting ass-backwards. Every trial, big or small, was a production with me. You put on your act and try to gauge the effect of it as you go along. You sense when your pitch is not scoring points and you adjust. You are playing to an audience even though that audience is the jury or the judge. No one else—because you are acting for no other reason on earth than to win your case."

In his thirties he had acted in a theatre group that put on plays at the Hastings Community Centre. He loves an audience, whether he is acting in a play, or as a standup comedian in a fund-raising event trying to put the audience in a generous mood, or before a jury. Stage fright has never plagued him.

In those years when Angelo Branca was at his best as an actor on the courtroom floor, another superb actor graced the bench. For seven years, before he moved on to take charge of MacMillan Bloedel, John Valentine Clyne linked his acting flair and his legal ability in an effort to raise the standards of practice in the British Columbia Supreme Court.

Judge Clyne believed that truth was more likely to emerge if witnesses sensed the majesty of the law, and that justice was more attainable if lawyers came into court totally prepared and mindful of court ethics and behaviour. He played the role of judge with that belief in mind. His court had the dignity of the High Court of England—he had studied at London University and taken his admiralty law in England. There was about him a hint of the awesome Lord Chief Justice Goddard, on whose bench he once sat as a guest.

No one took liberties in his court. When John Diefenbaker made a much-publicized appearance in Vancouver to defend a man charged with murder and tried some of the devices he used with such success on prairie juries, Judge Clyne quickly brought him into line. Diefenbaker was down on one knee dramatically re-enacting the death scene for the jury when the judge frostily reminded him that the jury was concerned with evidence—"and please come out from behind that table so that I, too, can see what you're doing."

Before Clyne became a judge, his prodigious ability had

led the federal government to offer him one of the country's biggest jobs, the presidency of Canadian National Railways. C.D. Howe, annoyed at his turning it down, said he was wasting his talents by burying himself in law in the backwoods of British Columbia. Howe's eastern elitism and low opinion of the importance of law offended Clyne, who felt moved to devote his talents to improving the justice system rather than the railway system even though it meant less than half the remuneration.

Clyne created his image of an autocrat in the courts as part of his campaign to raise standards. He was an experienced actor, veteran of twenty roles in university and other plays. When an English Shakespearean company playing in Vancouver was left short-handed through illness, Clyne deputized for a principal with such polish that the famous actor-manager Sir John Martin Harvey offered him a permanent job. Greatly though he loved acting, Clyne refused. He had talked to a member of the company who told him, "It's a dog's life."

When Judge Clyne embarked upon a heavy Assize in the Kootenays, it went on so long that after nine weeks Chief Justice Wendell Farris sent one of his characteristic telegrams, "Clyne what the hell you doing Chief." A long country Assize means a lonely time for the judge, and eventually Mrs. Clyne joined her husband. She is as stage-wise as he—they met while performing in UBC plays. Arriving in Nelson in midafternoon, she sat at the back of the courtroom, unobserved by her husband, while he dispensed justice. Later he related with relish, "The first thing my wife said when I came off the bench was, 'This show's been on the road too long, Jack Clyne. You're overacting. You can be very, very good when you play God, but today you were only pompous.' "

Off the bench, Clyne often belied his reputation as the hard man of the court and, later, the boardroom. Half a dozen incidents revealing his humanity come to mind but one will suffice.

A court reporter went into court drunk. During the evidence Mr. Justice Wood ordered, "The official reporter will please read back the last question and answer." The reporter, lurching to his feet, shouted, "You're goddamn right he will, Judge. You've got the goddamn best reporter in the province," and collapsed. He was fired. Judge Clyne heard of the incident and, learning the man was drinking because of troubles at home, he privately used his influence in Ottawa to secure him a new job in another part of the country.

Clyne's private compassion for people in difficulties did not extend to leniency for criminals in the narcotics trade. In 1955, Branca defended five men accused of maiming and nearly killing a rival trafficker. Having a poor defence and Mr. Justice Manson as the trial judge, Branca anticipated stiff sentences.

During the trial a newspaper report linked the accused with a feud for control of the illicit drug trade. The press's disclosure of this background, which the prosecution had correctly concealed from the jury, was highly prejudicial, so Branca cried, "Mistrial," and won a new trial. He thought the rehearing would come before a more lenient judge. He drew Judge Clyne who sentenced all Branca's clients to twenty years.

In the Assize Court one morning the reporters were anticipating drama. The cast included the imperious Clyne on the bench, bluff Tom Norris as prosecutor and the combative Branca for the defence.

During the previous week, Judge Clyne had privately castigated a lawyer for an alleged breach of ethics. The lawyer was aggrieved, believing he had acted correctly. Later he raised the matter in court, asserting that a former attorney general had assured him he was right. This brought from Judge Clyne an even more monumental rebuke, and the lawyer's application for leave to withdraw from the case was met with a refusal and a reminder that his first duty was to his client.

Branca noted counsel's anger and frustration. He knew that on Monday the lawyer was due to defend a murder charge before the same judge, and he wondered whether counsel would be at his best in a matter of life and death. Branca asked if he would like him to join in the defence.

"I only wish you could," said the lawyer, "but there's no money." Branca took home the transcript of evidence from the preliminary hearing as weekend reading.

On the morning of the trial, habitués of the Assize Court watched Judge Clyne as he took his seat on the bench and noted his surprise when he saw that, instead of the lawyer listed on his court sheet, senior defence counsel was Angelo Branca. Was this to be a day for "fireworks"?

With professionals like these in the key roles, we should have known better. The trial was a model of what a jury trial should be—justice at its most impressive. Evidence was led, and challenged. Objections were taken, argued and ruled upon. The jury asked to see the scene of the crime; Judge Clyne dictated a movement order by which the court was smoothly transported by taxis to the tug *La Pointe,* moored at dockside, and reconstituted in the crowded fo'c'sle where a young oiler had been fatally stabbed by a crewmate.

Back in the courthouse, the jurors listened to Norris for an hour, to Branca for nearly two hours and to the judge for one hundred minutes. They asked no questions and were back in half an hour with their verdict: not guilty of murder, guilty of manslaughter. Judge Clyne sentenced the accused to fifteen years in jail.

Branca had done what he felt called upon to do, and had no regret, but he reflected on the irony: Silvio Zanatta, the boy killed by the man he saved from hanging, belonged to a family he had known for years; and the reprieved killer was totally ungrateful. He blamed Branca for not winning a complete acquittal.

In Court of Appeal, the man claimed he had been denied justice because his lawyer had not let him go into the witness box to defend himself. Because Branca was not in court on the appeal, the chief justice took it upon himself to question the appellant's assertion. "Mr. Branca may have advised you not to give evidence," he said. "But didn't he say the decision was up to you?"

"No," answered the appellant. "All Branca said to me

was, 'You son-of-a-bitch, if you go in that witness box Norris will hang you.' "

Mr. Justice Robertson leaned over to the chief justice, and Norris heard him whisper, "That sounds like Angelo."

The jury must know nothing about any criminal record of the accused unless he chooses to give evidence on oath. Had this man given evidence, Norris would have been able to reveal that he had twenty convictions for violence, including rape and grievous bodily harm, and was a deserter from the U.S. Navy and a fugitive from justice. That surely would have tipped the scales when the jury deliberated between manslaughter and murder.

Judge Clyne's sentence was confirmed.

One judge feared by counsel with weak defences was Mr. Justice Alan Maclean. In his twenty-five years in the Attorney General's Department, he had acquired a concern for the interests of the public and a knowledge of criminal law that made him hard to upset on appeal.

Branca was defending in a case before Mr. Justice Harold McInnes in which the Crown's star witness was the newspaper columnist Jack Wasserman. His evidence told of an incriminating conversation with one of the accused in the Cave Supper Club, and Branca was grilling him relentlessly on that conversation.

The judge, knowing that only part of the conversation was admissible and that another part would be grossly prejudicial if heard by the jury, kept interrupting the cross-examination to make sure Wasserman did not blurt out the objectionable part. Wasserman became bewildered. Branca pressed on with his rapid-fire cross-examination. Finally Mr. Justice McInnes, whipping off his glasses and sending them skidding along the bench, cried, "Adjourn this court. Counsel to my chambers."

In his chambers the angry judge, pointing a shaking finger at his old friend from student days, said, "Damn you, Branca. I know your game. You want a mistrial. Well, you've got yourself a mistrial. You'll start this trial all over again Monday and I'll see to it your judge will be Alan Maclean."

Branca maintained that, since the conversation in the nightclub was the crucial evidence, he owed a duty to his client to negate it if he could, and that he had not overstepped the bounds of cross-examination nor would he. George Murray, the prosecutor, pointed out that nothing prejudicial had actually been uttered, so no ground yet existed upon which to declare a mistrial, whereupon the judge agreed to continue.

As they walked back to the courtroom, Murray said to Branca, "Go easy, Angelo. I've never seen the judge so shaken."

"Not half as shaken as I was," replied Branca, "when he threatened me with Alan Maclean."

That cross-examination was indeed caustic. Courthouse "regulars" were surprised to see Branca bearing down so heavily on Wasserman, knowing the cameraderie that existed around the courthouse and the Georgia Coffee Garden between the criminal law luminaries and the media personalities. But personal friendships never inhibited Branca once he was embarked on a defence.

In this instance, the friendship no longer existed. The two had often exchanged banter, but now Branca felt that Wasserman, by disclosing the conversation, had breached a friend's trust. Years passed before Branca allowed himself to speak to him again.

The judge, the defence lawyer and the witness were not the only shaken men in the courtroom that day. The official reporter making the record guessed ruefully that in the cross-examination Branca was at times shooting out words at nearly 300 a minute.

Many reporters considered Branca the fastest speaker appearing in the courts of British Columbia, but that would be hard to prove because he so often changed his pace. He probably averaged 200 words per minute—less in argument, much less when addressing a jury, more in cross-examination. In comparison, the biographer of the English defender Sir Edward Marshall Hall put his speed at 158 words per minute and that of his great rival Rufus Isaacs at 120. Qualification for a staff verbatim reporter in the British Columbia Supreme Court is a certified 200 words per minute. Those holding a 250-w.p.m. certificate receive extra pay. With Branca cross-examining, they would earn it.

A witness in Police Court, a building contractor, once complained that the speed at which Branca fired questions at him was making him dizzy. Magistrate Oscar Orr was sympathetic. "Mr. Branca," he said, "you talk like a machine gun."

The severity with which he sometimes questioned witnesses once disturbed his own wife. Viola had never before watched him in court, but with the girls old enough to be left and the Williams Lake Spring Assize falling in June, she travelled with him to visit and sightsee while he fought a murder case. Since the main spectator sport in Williams Lake was the Assize, she found herself in court watching her husband cross-examine an emotional woman. She had to tell him afterwards that she had found it so upsetting that she walked out. "I know," he said. "But I had to get the truth out of her. My man's life hangs on it." Helped by some favourable medical evidence, he won an acquittal.

Viola never watched another trial. The next time she would see her husband in court was during his investiture as a judge.

Williams Lake had early won a bad name for drunkenness and violence. An eminent British Columbian whose language was not normally noted for coarseness called it "the ass-hole of the province." People thought those days were long gone, but when Mr. Justice J.O. Wilson and three top defence lawyers arrived from Vancouver for an Assize calendar headed by three murder trials, they found the place in an alcoholic ferment. The lieutenant governor had set the Williams Lake Assize for the same time as the Williams Lake Stampede. Cattlemen came in droves for the stampede, and townspeople thought it was their civic duty to join in the carousing.

The drinking fever was contagious, and Judge Wilson privately cautioned the sheriff to guard against any drinking by the jury. The sheriff assured him that, as is normal in murder cases, the twelve jurors were duly segregated, confined by day to the courthouse and by night to their hotel rooms, shepherded at their meals by himself, and guarded by night-duty deputies posted in the corridor of the wing they occupied at the Ranch Hotel.

Branca was chagrined to find himself third on the trial list, facing days of waiting in his hotel room while fellow guests noisily celebrated. Henry Castillou, who could do no wrong with Cariboo folk, defended in the first trial and won a not guilty verdict, which brought cheers from a noisy gallery. Next morning, the sheriff had rounded up the jurors-in-waiting to start the second trial when word came that defence counsel Tom Hurley had caught the local contagion and was in no shape to fight a murder charge. Branca was asked if he was ready to have his case advanced to second place and gladly agreed. The judge again ordered the sheriff to ensure that there was no drinking by the jury. After a lively trial, Branca too saw his man acquitted.

Next day brought a revived Hurley, defending an Indian accused of murdering another in a drinking bout. This time the jury convicted the accused of manslaughter.

With liquor loosening tongues, a secret had little chance of remaining a secret: the sheriff heard stories, and found that jurors had been drinking despite all his precautions. Under cover of darkness, cowboy friends had used the fire escape to climb to the roof of the Ranch Hotel and had lowered bottles of rye with their lariats to jurors at their bedroom windows.

The drinking fever had spread even wider. Hurley, having appealed against the manslaughter verdict, ordered the necessary transcript. The official court reporter then confessed to the judge that on the trial's last day he had been in such an alcoholic haze that he could not write decipherable notes and so could not certify his transcript of the charge to the jury.

Lack of a transcript, and whatever Mr. Justice Wilson privately said in his report to the Court of Appeal, killed the conviction. The Appeal Court ordered a new trial, and when his Indian client was retried in another town, Hurley redeemed himself by persuading the jury to let his man go free.

Judge Wilson was then many years away from becoming chief justice of the British Columbia Supreme Court, but no judge was ever more zealous for the good name of the law, and he caused Williams Lake to be struck off the list of Assize towns. It remained off the list until, with growth and increasing diversity of its community life, it outgrew its ill repute as Cow Town.

CHAPTER TWELVE

The fifties, which for Branca became a decade of many courtroom successes, brought him other distinctions, including his appointment as a King's Counsel in 1950. His election as a Bencher of the Law Society, though it escaped public attention, was a more significant index of his recognition by his profession.

One reason he had so many successes in court was that he accepted so many briefs. His long working day enabled him to be almost constantly in court and still spend time on the thorough preparation that he claimed was "everything" in winning cases. He carried a prodigious workload, handling a seemingly endless succession of cases, big and small, for the Crown and against the Crown, civil and criminal.

He acted for and against both the federal and the provincial governments. He appeared for the Canadian Labour Congress and against labour unions. He fought a case for the Boilermakers' Union and another against the Fishermen's Union. No one could label him company lawyer or labour lawyer.

Nor was he less successful as prosecutor than as defender. As Crown prosecutor on one Vancouver Assize he had a spectacular record. Of twelve men charged in separate trials, two were sentenced to death, one went to prison for life, seven went for shorter terms and one received a suspended sentence. The jury found only one of them not guilty.

Six more times he prosecuted the Vancouver Assize.

When representing the State rather than defending the individual, he characteristically gave the State his best endeavour according to the law as it was and not as he thought it should be. For years he had advocated in public and private that the death sentence should be abolished, but, parliament having decided otherwise, he accepted it as Crown counsel's duty to ask for the death sentence against Walter Prestyko and William Worobec for the murder of an elderly man whose body and that of his wife were found in the bungalow they had just bought for their retirement. Both men were hanged.

The belief that he was only doing his duty as a lawyer never quite removed the uneasiness Branca felt about prosecuting capital cases. At any mention of the *Prestyko* case even now he feels the same stab of remorse he experienced on the day he opposed Tom Hurley's bid to save Prestyko's life in Court of Appeal, when the doomed man's mother thrust before him a picture of her son taken at his first communion at age seven.

(Branca would continue to campaign against capital punishment. A speech which he gave against capital punishment during a speaking tour of eastern Canada in 1976 was briefly reported in a Toronto newspaper. He immediately received from the Department of Justice an urgent request for the full text of the speech. A comparison with some passages in Hansard suggests it was used by government speakers as a source for argument in the ensuing capital punishment debate.)

During Branca's last Assize as prosecutor, Don Smith, the court reporter who recorded Judge Manson's "swan song," volunteered one of those occasional interjections which made him a "character" around the courthouse.

The court reporters then received only a nominal salary but made a good living if they worked "Branca hours" and if the attorney general and the lawyers ordered transcripts, for reporters were paid a fee for each transcript produced. They had a vested interest in murder because then transcripts were always ordered.

The case at bar was not murder but concerned an estranged husband and wife and the wife's father who intervened during a struggle for a gun. The father became emotional as he gave evidence of firing at his son-in-law to scare him. Excitedly he cried, "I wish now I'd killed him."

Smith looked at the witness and said, "So do I. We need the business."

As always when Smith perpetrated these outrages, after a few moments of dead silence the proceedings rolled on. But the light aside calmed the old man.

No trial lawyer expects to work nine-to-five days, especially during long-running cases. Many a transcript of the day's court proceedings has been delivered to lawyers between ten and eleven o'clock so that they could pore over it in the midnight hours preparing for the continued hearing on the morrow. Usually those were big cases, sometimes million-dollar civil suits, but lawyers also work unusual hours on smaller cases.

Acting for a Toronto woman in a matrimonial cause, Branca wanted to obtain the sworn evidence of her husband, who had moved to Vancouver, so that the transcript could be used in the Ontario Supreme Court. The husband evaded all appointments by pleading urgent business meetings that took him out of town. Branca called his bluff by serving him with an appointment requiring him to present himself for questioning at an unlikely time for any business meeting.

That was how three lawyers, the outwitted husband and I came to be in Branca's office at eight in the evening on 24 December 1953, and how Branca finally obtained his evidence while sounds of revelry floated up from the Christmas Eve crowd milling around Hastings and Main intersection.

Branca made demands on those around him, but he was not unappreciative. As I was leaving, he grinned at another noisy outburst from the intersection below and said, "When you send your bill, just double your attendance fee."

Headline writers revelled in the saga of a man they dubbed the "Love Bandit," until Branca entered the case. Police built up a file of thirty complaints against a man who broke into bedrooms of women living alone; he usually cut their telephone wires before entering by a window, always at night. Many of the women said he kissed them as they lay in bed and made suggestions to them, but there was no proven case of violence.

After three years of bafflement, police one night received a report from a woman who said a noise woke her and she saw a trousered leg protruding over her bedroom window sill. The rest of the intruder was hidden behind the drapes. A man's voice said, "This looks nice. I'm coming in." She screamed, and the leg disappeared. Police threw a cordon around the area but caught no one.

They had not been gone long when a young man, from his room, saw a ladder at the window of the same woman's bedroom, and a man halfway up it. By the time he ran down from his room and reached the ladder the climber was gone, but he searched the locality and seized a man who, he said, "seemed to be slinking away." The aroused neighbours, suspecting that the captive was the "Love Bandit," beat him so badly that when police arrived they had to take him to hospital.

The man proved to be the head of the Vancouver bicycle registration bureau and a former policeman of unblemished respectability. He was at first charged with breaking and entering and attempted breaking and entering the woman's bedroom. Protesting his innocence, he engaged Branca to defend him.

Although the capture was headlined as that of the long-sought nuisance, Branca asked City Prosecutor Gordon Scott what evidence there was to say that he was that man. It was true he had wire cutters when seized, but nothing to link him with the man on the ladder.

A team of experienced detectives pored over the reports and tried to link up clues, but all they established was that some garden hose found in the trunk of the man's car had been stolen from a residence occupied by one of the women complainants. Branca served notice on the prosecutor that he would challenge him to prove identification with the "Love Bandit." At the trial, the prosecutor withdrew the two charges relating to the climb up the ladder to the woman's bedroom, admitting that the only clue to identification was the voice that said, "I'm coming in."

The accused then pleaded guilty to stealing the garden hose and, after Branca told the court that the man was leaving Vancouver, he was fined $100. The complaints ceased.

Branca's trial diary for the year in which he was in his prime at fifty-two indicates his capacity for work. For much of 1955 he was counsel for the federal government in a campaign against retail price fixing by gasoline dealers. Anti-Combines Act inspectors and RCMP officers, after investigating for a year, laid before him evidence against nearly 500 gas station operators in B.C.'s Lower Mainland.

While co-ordinating this evidence and reducing the long list of allegations and the piles of accounting records to triable proportions, Branca was handling his usual load of trials as defence counsel.

To consider only his high court work in that period: he was defending in the Assize in January and February; in March came the case in which he was ejected from court for the second time by Mr. Justice Manson; then followed three weeks of preliminary hearings in the price fixing case, after which came a long preliminary in an attempted murder charge which he was defending.

In June he secured the acquittal of a young man charged with attempted rape, and he went straight from the Assize Court to argue a case in Court of Appeal. Another long preliminary hearing in a drug trafficking case followed.

Having in his out-of-court hours reduced the price fixing case to indictments against twenty-six dealers and two trade associations—the associations pleaded guilty—he spent twenty-three days in court, obtaining convictions against all.

That trial ended on a Friday night, and on Monday morning Branca was back in Assize Court, this time as a defender in an attempted murder case and in a complex charge concerning the issue of false company prospectuses.

Then he went over to the prosecution side again, arguing unsuccessfully in Court of Appeal in the Anti-Combines Act case. Soon he was back defending in Assize: he and Hugh McGivern appeared for five men charged with attempted murder.

Branca's record of defending sixty-three persons on murder charges with only four being convicted of murder and only two hanged is remarkable. An officer of the Canadian Bar Association once described Branca as "British Columbia's if not Canada's version of a Marshall Hall or a Clarence Darrow." Sir Edward Marshall Hall, Britain's most celebrated criminal defender of this century, defended twenty-five murder cases and lost ten of them. Figures of Clarence Darrow's murder cases are not known. He claimed to have saved one hundred persons from the death sentence but those included acquittals from rape as well as murder charges. And Darrow, who had fifty-seven years at the bar as against Branca's thirty-eight, was still defending alleged murderers at seventy-five.

The recital of Branca's court activity creates the image of a perpetual criminal lawyer. Yet Branca estimates that eighty per cent of his income came from his civil practice.

Two paradoxes of Branca's career distort the image. First, the feisty fighter in the criminal courts was a settler in civil cases. He doubts whether ten per cent of his civil actions—even five per cent in some years—reached the courtroom. Many were settled "on the courthouse steps." These were often personal injury claims arising out of car mishaps, in which insurance companies would belatedly take their counsel's advice to accept Branca's final figure.

Remembering all those cases that went to trial because some people regard being hit by a car as almost equal to winning a lottery, I asked him, "How did you persuade the greedy ones to talk in the same ballpark as the insurance companies?"

"I made the terms," he said. "I researched what the

claim was worth on the basis of the courts' awards in similar situations. When I set a figure, that was it. If the client wanted to go for broke, he could try elsewhere."

The other paradox about the Branca practice is that the advocate whose fame came from success with juries never asked for a jury in civil actions. This form of trial is available to the parties in many kinds of civil litigation, with a jury setting the degree of blame and the amount of damages. Personal injury claimants, expecially before "no fault" insurance, often chose trial by jury on the theory that judges are less lavish with insurance companies' money.

Branca considered that the chance of higher awards was outweighed by the risks. "Juries are superb at applying their good collective common sense to yes-or-no questions," he says. "When several issues had to be decided in order to arrive at a judgement and make an award, I always felt happier putting my case to a judge."

Of his few civil cases tried by juries, two produced verdicts that illustrate the gambling element he disliked about civil jury trials. Not his gambling: in neither case had he asked for a jury.

In one, his client claimed that under promise of marriage she lived with a man and with him operated a Vancouver hotel, until he jilted her for a younger woman. The jury took to their room a list of the issues, and came back with a written verdict that gave her a one-half interest in the hotel plus the unusually high award of $5000 damages for breach of promise to marry.

Senator Farris, the man's counsel, quickly pointed out the lack of any evidence of marriage talk on the date specified in the verdict. Branca argued in vain that sheer inadvertence had led the jury to use the wrong date and that they could have picked any one of half a dozen other dates to which evidence of marriage promises related. The judge ruled that part of the verdict defective, and the woman lost her $5000 damages. In this instance the error was not ruinous, because the declaration of entitlement to a one-half interest in the hotel still left her an award worth $250 000. It does show how jury fallibility in compound issues can turn a lawsuit into a lottery.

The only matter in which Branca acted for an insurance company against a personal claimant also involved a jury verdict. A teen-age girl received injuries in a car accident which left her with an oddly shaped purple mark on her forehead. Instructed by the insurers' lawyers, Branca questioned the girl on oath in examination for discovery, then recommended they offer $10 000 in damages and costs. This offer being refused, the insurers' lawyers, without Branca, fought the case in Supreme Court, where the jury awarded the girl $35 000 damages.

Branca recommended an appeal, and the insurance company, though skeptical about their chances, agreed. In Court of Appeal, he argued that the jury had inflated the award on the strength of evidence by a doctor that the girl continued to suffer mental anguish because of the mark on her forehead. The doctor said she had told him that what especially upset her was her belief that boys would see the mark as a sign that she was sexually available. What a patient tells a doctor can be important, but Branca challenged the admissibility of this evidence on the ground that neither in examination for discovery nor in court did the girl make any such reference, about either its truth or saying it to the doctor. That, he contended, made the statement hearsay.

The Court of Appeal quashed the award and ordered a new trial. Branca advised his principals to repeat the original offer of $10 000 with an added $1000 towards the trial costs. The girl's lawyer accepted. One can safely assume that the girl's costs exceeded $1000 and that, having gone through a trial, she was worse off than if she had taken the first offer.

Between trials Branca ran his office practice in a style that was peculiarly his own. Normally, he did not make appointments: you inquired when he would be seeing clients, then took a seat in his reception room with three or seven or ten others. Staff members of those days recall clients overflowing onto the stairs. Branca would sit in his office facing the door and, as a client departed, would bark, "Next."

Lawyers who thought his system was extraordinary talked of "Branca holding court," and certainly by today's practices it seems prodigal of clients' time. One of them tells of sitting in the reception room when the visitors—including two of Vancouver's business giants, Jack Diamond and Sam Cohen—waited while the lawyer reminisced with an earlier arrival, a down-on-his-luck ex-boxer who had come in only for his regular handout.

Actually, the waiting room was mainly for new or run-of-the-mill business. Branca found that many of his important clients were as happy to have a 7:00 A.M. or 9:00 P.M. conference as he was, especially since he then would be glad to go to them.

The interview diaries for those years show days when he saw up to fifty clients. His notes of the interviews are generally just a few lines, but his memory was such that reading them could recall to mind all that had been said. Different-coloured crayons indicate the category of legal service into which each interview fell, and those requiring litigation are further colour-coded to indicate Supreme, County or whatever court. Symbols point to where interview entries were expanded later from memory. "It was my own system," he says. "It worked."

Amid the pressures of this schedule Branca still kept his reputation for being always available to younger lawyers with problems. Once when he was interviewing clients, a call came from a young lawyer who said he was being held in the police lockup at Matsqui and wanted out.

The lawyer was Victor Stephens, who was gaining a reputation as a fighter in court, and who a dozen years later would be for a while leader of the B.C. Progressive Conservative Party. Stephens explained that he had been defending a client before Police Magistrate William Walker, who found fault with his vigorous cross-examination, warned him, then declared him in contempt of court and had him arrested.

Branca dropped what he was doing and called the magistrate. The outcome was that his worship finally said, "If you tell me that's the law, OK, it is." He released Stephens, who proceeded with the defence of his client, and Branca resumed his interviews.

Branca and Walker were old friends. The lawyer had known Walker when he was fire marshal, and now he was one of those citizens without law degrees who formed the major part of the Provincial Court bench in British Columbia until 1974, when it became restricted to the legally trained. Some of the "old school" were not good judges but many of them Branca respected, believing they achieved a creditable standard of fairness. Walker was one of those.

Here again all friendship was thrust aside when magistrate and lawyer faced each other in court. Often they clashed. Branca once asked the Matsqui magistrate to adjourn a case because a witness was not available, but Walker refused because he was going on vacation and did not want to leave unfinished business. Branca asked him to stand the case over for just one day, but the magistrate explained he was leaving that day "and I have to be out of here by 3:30."

The prosecution evidence was soon given and it seemed the case would be quickly finished; Branca began to cross-examine the last police witness, who probably expected no more than a dozen questions. The cross-examination went on and on, without any sign of ending. After three hours, the magistrate rose and exclaimed, "This case stands adjourned for four weeks," then left the bench.

"God knows what I cross-examined about," said Branca afterwards.

Many lawyers tell stories of Branca's helpfulness when they were young, even though he gave them a rough time in court. Bryan Williams, who became B.C. president of the Canadian Bar Association, was an articling student anxious to prove his merit when his principal sent him to obtain evidence that a certain man lived at a certain address. The man was an old hand at evasion, and Williams found himself in the witness box, cross-examined by Branca, and unable to say by his own knowledge that the man lived there. "But I'd learned something at the door from another person," he says, "and I wanted to be damn sure I got that information out. And I did. Branca objected, and the judge severely reprimanded me. Then Branca took me out to lunch and carefully explained to me what self-serving evidence was all about."

When a man named Heathman, who had been acquitted of murdering a boy in a "hobo jungle" at Vernon, later confessed to the crime, a conscientious lawyer who had acted in the case was concerned about the implications and wanted some independent advice quickly. It was almost noon on a Saturday, and he did not know Branca at all well, but he called his office. "Sure," said Branca, "I'm tied up now but come in at four o'clock."

The lawyer found Branca winding up the day's interviews. Thus he learned of Branca's Saturday sessions, during which he closed the doors at one o'clock but stayed at his desk for as many hours as were needed to hear everyone who was still waiting.

Many mornings he and the office staff arrived together just before nine o'clock—they to start the day's work, he returning from visiting his mother. During all the years she was a widow, unless his practice took him out of Vancouver, Branca rarely missed a daily visit with her. His routine was to arrive at the office about seven, work for an hour and a half, walk the few blocks to and from her home and be back at his office to meet staff and clients. If the rest of his day had to be spent in court, the early morning dictation enabled him to leave material to keep two or three secretaries busy.

One escape from the pressures of his practice was an occasional trip to the northern inlets in pursuit of salmon, but those were difficult to fit with his court calendar. He accepted a long-standing invitation for a fishing trip after a federal prosecutor told him that a case he was defending would have to be adjourned, leaving him free of court engagements that week. On returning he was appalled to find a newspaper headline awaiting him which read, "Court Annoyed. Postmistress Trial Delayed. Her Lawyer's Gone Fishing!" The Justice Department, though it told him it was arranging an adjournment, had not told the court.

Next morning, still smarting from the unjust blame, Branca said in Magistrate Oscar Orr's court, "The report was absolutely disgraceful. Thousands of people read it. If that's the way the press is going to distort things, it's high time they were muzzled." His disclaimer was duly reported, but not in the way he would have preferred. It began, "Angelo Branca thinks the press should be muzzled."

One memorable fishing trip took him to Rivers Inlet as guest of Sam Cohen, founder of Army and Navy Stores. Branca was one of three anglers who all had exceptional specimens in the day's catch of thirty salmon. The largest, caught by Dr. Reuben Rabinovich, Montreal neurologist, was only eight pounds under the world record.

Rabinovich and Branca had more in common than catching big fish. The doctor was the author of a textbook on the effects of alcohol on the human system, and certain passages were much used by defence lawyers in alcohol-related prosecutions. So successfully were such cases being defended that the RCMP sent a sergeant to take long and specialized training to qualify him as an expert on the effects of alcohol, after which he testified in courts all over western Canada. He was highly competent, but overzealous in his criticism of the Rabinovich textbook.

Cross-examined by Branca, the sergeant elaborated all his answers with attacks on the Rabinovich book. Finally Branca looked appealingly to the trial judge. Chief Justice Wilson was apparently waiting for this and he said, "Sergeant, I'm sure the jury is suitably impressed by this public flogging of poor Dr. Rabinovich. Now just answer the questions."

Branca has been a fortunate lawyer in a number of ways, not least in being favoured with unusually talented and long-serving staff. After he finally lost the remarkable Miss Trasolini of "The Flying Seven" following her marriage, he wondered aloud in the barristers' room where he would find another so competent. Paul Murphy, his family growing up, thought his wife might be cajoled into helping temporarily. She had been secretary to some distinguished lawyers, including Brig. (later Chief Justice) Sherwood Lett and the redoubtable Neil Hossie, K.C.

Winifred Murphy agreed to help but only for two weeks. She stayed for years, managed his office, studied law at night, articled with him, was called to the bar, and left only when she was appointed judge of the Family Court, where she presided with distinction until retirement. Coping with the pace set by her employer in that busy practice and reading for the bar until late at night would be good conditioning for the pressures that bear down on a Family Court judge.

Mr. Justice Manson was not the only judge who told Branca he worked too hard. Mr. Justice O'Halloran, after delivering a judgement in which he ruled against Branca but noted his "valiant efforts," called him into his chambers and gave him fatherly advice about the dangers of overwork. Judge O'Halloran spoke feelingly. He had impaired his own health and tired his brilliant mind by overwork as a judge of Appeal.

What did Angelo Branca gain from all this unremitting effort? "Happiness," he says. "I wouldn't want to be doing anything else." He had, of course, the financial rewards— "There's money to be made in law"—though seeing the fees that can be commanded by the top lawyers today, he jokes about being able to earn $400 000 a year if only he had not been born too soon. He had the gratification that comes from professional success, and certain other satisfactions, as these three cases illustrate.

Having experienced some of the great days of the Wigwam Inn, the once famous resort on Indian Arm at the head of Burrard Inlet, Angelo Branca lamented its fall into disrepute. Before the First World War it had entertained tycoons like J.J. Astor, just before he went to his death in the *Titanic,* and J.D. Rockefeller, as well as a twenty-year-old German named Joachim von Ribbentrop. In 1960, when the inn had fallen on hard times, plans were secretly made to turn it into a casino. A smart young

Vancouver lawyer was implicated in a plan to pay bribes for police connivance in the gambling. Branca's spirited defence was not enough to save him from a six-year sentence. After Branca became a judge, he received a letter from the young man in prison saying:

Your appointment was particularly significant to me inasmuch as you represent something I would very much have wished to be like. Unfortunately I had neither your talent nor your wisdom.

I am confident that you will lend something to the Court that I have always felt it sorely needs, that is, a touch of reality and understanding of human affairs.

Branca has derived satisfaction from knowing that this lawyer, his sentence served, carved out a new career for himself, made a success of it and became a respected and prosperous citizen of another city.

In the second case, three brothers were charged with beating a man to death in a quarrel over money which they believed he had stolen. One brother was sentenced to death, and his family went to Douglas Wetmore (then a lawyer in Trail, later County Court judge in Vancouver) and asked him if he could get Angelo Branca to appeal for his life.

The execution date was set, and Wetmore hurried to Vancouver as soon as he received the 800-page transcript of the trial. He described the interview: "Branca said, 'Have a seat.' He flipped through parts of the transcript, then settled on the judge's charge to the jury. He stabbed a paragraph with his finger and said, 'That's fatal. I'll get you a new trial. Nice to talk to you, Doug. See you in Court of Appeal.'" He saw Wetmore out as his next client was on his way in.

Branca won the appeal, but the new trial did not go as he hoped. Mr. Justice Norris, who gave some of the best jury charges I have heard, delivered in this trial what may have been his worst. Again Branca's client was sentenced to death. Again Branca went to the Court of Appeal, citing so many errors in the judge's charge that anyone not knowing these men would wonder how Norris and Branca remained friends.

Opening his argument on the appeal, Branca said he would present seven main grounds why the death sentence should be quashed. He took about half an hour over his first ground and was about to start on his second when the judges of Appeal stopped him and asked how the Crown proposed to meet the first argument. For the rest of the day, Crown Counsel George Murray, Q.C., replied, first to Branca's argument, then to all the points raised by the judges. At the end they were still not satisfied and invited Murray to search and consider the law further overnight. Next morning Crown counsel said he could add nothing to what he had said. The court congratulated him on his fight but, without hearing Branca's six other grounds, quashed the death sentence and ordered a new trial.

For the client's third trial he was charged only with manslaughter. He came before Mr. Justice Wilson and was sentenced to five years in jail. The last word Branca had of him was that, when serving his time, the young man was influenced by a prison chaplain, became interested in social work connected with a religious organization and decided to make that his career.

As part of that thoroughness of preparation which, according to Branca, is fundamental to success in law, he attaches great importance to examination for discovery, the procedure in civil cases by which each side can compel the other to attend before an official reporter and submit to cross-examination by the opposing lawyer, with the right to use the transcript at trial. The third case illustrates the rightness of his view and also the satisfaction he derived in helping people in trouble.

A mother whose young son had been struck by a car and seriously injured called on Branca in despair because the insurance company refused to pay compensation or medical bills on the ground that the driver was blameless. When he read the driver's statement, Branca found no evidence on which blame could be ascribed to the driver. Nor could he find any independent witness who had seen what happened. But he found it hard to accept that because a child may have behaved childishly there should be the double penalty of injury and financial loss.

Knowing that if the driver's statement was the whole truth the family could get nothing, Branca in the examination for discovery questioned the driver in the most minute detail until there were several hundred questions and answers on the record. Right at the end, two answers contained admissions of what might be construed as negligence by the driver.

The intensity Branca put into that examination so impressed me that I later asked him what had happened to the case. "After that examination for discovery the other side offered $60 000," he said. "I grabbed it. Had we gone to trial without those two admissions, we wouldn't have got a nickel. Even with them we still might have lost."

Remembering the evidence of medical bills and that the child had some brain damage, I asked how much would go to the family, and Branca replied, "They'll get the $60 000. I was so pleased with myself I'm not sending them a bill. Their grief isn't over yet."

There are more satisfactions to the practice of law than winning cases.

There are distinctions, too, for the successful. In 1950, Angelo Branca was named "one of His Majesty's counsel learned in the law," with the title of King's Counsel; though how much distinction the suffix K.C. (now Q.C.) carries in Canada has been disputed for sixty years, because most provinces diluted the old English honour by lavish distribution and tainted it with political patronage.

In 1922 when Senator Farris celebrated his resignation as attorney general by announcing a list of new K.C.s, two lawyers rejected the honour, "not wishing to be associated with a list savouring of political preferment." A newspaper called the 1928 appointments a scandal. The Law Society denounced the system in 1944. When Branca received his K.C., one Canadian lawyer in every three outside B.C. had it.

Yet that statistic is no measure of the status of K.C. or

Q.C. in British Columbia, because this province more than any other has kept the honour exclusive by restricting the number of appointments. During the days of coalition government in the late forties, two powerful provincial ministers, the Liberal Gordon Wismer and the Conservative Herbert Anscomb, fought bitterly over Wismer's plan to take some sting out of the charges of favouritism. At that time the appointments were recommended by the attorney general and made by the cabinet, and Anscomb wanted to keep it that way. Wismer finally forced through legislation which required that appointments be made in consultation with the chief justices of the Appeal and Supreme Courts and two representatives of the Law Society.

While the politicians argued, six years went by without any King's Council appointments in B.C. "If Police Chief Mulligan would look the other way," wrote columnist Tom Jarvis, "they could get a good lottery going on the forthcoming creation of a new batch of K.C.s. I'd buy tickets any day on Angelo Branca." The first list under the new law duly included Branca.

That reform remains on the statute book today, but the criticisms occasionally recur. In 1966, the future Mr. Justice Alan Macfarlane, then an M.L.A., suggested that names recommended by the chief justices and Benchers had been discarded "in favour of political hacks." Left-wing lawyers are scarce among the Q.C.s. Alex MacDonald told the legislature that he would not accept a Q.C. under "a system heavily interlarded with politics." He sports the letters now, but only because by law every attorney general becomes a Q.C.

Lawyers sneer that one Toronto office tower has more Q.C.s than all England. Philip Collings (later a Provincial Court judge) wrote, "In B.C. it is at least fairly rare to be a Q.C. But rarity is a quality our Q.C.s share with the whooping crane and the Tasmanian marsupial cat—it isn't in itself a guarantee of worth."

Branca used the one practical advantage conferred by the distinction. Q.C.s who argue cases in the Supreme Court of Canada have the privilege of speaking several metres closer to the bench of nine judges than their lesser brethren. But many Q.C.s never have the opportunity.

(Winning distinctions with their consequent publicity can bring unwanted results. In 1955 a nineteen-year-old youth, having driven a car into the back of another, jumped out and told its driver, "You've heard of Angelo Branca, the famous criminal lawyer. Well, I'm his son, and this will cost you $165 unless you admit you're in the wrong." The other driver happened to know that Branca had no son, and the police established that the lawyer had never heard of the young man. He was fined $50 for driving while impaired by alcohol.)

The members of his profession made Branca a Bencher of the Law Society of British Columbia in 1959. The Benchers are those few lawyers (there were then fewer than twenty elected Benchers) in whose charge the legislature places the honour of the profession. They sit on the discipline committees that pass judgement on their brother lawyers in matters of professional misconduct and they have the power to disbar and strike off the rolls a member who transgresses. Except for election to the treasurership of the Law Society, electing a member as a Bencher is the highest accolade lawyers can bestow.

Branca's preferment in this field was in those days an exceptional event because his fame was so commonly identified with the criminal law. Until recent years, the profession reflected the public's own ambivalence towards "criminal lawyers." In the fifties, Mr. Justice Kay Collins, whose background was certainly not sheltered—he served in the trenches in the First World War and practised law in the mining towns of southeastern British Columbia—recalled that after his first big criminal case on moving to Vancouver he so feared crime's corrupting influence on his Baptist ethics that he resolved never to take another criminal case. (One result was that when made a judge he had to devote all his spare time and his two months' vacation to refreshing himself on criminal law.) Similarly, after a distinguished career in civil law, the widely respected Reginald Tupper, while heading a Royal Commission, was visibly shocked by revelations of the amoral climate in which Vancouver law enforcers were working.

The fact that some of the best criminal lawyers were spectacular drinkers did not help the reputation of that section of the bar. In general, the members of the legal profession refrained from electing the so-called criminal lawyers as the guardians of their honour.

They elected Branca, and when his term of office expired they re-elected him. He continued to function actively as a Bencher and a member of disciplinary committees until his judgeship made him ineligible. To have been chosen by his peers to sit with the few who set the standards for such a proud profession, and to have come to the honour by his particular route, may have been Branca's most gratifying achievement.

CHAPTER THIRTEEN

Angelo Branca played a role in one of the crucial episodes in the history of the Doukhobors in British Columbia when he prosecuted Michael the Archangel and secured convictions that put 488 members of the Sons of Freedom in jail. Thirty years later it becomes clear that he had a part in the beginning of the end of the years of bombing, burning and nude parading in West Kootenay.

Because of an epidemic of these outrages in 1947, the provincial government set up a Royal Commission under Judge Harry Sullivan. His tour of the Doukhobor areas began amid more explosions and burnings. The judge hastily wrote an interim report diagnosing "a conspiracy wherein all active members of the Sons of Freedom have combined with seditious intentions" and recommending prompt action against them. He adjourned the hearings indefinitely.

Attorney General Gordon Wismer doubted that prosecuting "all active members of the Sons of Freedom"—perhaps 2500 out of about 9000 Doukhobors in British Columbia—was the answer. Prosecution was what the Freedomites wanted. They deluged the commission and the police with confessions. For nearly two years Wismer wrestled with the problem and watched the reports of depredations mount. To the clamour of West Kootenay residents that the government do something was added that of voters closer to Victoria. People in central Vancouver Island were shocked at reports of nudism and spouse swapping in a breakaway colony of Freedomites near Nanaimo.

Wismer assured the cabinet that the police were prosecuting all the terrorists they could catch and that nothing in the criminal code prohibited rotating wives. The cabinet demanded that an example be made of the ringleaders. Wismer asked Branca to accept the assignment of special prosecutor and counsel in Doukhobor affairs to the federal and provincial governments.

Branca embarked on a six-month study of the history, customs and beliefs of these descendants of Russian peasants who in the eighteenth and nineteenth centuries shunned the Orthodox Church and adopted a form of Christianity that favoured communal living, pacifism, vegetarianism, antimaterialism and universal brotherhood, having no priests, churches, icons or Bible—except an oral "Living Book"—and only vocal music.

Their opposition to the State Church in Russia and their refusal to bear arms in the Czarist armies brought severe repressions and exile to penal colonies, which persisted for generations, until the writer Tolstoy took up their cause. Mainly through his efforts, about 7500 of them, probably about half the sect, came to Canada in 1899 and settled in communities on 400 000 acres on the prairies. They were soon in dispute with the authorities, with other settlers and among themselves, and lost much of their land.

In 1903, the more communal-minded of them began moving to British Columbia to settle on lands they bought near the confluence of the Columbia and the Kootenay rivers at a place they called Brilliant, and in the Kettle Valley near Grand Forks. By 1914 there were nearly 4000 Doukhobors in West Kootenay.

Branca became so fascinated by their extraordinary odyssey that long after his official connection ended he was writing articles and speaking in public in an attempt to clear up misconceptions about the Doukhobor enigma.

He noted their historical tendency to split into hostile sects while remaining within Doukhoborism. In Russia there were feuds between the Large Party, the Middle Party and the Small Party. In Canada there were the

Orthodox, who were community-minded and staunchly pacifist, the Independents who practised a more Canadianized way of life, and the minority Sons of Freedom, the bitterest opponents of everything savouring of government coercion such as compulsory schooling and the registration of births and marriages. Branca particularly noted the perpetual hunger for a spiritual leader, a compulsion which in Russia as in Canada drove them to internal strife and lawbreaking.

All these things Branca felt he needed to know thoroughly, because he believed the existing void in leadership was the cause of the turmoil that he was going to have to explore through Doukhobor witnessess in the courtroom. His notes read like raw material for a Russian novel. He compiled biographies of persons worthy of being Dostoevski characters. Among them were nine who figured, in frequent allusion or in person, in the prosecutions which he conducted in Nelson Assize Court. What follows here is the barest outline of the details he noted about the nine.

Peter ("The Lordly") Verigin—Peter I (1859-1924)—started the movement of Doukhobors from the prairies to the Kootenays. He was a powerfully built, handsome man of imperious manner and great ability. During his sixteen years' rule, the Doukhobors prospered, quarrelled and fell upon hard times. He tried to sell their West Kootenay community lands in the hope that he would lead a mass return to Russia, when dynamite planted close to his seat on a CPR train near Castlegar blew the coach to pieces and killed Peter and eight others. Who was responsible remains a mystery. Many Doukhobors blamed the Canadian government. Some Canadians theorized that Soviet agents had been sent to get rid of him, much in the way they murdered Leon Trotsky in Mexico. Another theory said that a jealous lover of Mary Strelieff took revenge. Twenty-year-old Mary, sitting next to Peter, was killed with him.

Peter ("The Purger") Verigin—Peter II (1880-1939)—was the Lordly's son but had been abandoned by him before birth, the twenty-year-old father having been persuaded by the sect's revered prophetess, Lukeria Kalmykova, to leave his pregnant young wife so that Kalmykova could train him for future leadership. Peter II, left behind in the exodus to Canada, was in a Moscow jail when the British Columbia Doukhobors, following the murder of his father, petitioned that he be allowed to come to Canada to succeed him. Such a concession by the Soviet authorities was almost unheard of, but amazingly it was granted. He assumed leadership of Canada's Doukhobors in 1927, settled in West Kootenay, acted even more autocratically than the Lordly but with less ability, and shamed them by his behaviour in the beer parlours of Nelson. He was a drunkard, a loser as a gambler and given to violent rages, but he was a Verigin, and though the fortunes of his people waned, he remained their controversial leader until his death in 1939.

Peter ("The Hawk") Verigin—Peter III (1904-1942)—was the son of the Purger but was left in Russia when his father came to Canada. Although he had been missing since the Stalinist purges of religious dissenters in the thirties, the British Columbia Doukhobors, in a typical gesture of faith in prophecy, elected him to succeed his father. They never traced him. Twenty years would pass before it was learned that he had died of starvation in Siberia.

John J. Verigin (born Voikin) interested Branca as being spokesman for the Orthodox Doukhobors of the Kootenays rather than a recognized aspirant for spiritual leadership, and as the main target of attacks by the Freedomites against their less radical brethren. His authority stemmed from his being a grandson of the Purger in the female line, who followed his grandfather from Russia in 1928 at the age of seven.

Michael ("The Archangel") Orekoff was a third cousin of the Lordly in the female line. Born in Russia, he left his Saskatchewan Doukhobor village as a young man and was running a rooming house in East Vancouver when Peter II died, whereupon he emerged claiming the leadership in fulfilment of an ancient prophecy. Branca's critical examination of this prophecy would make headlines during the trial. (In the witness box Michael swore that before he offered himself for leadership he talked personally with God for three days, but refused to say where the interview took place.)

John Lebedoff was one claimant to leadership who was not of Verigin lineage. He was revered as a descendant of a Doukhobor martyr who, when a corporal in the Czarist army, inspired a mutiny by throwing down his rifle. When Branca had him arrested, Lebedoff had five wives, which was to have unexpected legal consequences.

Stepan Sorokin, calling himself a Baptist missionary but looking, with his piercing eyes and black beard, like an Eastern Rite prelate, complicated the leadership puzzle just when Branca was unravelling it. He was born a non-Doukhobor in the Ukraine in 1902. After his family lost its land in the 1917 revolution, Sorokin wandered through Asia Minor and then westwards. He seems to have had training in many kinds of belief, Christian and Asian.

In 1949 he reached Toronto as one of a group of displaced persons from Germany. A year later he addressed a mass gathering of Doukhobors at Grand Forks. His offer to lead them into a new future did not impress the Orthodox and Independent Doukhobors, but the Sons of Freedom, spurred by rumours that this mysterious stranger was their long-awaited Peter III delivered from exile, elected him their leader. He always denied he was a Verigin, and circulated an open letter reproving Freedomites who looked for marks on his face and scars on his body to prove he was the missing Peter.

After the trials his followers would finance his trip to South America to find a new homeland for them, and would support him when he settled on an estate in Uruguay. The relocation of the Sons of Freedom in the new homeland never happened, but Sorokin remained there as their absentee leader.

Florence Lebedoff, one of the five wives, figured repeatedly in Branca's notes. At seventeen she had been the Archangel's so-called Virgin Priestess. She transferred her loyalty to Lebedoff and with him set off for Turkey to seek a new homeland, but they were turned back in

Ottawa for lack of visas. When sect members vied with each other in volunteering confessions, she outdid them all by supplying Branca with the names of 364 individuals who she said had taken part in acts of violence, and he marked her down as his star witness. (After the trials she was next heard of as a follower of Sorokin at his little colony in Uruguay. Years later, when RCMP officers went to a home in the Kootenay Valley to question a suspected bomber, they were admitted by a woman they took to be his wife. An officer said he recognized her as the one-time Virgin Priestess.)

Lukeria Kalmykova (1840-1886) was the only woman leader and perhaps the greatest personality of Doukhoborism in Russia. She selected Peter I, when still a boy, as one destined to be the sect's great spiritual leader. The authority of the Verigin dynasty down the years stems from her consecration of it as perpetuated in a tradition still known among Doukhobors as "the sayings of Lukeria."

What relevance had the sayings of a woman in the Caucasus seventy years before to the investigations of the prosecutor in a trial in British Columbia in 1950? Branca suspected plain fraud in Michael's use of her supposed prophecy to establish his leadership claims. The prophecy that Michael relied on was not in the earlier versions of the sayings of Lukeria, yet many Freedomites believed it was. Branca tracked its origin to an old man named Sam Savenkoff, who had related to the Freedomites' fraternal council that, when he was a boy in his native village in Russia about 1885, he was passing down the street at midnight when he saw on the roof of a house two angels, one with the face of Lukeria and the other resembling an earlier famous leader. The female angel alighted by him and asked if he knew who she was, and he replied, "Lukeria." She then told him, "In this house is a newborn child. He will be called Michael and he is the Archangel who will lead the Doukhobors to salvation." In the house there was a newborn child who grew up to be Michael Orekoff.

Branca believed that Orekoff had suborned the illi-

terate old man, by this time over eighty, into spreading
this myth. He was even more skeptical about the series of
events that led to Michael's accession to leadership of the
Sons of Freedom. A year after the Purger's death, Orekoff
appeared at a gathering of Doukhobors in Grand Forks
and claimed he was the foretold Michael the Archangel
who would one day lead them out of their sufferings—but
only when there was a pillar of flame from the ground to
the heavens at Brilliant. He returned to Vancouver.

One night in 1943, at Brilliant, fires destroyed the co-
operative packing plant, the jam factory, the meeting
hall, the general store and other Doukhobor buildings and
six CPR boxcars. In a few days Orekoff (now calling himself Verigin) arrived in West Kootenay; he said that while
walking in the streets of Vancouver at midnight he had
seen a pillar of fire from the ground to the heavens in the
direction of Brilliant, so he knew that the time of the
Archangel had come. The Freedomites (but not the
majority of Doukhobors, who by now accepted the tempo-
ral if not the spiritual leadership of John J. Verigin) proclaimed him as the Archangel foretold in prophecy.

He set up a communal home in the Sons' settlement of
Krestova. The ritual there provided for the sharing of
wives by night and nudism by day. One of the women left
the home and went back to her husband. Hearing a noise
in the night she opened the door, and someone drenched
her in gasoline and threw a lighted match at her. Her
murderer was never identified.

Branca received statements from many Freedomites
that Michael instigated terrorist outrages, but it was suspect evidence because the main body of Freedomites had
turned against Michael, who scandalized these believers
in communal ownership by opening a store for his own
private profit. They burned his store to the ground, and
tied him to a tree and beat him. He and sixty-five
adherents, mainly women, were driven out; they moved to
Hilliers on Vancouver Island, where they set up what
became known as New Jerusalem.

Branca concluded that Orekoff was a charlatan and an
opportunist who counselled terrorism to establish his

leadership. He had evidence that Lebedoff, who became leader of the Freedomites when they drove out Michael and his followers, was involved. He ordered both arrested. Then he started drawing up charges against the rank and file followers. The preliminary hearings and the trials went on for months.

Meantime, homes and buildings burned day and night in the Doukhobor villages of West Kootenay. Nude parading became a daily occurrence. In courtrooms policemen picked up clothing and tried to wrap it around demonstrators as fast as they discarded it. Then the police took blankets into court. As soon as demonstrators, usually women, began disrobing, they were wrapped in the blankets and hustled away to detention. The Freedomites countered that. When Branca called a new witness to the stand, she said, "The only evidence I have is this," and began stripping. Police were quickly at her side with blankets, whereupon in the public gallery three women stood up and used pull-cords to shed their clothes in seconds. By the time the police reached them the women were chanting, "We came into this world unclothed." They went to prison clothed.

Nude paraders filled the jails and clogged the court lists faster than Branca could get the real terrorists committed for trial. He mobilized local magistrates and special prosecutors to deal with these offenders while he worked on the conspiracy and terrorism charges. Three hundred and ninety-five nude paraders had been sentenced to between two and three years' imprisonment apiece by the time the main trials of the leaders and bombers and arsonists started at Nelson Special Doukhobor Assize in 1950.

In his opening address, Branca revealed the government's method of attack—to establish conspiracy by the leadership and to jail not only those guilty of planting bombs but also those who sent them. He said the Crown would show that the motive of the leaders was not religious but financial; that these leaders plotted to keep their followers in fear and ignorance in order to be able to squeeze money out of them; that they were not spiritual leaders but gangsters living off racketeering; that they demanded lawbreaking by their followers in order to have a hold over them. He cited Michael's institution of the practice of nude baptism for all his adult followers, for which he charged twenty-five dollars each, as only one of his money-making schemes.

Bringing out the evidence to establish conspiracy was a frustrating exercise in digging and backfilling. The evidence was there in abundance. Eliciting it was the problem. Poor use of English by Doukhobor witnesses as well as translation difficulties when they used Russian made it necessary to canvass points of evidence over and over again. Simple questions rarely brought simple answers, and rules of evidence meant nothing to most witnesses.

It was as difficult for the defence. On Michael's preliminary hearing, convicted arsonist Zakar Barisoff declined to answer questions by defence counsel about the sayings of Michael because "You are not such a wise man, so you wouldn't understand him. He is very wise." The lawyer thus unfavourably compared was Nathan Nemetz, who would become chief justice of British Columbia.

Only patience and persistence produced evidence out of long, roundabout statements about the planning of incendiary raids. Evidence of nude parading was more easily obtained. One woman, replying to Branca, contributed this to the record:

Q And you agree with nudism?

A I didn't even want to come here dressed but you wouldn't let me come other way.

Florence Lebedoff was the first of several who testified that Michael gave the orders for the terrorist raids. She also gave a piece of evidence that would later have a curious effect in Court of Appeal: "I am one of John's wives. I have no objection to him having five wives. I consider wife-sharing a good idea."

Branca challenged the first defence witness to say whether she had given her real name to the court. She admitted she had given her maiden name, and said she had been the wife of the arsonist who started the Pillar of

Fire blaze at Brilliant but dropped his name when she joined the Archangel's community. Having said she believed Michael was the Archangel and had a divine mission, she agreed that he had amended the Ten Commandments to the Three Commandments, but said she believed all thirteen. Branca asked her how she reconciled the commandment against coveting one's neighbour's wife with the community's wife-sharing practices. She answered, "Once they went in there the husband and wife business was annulled."

JUDGE COADY: If a man and wife went into this residence, immediately they crossed the threshold they were no longer man and wife?

THE WITNESS: Yes. They came to the table and each one said that for themselves.

JUDGE COADY: Once they entered that house they were no longer man and wife?

THE WITNESS: Yes. No ties.

Branca fulfilled his instructions to obtain convictions against leaders and followers alike. Both the Archangel and Lebedoff were sentenced to long prison terms.

Michael won a new trial when the Court of Appeal ruled that the trial judge had not sufficiently warned the jury of the danger of convicting on the evidence of self-confessed accomplices. Branca was preparing for the new trial when Michael suffered a stroke. He survived, but doctors told Branca that another ordeal in court might be too much for him. Plans for the retrial were suspended indefinitely. Michael died the next year.

Lebedoff's sentences were cut to three years on appeal, and his counsel came close to having the term reduced to one year on a curious legal technicality. One conviction was for seditious conspiracy with three named women. Paul Murphy argued that all three were Lebedoff's wives by Doukhobor custom; that long-established English common law holds that man and wife are one, and that there cannot be a conspiracy of one.

The court seemed disposed to accept Murphy's argument, but finally adopted Branca's submission that since a fifth person was involved as signatory to a document filed as an exhibit, and since that person was a man, the conspiracy definition was valid.

With the rival Freedomite leaders convicted, Branca stepped up the pace of the proceedings against the ninety-two other alleged terrorists. The old Nelson Assize Court saw justice in high gear. The cases differed from one group to another, with different circumstances and witnesses. Disposing of them without becoming bogged down in interminable procedures required detailed planning for the orderly presentation of evidence and exhibits. Juries were switched in and out of the jury box like trains in a subway junction.

By sitting long hours, often from ten in the morning to ten at night, sometimes till after midnight and on Saturdays, the court tried ninety-four accused in three weeks. All except one were convicted. Sentences ranged from one and a half to fourteen years, and they totalled more than eight hundred years.

What looked like an abject flip-flop by government followed almost immediately. All but the most serious offenders among the 494 Freedomites in jail were offered parole. Many were released at once. The public never suspected that this dramatic policy change could be fairly ascribed to a phenomenon: almost all non-Russians who went to West Kootenay to work on this sociological problem found themselves developing a real affection for the rank and file of the Freedomites.

The general Canadian view of the Doukhobors divided them into "goodies" and "baddies" as sharply as if the Orthodox wore white hats and the Freedomites black. Experience with them soon proved it was never as simple as that. Many Freedomites had attractive qualities. Even members of "D" Squad, the antiterrorist unit set up by the RCMP, investigating in the communities by day and patrolling at night, would say, "Sons of Freedom, sons-o-bitches. But you can't help liking 'em."

By old-fashioned standards of commerce they were models. Their word was their bond. They abhorred debt, and were almost painfully honest. Litigation-loving

Doukhobors of all sects ordered trial transcript by the yard, and it fell to me for some years to handle such orders. A small matter but perhaps revealing: the Sons of Freedom always paid immediately. (Some of the others embraced the North American tolerance of long credit to the extent of never paying until forced.) People who came to know them through working around the courthouse or in the villages found it easy to forget that these good, likable people were the lawless Sons.

They charmed an official court reporter who went from Vancouver to Nelson to take a turn recording the trials. Bothered by the unusual names and the unfamiliar Russian idioms, Don Smith supplemented his verbatim notes with a tape recording. (Those idioms were truly exotic. We all know "You can't get blood out of a stone," but only a Doukhobor could tell a Nelson court that "You can't get a featherbed off a chickadee.") One afternoon the Sons' fraternal council ordered a transcript of the day's court proceedings for study at a special meeting that night. The reporter said, "I can't get it out in time," but felt so badly about disappointing his new friends that he smuggled the official tape out to them, swearing them to secrecy.

At breakfast in the coffee shop next morning he found D Squad officers talking about their big raid on Freedomite villages during the night, in which dozens of police had seized loads of exhibits, from inflammatory writings to incendiary supplies. He dared not ask if a tape recording had also been seized, and spent the day worrying how he would explain to his boss, the deputy attorney general, why the official court tape was found in a Freedomite home in Krestova.

Before supper, responding to a tap on his hotel room door, he admitted a man who looked like Nikita Khrushchev but was Bill Moojelsky, secretary of the fraternal council, who brought out from under his coat the official tape. "How come?" gasped the relieved reporter.

"Not to worry," said Moojelsky. "When the raid hit, first thing we thought of was you. We slipped the tape under Anastasia's mattress. Those Mounties are good boys. They wouldn't disturb a nice old babooshka who's been bedfast for ten years."

That the Freedomites could so quickly win the sympathies of a cynical old court reporter like Don Smith should help explain some curious behaviour of Angelo Branca in West Kootenay. Cabinet ministers would have been scandalized if they had seen their special prosecutor with a group of prominent Sons enjoying a borscht supper in one of their homes. This was no potluck meal but a formal occasion; only men were at the table, and the wives bustled around acting as hostesses in the tradition of hospitality that they had brought from Russia. Police top brass would have been even more surprised to learn that Branca had persuaded one of their investigators to go as a fellow guest.

The hosts, when they extended the invitations, knew their guests would be busy the following week presenting evidence that would send some of them to jail. It took an unusual lawyer as well as an outgoing personality to flout the conventions of prosecutor versus accused and fraternize so happily in the enemy camp on the eve of battle. Having concluded that winning the hearts of these people would achieve more than winning legal victories from them, he saw nothing wrong in breaking bread with John Lebedoff and three of his wives even though he had ordered him arrested.

When it seemed that the Nelson trials would interfere with their wedding anniversary celebration, Viola joined her husband and they spent the evening of their twenty-second anniversary as guests in a Sons of Freedom home. He was not playing favourites. When the Orthodox heard that his daughter Dolores was visiting him, they hospitably invited father and daughter to hear a concert by the unique Doukhobor Choir. Branca still rhapsodizes over those haunting Russian hymns and folk songs.

His experiences among the people disabused him of some misconceptions that many Canadians held about the Doukhobors. One, that the women were treated as drudges, arose partly from a widely published picture of twelve women yoked together in pairs, straining at a plow like a team of oxen while a bearded giant masterfully steered it. Newspapers reprinted that picture for years, never explaining that in the early days of settlement before their communities had draft animals, the women worked the fields to free the men for heavier tasks. In fact, as one incident showed, the women held much power in Doukhobor affairs.

Although in court Branca used an official interpreter—a former officer of the Russian navy—he chose for contacts with the people a native Doukhobor who had impressed him: Anton Kolesnikoff, better educated than most and articulate in both languages. His investigators warned him that Kolesnikoff was a suspect in the Pillar of Fire and the dynamiting of Peter's tomb six years before, but Branca felt he was gaining some insights from the man, and kept him on as interpreter.

One day Kolesnikoff did not report for duty, and word came that his house had burned down. He seemed reluctant to face Branca again, but finally explained, "My wife said, 'Anton, we have to burn.'"

Branca, knowing the home, which was not much more than a shack but well built and well kept, said, "But, Anton, your neat little home? Didn't you tell your wife it was wrong?"

"How do we know it's wrong?" was the answer. "I didn't want to do it, but she convinced me God wanted it. I said we should take a few things out before we burned— our silver teapot that was our wedding gift—but she said, 'No. Everything goes.'"

Yet Kolesnikoff was a man of authority, a descendant of the Kolesnikoff who was the Doukhobor leader when Catherine the Great ruled Russia nearly two hundred years before. Two years after he burned their home at his wife's word he became Sorokin's right-hand man in the pilgrimage to Uruguay.

That the Freedomite women were a greater power than officialdom realized became clear a few years later when the Women's Council of Thirteen seized control from the fraternal council, and Big Fanny Storgeoff led a march to the coast.

The more Branca learned about the problems the more he questioned the government's policy. He decided that the terms of his appointment required him to advise strongly as well as prosecute with vigour.

He was much impressed by two senior police officers who prepared a report on the Freedomite problem, and whose experiences among the people had aroused in them much the same sympathies as his own. He urged Wismer to adopt their suggestion that the services of the University of British Columbia be enlisted to seek a scientific rather than a legalistic solution. Out of this came the setting up of a research team and a consultative committee, and these produced recommendations that led to the generous program of parole.

George Woodcock and Ivan Avakumovic, the authors of the best book on the subject, *The Doukhobors,* published in 1968, noted the diminishing barriers between Doukhobors of all sects and their Canadian neighbours, and wrote, "If any single event marks the beginning of this change in relationship it is the request that Attorney-General Wismer made to President Norman Mackenzie of the University of British Columbia."

In the late fifties outbursts of terrorism recurred, but they involved only a few hard-core lawbreakers. There may be echoes in the future, but by the eighties Sons of Freedom fanaticism was no longer a British Columbia problem.

CHAPTER FOURTEEN

Policing the city of Vancouver produced scandals with deplorable frequency in the first half of this century, so Angelo Branca needed no time for special study of the background whenever he was retained for hearings concerned with police, gambling and corruption.

About the time he was born, the Drake Inquiry learned that the chief of police and his deputies took money from those brothel operators they did not prosecute and pocketed part of the fines levied on those they did. When Branca was a young lawyer, the Lennie Commission heard Gerry McGeer's demand that the chief of police and some assistants be indicted for "conspiring with the over-lord of vice, Joe Celona, and the king of gambling, Shue Moy." In the thirties, two separate inquiries into corruption both led to dismissals and what were called "shake-outs" of the police department. In the year Branca became a King's Counsel, an inquiry directed by the Board of Police Commissioners was investigating allegations of bribery in the high ranks.

Five years later, in 1955, Branca was taking part in the Tupper Royal Commission hearings inquiring into alleged corruption and lax enforcement of the law by the Vancouver city police.

Gambling and prostitution supplied the funds which made it possible to corrupt law enforcers. Betting was widespread. In 1951, after 565 convictions in six years against betting shops in downtown Vancouver, the trade was flourishing as never before. If bribing policemen and city politicians did not keep them out of court, the book-makers hired the best lawyers in town to keep them out of jail.

When Mayor Fred Hume ordered a crackdown and had all the leading bookmakers charged, they retained the greatest array of legal talent ever assembled in Vancouver for the defence of a single case. Their lawyers included Senator Farris and four future high court judges, Branca among them.

The mayor was applying to gambling the same reasoning that the government used in the Doukhobor crisis: jail the generals, not just the foot soldiers. Prosecutor Gordon Scott said, "The law enforcement officers of this city have become sick and tired of bringing front men and hirelings to court while the kingpin operators grow fat on the profits."

The prosecutor planned to translate the gambling operation into a conspiracy by proving that groups of betting houses were linked by joint rentals and common use of wire services and information sheets. The gambling squad, reinforced by constables from general duties who were not known to the betting fraternity, went on raids which produced the biggest gambling conspiracy case ever heard in Canada. Thirty-three men and one woman appeared for preliminary hearing; Branca would defend eight of them. By the time two weeks of preliminary hearings were completed, he had secured acquittals for two. The rest were sent to stand trial: E. Massie White, the man who owned the wire service; Laura Cook, who published the information sheets (the "scratch sheets"); her husband, who published *The Analyst;* and twenty-three alleged bookmakers. The best-known of Branca's six clients was Bruce Snider, businessman, racehorse owner and well-dressed man-about-town, who had never been convicted of any betting offence but who, the Crown alleged, was one of the three kingpins of local betting.

When the trial opened in Assize Court in February 1952, it was necessary, because of the large number of challenges open to so many accused, to call a jury panel of 400 citizens, most of whom hoped not to be selected for a trial which it was thought might last two months. Jurors were paid six dollars a day in 1952. Merely picking a jury took a whole day, but finally ten men and two women occupied the jury box.

Day after day they listened to Crown evidence of undercover operators in betting parlours and of police raids on seemingly innocent premises—a music studio which had no piano, a public stenography office with no typewriter, and a dressmakers' establishment with no sewing machine. All had telephones in abundance.

A retired bookmaker gave Crown evidence about links between betting rings and sources of racing information, and described a loudspeaker system in a betting shop which was connected by telephone to American race-tracks so that patrons could hear running commentaries. He went home with his evidence uncompleted. As he entered his luxurious West Vancouver home, he was badly beaten by two masked men toting guns and was robbed of $300. Police never traced them.

Seventeen days were needed to hear the sixty-five prosecution witnesses. The cross-examination of the gambling squad officers was searching and hostile. Branca sharply attacked the evidence of one police officer who admitted he had spent an average of $100 a month throughout his twenty-four years' service on an estimated 20 000 illegal bets. To another officer he suggested that the betting house operators, far from conspiring together, were distrustful of each other. The witness replied, "I doubt if they trust themselves to play solitaire."

Branca told the jury, "If the authorities wanted to stop bookmaking all they would have to do is take proceedings under that section of the criminal code which prohibits landlords from knowingly permitting premises to be used for gambling. You have been told of betting shops where three convictions have been secured against the same rented premises. How can the landlord not know? Yet they have not gone after the landlords."

Excitement ran high when the jury went out after twenty-two days of trial. Expectations that the massive volume of prosecution evidence would convince the jury had been shaken by the success of the defence lawyers in cross-examination.

That night front-page headlines announced the not guilty verdict.

The defeat demoralized the forces of law. They had a second line of attack in the form of additional charges already laid against seven of the bookmakers, and Branca was ready to conduct the defence of Snider all over again. The prosecution asked that these charges be stood over to the next Assize, then quietly abandoned them.

The defendants told the press that their defence had cost them more than $100 000. What the prosecution cost the City of Vancouver in police time alone will never be known. Hindsight suggests that going after the landlords would have been more effective and would have cost less.

The last of the long series of inquiries into police collusion in crime was the Tupper Royal Commission of 1955. Branca joined the battery of lawyers who represented some of the 126 persons called to testify, from petty gamblers to the attorney general, an ex-mayor and a judge. One witness was an alderman and ex-M.L.A. who admitted trying to protect a bookmaker from police investigation.

Among those whom Branca represented at different stages of the inquiry were a detective sergeant alleged to have accepted a thick wad of bills from a man in a drugstore; Bruce Snider, whose acquittal he had obtained in the bookmaking conspiracy trial; and Joe Celona.

The Celona of 1955 was a much chastened character compared with the crime boss whom Branca had watched being sentenced to twenty-one years in jail in 1935 as head of a prostitution ring. Gerry McGeer had kept his promise made in his election-winning slogan, "I'm Going to Barcelona." Branca had not represented him then and thus had no part in the controversy that swirled around local Liberals in 1940 when Celona was quietly freed after serving only five years and three months. It was Jack Henderson, Branca's friend and partner in community projects, who disclosed that Celona was free and started a storm of protest that was taken up in the House of Commons.

Rumours of a deal spread and led to a public outcry of "Liberal politics." The Liberals, with an election coming, knew where their best interests lay. The minister of justice cancelled Celona's ticket of leave and he went back to jail.

In 1955, released from prison, Celona was running a bootlegging establishment on East Hastings Street, and he was ordered to appear before the Royal Commission after witnesses testified that he had inside knowledge of police plans. Two officers gave evidence that on separate occasions when they were checking Celona's premises, he told them they were going to have a change of duties. Neither believed him or thought it likely, but in two or three weeks they were notified of the exact transfer Celona had predicted. This evidence sorely perplexed the commissioner, who demanded a full investigation but in the end could only report, "It is mystifying and aggravating."

Celona's explanation for the admitted presence of various other police officers at his bootlegging establishment was that he was helping them with their investigation into the murders of Danny Brent, a club waiter, and William Semenik, a drug ring operator, both linked with the Vancouver underworld.

(This was reminiscent of Celona's defence in an earlier case in which he and Chief of Police John Cameron were charged with "conspiring to effect a public mischief, to wit, to prevent the closing of certain bawdy houses." On that occasion Celona admitted he had been with the chief on the police boat in Howe Sound, but said he was helping the police track down American gangsters who were planning to rob a B.C. Electric armoured truck carrying money bags. The gangsters, he said, were on Bowen Island planning the raid. Why a bagpiper serenaded the boat party during the operation was not explained.)

That police might legitimately associate with criminals was accepted by Commissioner Tupper. He was impressed by the evidence of Inspector Ben Jelley, who said, "Sherlock Holmes may have been a wonderful character but I don't think he would have solved many present-day crimes. These are solved by policemen who know what's going on. It's conceivable they would find themselves in places where they might find it difficult to explain why they were there. You're not going to get the information that puts a killer behind bars by attending a church service." This evidence gratified Branca because it echoed the argument he used in a long and successful battle against Mayor Gerry McGeer and the Police Commission to secure the reinstatement of seventeen policemen discharged in one of Vancouver's periodical "cleanups."

Cross-examination being a Branca specialty, he was in his element at the Tupper Commission hearings. Witnesses gave evidence linking his clients with exchanges of money or indicating them in suspicious associations. He did not have to prove a case but to destroy the credibility of the accusers.

Branca could be cruel in cross-examination. He was merciless with one witness who testified against his clients. Early in his questioning, the witness drew laughter from the crowded gallery in this exchange:

BRANCA: Your conviction in July 1945 was for possession of an offensive weapon. What was that offensive weapon?

THE WITNESS: You ought to know. You defended me.

Encouraged by the laughter, the witness tried it again.

BRANCA: You were convicted of contributing to juvenile delinquency. What were the details?

THE WITNESS: You ought to know. You were my lawyer then.

BRANCA: Today I am not. You may wish I were.

Branca proceeded to catch the witness in lie after lie and to destroy his evidence line by line. With a recess approaching, he intimated that he would continue his cross-examination on the resumption. When the hearing resumed the witness could not be found. Word came that he was in jail, having been picked up drunk. On leaving the witness box he had consumed most of a bottle of rye and was in no condition to continue his evidence. The commissioner rejected all his testimony as "worthless."

Branca so convincingly cleared the detective sergeant who was alleged to have been seen taking money that the Police Commission promoted him to inspector without waiting for the Tupper Report to vindicate him, which it did.

Sensation dogged the unfortunate Tupper Commission.

The head of the police antigambling squad shot himself, but he recovered and testified that he shared protection money from gaming house operators with the chief of police.

Chief of Police Mulligan left the country.

A police superintendent killed himself when about to be cross-examined.

A lawyer, Tom (later Mr. Justice) Norris, quit the proceedings on a personal point of principle.

Another, John G. (later Mr. Justice) Gould, withdrew after making eleven objections against the conduct of the inquiry.

Angelo Branca was prosecuted.

An incident that occurred as the commission recessed for the day led to Branca's prosecution. Word had gone round the newspaper offices that Celona was about to give evidence. He was notoriously difficult to entrap into being photographed, and cameramen assembled in force. He was not called to the stand, and the afternoon went by with no sign of him in the witnesses' room.

The ever-alert Simma Holt, later author and M.P., was reporting the hearing for the *Sun*. At the adjournment she cast a last glance around the room and spotted the burly figure of Celona leaving the public gallery. The cameramen's hunt was on.

Photographer Brian Kent, then a slight twenty-six-year-old, intercepted Celona and his lawyer Branca in a corridor, and bravely got his picture at the expense of a bruised head and a broken camera. As a result, Branca and Celona appeared separately as defendants at Vancouver Police Court. Celona was charged with common assault. He said, "I became very angry. I called them blackmailing rats." He was fined twenty-five dollars.

Branca was charged with doing wilful damage to a camera. His defenᵤ ᵥas that there was nothing wilful about it, that the first flash went off when he was less than five feet away and he stuck out his hand before another went off. Magistrate Gordon Scott (former prosecutor against many of Branca's defences) ruled that Branca was trying to prevent his picture being taken and had no intention of damaging the camera. He dismissed the case.

It was Joe Celona's last "Hurrah!" After another little brush with the law he told a reporter, "There's no dough left in bootlegging. All the bawdyhouses are closed. Now they stop a man taking a few honest bets." What was left for a man like Celona to live for? He went into hospital and died there in March 1968, aged sixty.

Betting ring operators like Bruce Snider and others who paid fees to Branca to defend them never had a chance to recover their money from him through gambling. Branca, who will readily wager with a friend, will take no part in gambling involving bookmakers or syndicates. He explained his distrust to a gathering of lawyers and the public when the Canadian Bar Association, during its national convention in Vancouver, hosted a panel discussion in which six representatives of law enforcement, the church, the legal profession, the press and radio debated controversial topics. The inclusion of disputatious speakers like Branca and Jack Webster of broadcast fame promised conflict, but on the subject of gambling, at least, the two were united.

Webster questioned whether there was any evidence that even the most widespread gambling, when it was for modest stakes, damaged the moral fibre of a nation. Branca said, "By all means let's have lotteries but keep them in public ownership, run only by governments for good causes. If you legalize them for private profit you open the door to crime and gangsterism." An amalgam of the Branca and Webster opinions advanced on that occasion in the late fifties would read like the parliamentary arguments justifying government lotteries which in the late seventies became a feature of Canadian life.

CHAPTER FIFTEEN

It was one of those things that make the life of a court-room lawyer exciting—a telephone call from a leading Vancouver law firm asking him if he would accept their instructions to defend Minister of Lands Robert Sommers on bribery charges. That was Branca's introduction to the celebrated forestry licence bribery case of 1958. Branca refuses to call it his most important case, but it confirmed his status, long accepted in the public mind, as the top criminal lawyer in the jurisdiction.

Around the Vancouver Court House everyone wondered who was paying Branca. This was no legal aid case. Ready as Branca might be to donate his services in needy cases, he normally commanded high fees. Sommers—it would be part of his defence—was not a moneyed man. Branca does not know today where the money came from, only that it came through a law firm above reproach. Inadvertently he did learn that the money came from a man not known at all in politics but known in industry. He never heard his name.

Branca's preeminence in his profession can be the only reason he was chosen. He had never met Sommers. He had no Social Credit affiliations. He was a friend of the two Liberals who brought the scandal into the open— Gordon ("Bull of the Woods") Gibson, Sr., then an M.L.A., who first charged that "money talks in forest licence applications," and lawyer David Sturdy, who particularized the allegations.

Political wrangling for two years inside and outside the

legislature preceded the longest criminal trial in the history of the province to that time. Seventy-three days of evidence, apart from days of legal submissions, extended over six months. Ten leading lawyers disputed before the chief justice of the Supreme Court and a jury whether Sommers, three other individuals and three forestry companies had engaged in a conspiracy and whether the minister of lands and forests had accepted bribes to show favour in issuing forest management licences. A former accountant of one of the companies swore this to be true. So did a dismissed senior officer of a big lumber firm not implicated in the charges.

Lawyers for the companies sought to show that the monies were normal contributions to party political funds. Sommers's defence as presented by Branca was that the monies he received from a coaccused were personal loans from an old friend to enable him to live in a style befitting a cabinet minister, and were being repaid.

Other defence lawyers implied more sinister motives. One suggested a nefarious plot by Liberal and newspaper interests to destroy the Social Credit Party. Another alleged that the Crown's strongest evidence came from a dismissed executive actuated by wounded pride. A third tried to show that the affair had started in a plot to blackmail leaders of the cabinet. The judge invited the jury to consider whether these allegations were red herrings.

Crucial to the Crown's case were the evidence of Charles Eversfield, former accountant of one of the accused companies, and the 253 documents he had taken with him on leaving its employ. After giving Crown evidence for four days, he stood up unshaken to six days of cross-examination by some of the most incisive interrogators in the country.

When Alfred Bull found that his usual smooth and ingratiating cross-examination was not gaining any admissions from Eversfield, he tried to shake him with a display of hostility and drew a rebuke from the judge. J.R. Nicholson put promissory notes, cancelled cheques, vouchers and travel tickets to the witness and explored their significance in minute detail. Eversfield was in his ninth day in the witness box when he faced Branca, and he knew that still waiting to grill him were either Walter Owen or Douglas McK. Brown, and E.E. (later Mr. Justice) Hinkson.

These early questions and answers made it clear that Branca was not going to win favourable replies easily:

Q This Terminal City Club bill—why did you take it?

A Because in my mind it was connected with these transactions.

Q Well, how? In what manner was it connected?

A It is not up to me to say how.

Q But you say you formed a connection between this bill and these transactions. Why?

A I wasn't blind enough that I didn't put some connection between it and these transactions.

Q Why?

Branca went on asking the same question in different form for what amounted to, by a newspaper reporter's timing, twenty minutes. Once Eversfield replied, "I'm telling you for the sixth time," to which Branca said, "But you are not telling me why."

Q Was it because you saw an endorsement on the back, "Entertainment for the Minister of Lands, eight people"?

A Entertainment for the Minister of Lands, eight people.

Q So you thought this thing may have had its origin way back in April of 1953?

A I did not so state.

Q There is no question about it, is there?

A About what?

Q About that thought going through your mind.

A I didn't say that. Some thought like that could have gone through my mind.

Hour after hour Branca pressed him. Eversfield kept his composure.

Q Exhibit 617 is an expense account for the Cave Supper Club, dated December 21 and 22 of 1953. I suppose you took it for the same reason as the last one we discussed?

A I made some connection in my mind and I took it. The prosecutor evidently has made some connection in his mind with the case.

Q The prosecutor was not there when you took that, back in December of 1954 and the first two months of 1955, was he?

A No, he was not. My thoughts at that time and his thoughts now, I surmise, are in common.

Q Give me your thoughts at that time. I am not concerned with the prosecutor's thoughts now.

A I'm sorry, I can't reconstruct my thoughts at that time.

Q Didn't you take it because you saw that R.E. Sommers and his wife were entertained at the Cave Supper Club by your principals?

A Yes. I have extended my explanation to say that I made some connection in my mind between this—or the circumstances there and these transactions.

During questions about Eversfield's purchase of travel tickets for the Sommerses on a trip to Toronto, Branca tried to upset the witness's stance of absolute assurance:

Q How much did you pay for the tickets?

A The exact sum that Gray gave me was what I paid for the tickets.

Q That's $1250, isn't it?

A As I recall it, it was $1250, and, as I recall it, it was $1250 exact.

Q That's what I wanted to know. It was $1250. Isn't that so?

A According to my recollection it was.

Q You are a man of meticulous care in dealing with your accounting. I suppose you got a receipt from them, because this was rather a large sum of money.

A I did not get a receipt. I got the tickets in lieu.

Q Are you sure you didn't get a receipt?

A I could have. I should have. I don't recall at this moment that I did.

Q You should have. Because you even want a receipt for a ten-cent piece?

A Five cents. Yes.

A You even want a receipt for that. You would certainly have wanted a receipt for this sum of $1250 which you say you received from Gray and paid for these tickets. Did you get one?

A It's likely I did. As I say, I can't recall it.

Q We'll see if we can refresh your recollection. Take a look at that document, please. Is that a receipt given to you by this travel agency?

A The date is October 31, 1953. As I recall it, that's about the time of it.

Q And is that the receipt you got from them for these tickets?

A This is a receipt for $948.20.

Q But, you see, you had $1250.

A I recollect I had $1250. If my recollection is correct I paid out another approximately $300. I do not recall the explanation for the difference in the sum.

The witness insisted on his right to have all questions completely clarified, as passages like these indicate:

Q You don't know of any portion of these funds finding its way to Mr. Sommers?

A My answer would depend on the interpretation of "finding its way."

*   *   *

Q When you say they are carbon copies, they were the duplicate copies of the originals you left with the bank when you made the deposits?

A I would say that is synonymous with carbon copies.

Branca tried to penetrate Eversfield's guard by springing a surprise on him:

Q In giving your testimony in the court below you insisted that the bank manager marked that promissory note with a red mark.

A He had a red pencil in his hand.

Q He made a mark?

A He pointed out where it would be signed by Mr. Sommers and indicated with a red X.

Q He made a red mark on the document?

A That is correct.

Q You saw that?

A Yes.

Q It was done in your presence?

A Yes.

Q I show you a document. Would you please look at this and tell me if that's the document that was written out on the occasion that you speak of?

A (No reply.)

Q Mr. Eversfield, does it take you that long to inspect this document?

A This does not have a red X on it.

Q I thought you would spot that.

A I had it very firmly in my mind that the one I saw had a red X on it.

Q You have sworn on oath on numerous occasions that it did have.

A And as a result of that I would not venture to say this is the note I saw him make. The balance of the information appears to be the same.

In support of the defence that they were legitimate loans, Eversfield was pressed on every transfer of money to Sommers, and here Branca won a small advantage.

Q You had some discussion with Mr. Gray about remitting $2500 telegraphically to Mr. Sommers in Victoria, and the gist of that conversation was to do it as surreptitiously as possible so that it could not be traced, according to you. Is that right?

A That was the general conversation.

Q You knew, of course, as an accountant, if you telegraphically transmit money through a bank, that records are kept?

A   I am aware of such circumstances.

Q   And in connection with this particular transaction, although it was desired to keep it secret, there was the cheque, Exhibit 12, a personal cheque of H.W. Gray?

A   There was this cheque.

Q   And then we had the charge of $13.50, which is Exhibit 13?

A   I recall the charge for transmitting it, $13.50.

Q   So insofar as this particular transaction is concerned there were at least three written records of it. Correct?

A   It would so appear.

A full day and a half of cross-examination by Branca and another day by the remaining defence counsel left Eversfield still composed. More than fifty days of trial remained, but already some observers could forecast the trial's result. As Eversfield stepped out of the witness box for the last time and the court took a short recess, an experienced court reporter remarked to Branca's associate counsel Nick Mussallem, "There goes the ball game."

As the end neared, people around the courthouse speculated whether a lay jury—in this instance, nine men and three women—could do justice in such a long and complex case requiring so much accountancy evidence and the production of 1060 documents.

Throughout, Chief Justice J.O. Wilson did everything possible to clarify the case for the jury. Once, with the jury excluded, he ruled a certain matter as being irrelevant and therefore inadmissible. "And," he added, "it would only confuse the jury."

Immediately, that most urbane advocate Alfred Bull said, with mock gravity, "Your lordship would not want to take from us the last refuge of defence counsel—the right to confuse the jury?"

When all the evidence had been heard the trial watchers were saying that only a masterpiece of pleading in the addresses to the jury could avoid convictions. This jury did not go to its deliberations within two or three hours of hearing the final submissions from the defence. A weekend intervened, then the volume of evidence required that the judge spend three days reviewing it for the jury and defining their responsibilities. A contemporary estimate of the number of words he used puts it at three times the length of this book.

Having lived with the case for six months, the jury themselves established a provincial record by taking three days to arrive at their verdicts. They found some charges proven, some they dismissed and on some they could not agree.

Sommers, a former elementary school principal, was sentenced to five years in jail for conspiracy and for receiving bribes in cash, bonds and rugs of a total value of $7100. H.W. "Wiggy" Gray, a timber broker and wartime bomber pilot holding the Distinguished Flying Cross, from whom Sommers said he received only loans, was also jailed. The other individuals and the companies were cleared on some counts, and those the jury could not agree upon were abandoned.

Branca could find no fault with the conviction of his client, nor the sentence. Had there been a chance of success on appeal, he was ready to fight the case all over again. He thought he had taken some of the sharp edges off the Crown's case but enough remained to make the verdict reasonable. The convictions were never appealed.

For the first time in the history of the Commonwealth a man was sent to prison for having taken bribes while a minister of government.

For a lawyer to defend two cabinet ministers against unrelated charges may be a record. The other minister Branca represented—not in a trial but in a statutory inquiry—was Philip Gaglardi. It was Branca's last tour de force of advocacy, a fitting farewell performance before going to the bench. If ever a client went to court under a cloud of public suspicion and came out cleared of all allegations it was "Flying Phil."

A man who adopts methods as flamboyant and achieves results as spectacular as those of Gaglardi when minister of highways naturally inspires legends. Some of the stories that circulated, as he wove a web of blacktop across the province like a demonic spider, were amusing. Some were bandied around the province for years without any substantiation. Some were affectionate parodies of the minister's unconventional style. They ceased to be jokes when lawyer Gordon Dowding, later speaker in the NDP government, tabled an affidavit setting out some of the stories as serious allegations, and adding new and more serious ones, such as that a contractor had been paid $135 000 for work which was never done. An inquiry by a select committee of the legislature was ordered by the government.

The source of the allegations was a highways contractor from Montana who said he lost $200 000 on a contract and blamed the Department of Highways. The New Democratic Party leaders, when they pressed for the inquiry, believed there had been wrongdoing, and that the charges made by this contractor would be supported by the evidence of another American who had been concerned in the same Contract 819.

Branca, given his command of the techniques of cross-examination, was always at his best when called upon to reduce emotional, self-serving evidence to hard facts, and this proved to be an exercise in that art. He showed that the evidence of the two contractors was that of speculators aggrieved by failed projects, and was in fact contradictory. Branca met each allegation by going into it in detail in cross-examination and then asking: Did the minister or his officers extend any favour? Did the minister or his officers receive any favour? Was there any wrongdoing by the minister or his staff? The transcript—almost half a million words—has long interrogations of the principal accuser in which he was constantly confronted with questions like, "Do you know of any favour ever done by the Minister or anybody in the department, for you personally or for any company you were associated with?" Nowhere is there an unqualified "Yes." More typical was:

Q Are you aware of any possible loss to the taxpayers on Job 819?

A   No. I think we saved them half a million.

Q   Due to no effort on your part? Due to reasonable efforts on the part of the department?

A   Due to the efforts of Mr. Gaglardi getting us to move in and finance this.

This was the contractor whose allegations had brought about the inquiry. The second contractor, asked if he knew of any favours to contractors, said that only idiots would try to implicate Gaglardi in graft or favouritism.

Only when he could not destroy the evidence by securing admissions from the accusers did Branca call evidence to rebut them. One witness he called was a woman who was alleged to have received $350 a month through a contractor's payroll for playing the organ in the minister's Calvary Temple at Kamloops. She testified that she had never received a penny and could not play the organ.

The proceedings were long and acrimonious. Hostile exchanges occurred constantly between the politicians on the committee and the lawyers. A member complained that the first hour and a half of each two-and-a-half-hour session was taken up by political fighting.

After seventy-two sessions extending over six weeks, Branca was so sure he had demolished all the allegations against Gaglardi that he advised him he had nothing to answer and need not go into the witness box. This was not Gaglardi's way. Opposition members wanted to attack him, and he chose to face them.

As a witness his main contribution was to answer the charge that two men had worked for six months on building an auditorium at his church and had their wages paid by the contractor. While pointing out that he had been too busy running the highways department to oversee details of the building project, he said all church extension was financed by donations in response to appeals and that this was just one more instance of "the power of the pulpit."

He and his officers were cleared of the charges. The

committee that conducted the inquiry consisted of eight
Social Crediters, four New Democrats and one Liberal. A
majority report signed by seven Socreds said, "No wrongdoing. The Minister and his staff should be commended
for their conduct during the course of Project 819, for
their devotion to duty and for their tireless efforts on
behalf of the people of B.C." The minority report, signed
by the four New Democrats, the Liberal and one Socred,
said, "No impropriety," but criticized some aspects of the
department's methods in regard to contracts.

One principle was established by the inquiry: after the
wrangles that marked this one, never again should a matter of this gravity and complexity be sent for decision to a
select committee of the B.C. legislature.

An interesting sidelight was the association of Gaglardi
and Branca, two men with some similarities but so basically similar. Both had Italian immigrant fathers and
were born Catholics; both have the zest for life of the
Latin temperament. From there on the parallels end: the
man of law, ardently identified with the Italian community and the Catholic Church; and the man of politics,
embodying North American fundamentalism.

During the inquiry the two found each other's company
stimulating, and for long afterwards people might occasionally see them lunching together in the Hotel Vancouver or taking a noontime stroll on Georgia Street, chatting
away and laughing like schoolboys at each other's jokes.

CHAPTER SIXTEEN

Gold established the Brancas in the New World when Filippo became one of the lucky seekers in the Klondike. Gold figured in many of Angelo's most interesting criminal cases. And his hobby of collecting gold coins involved Angelo and Viola in an unnerving experience.

Branca's court cases having to do with gold were all "upcountry" and are a reminder that his practice was province-wide. He did much of his criminal code pleading in the fifteen Assize towns, most of them far from the Lower Mainland, often in the old courthouses that had their great days before he was born.

For Branca, going on court business to the mining towns in the interior of the province was like going back to pioneer days. Particularly was this true of Lillooet, where he loved to fight cases in the old courthouse with its Hanging Tree at the back. Tradition, nowhere documented, says that among those hanged from this tree were four men who killed a miner for his gold.

When Branca first defended a gold thief at Lillooet the magistrate was George Sumner, a legendary character who had been around the gold fields of British Columbia since 1870. He had been miner, prospector, mine paymaster and assistant gold commissioner. His acquaintances ranged from premiers down to Bill Miner, B.C.'s only genuine Wild West train robber. The room that Sumner used as judge's chambers had once been the office of Andrew Elliott, who was gold commissioner in 1867, nine years before he became premier of the province. Branca, whose reputation overawed many country magistrates, did not overawe old George Sumner, who sent his client for trial.

One local person in that courtroom would become more of a legend than Sumner. Reporting the hearing for the *Bridge River-Lillooet News* was the owner-editor, a sprightly woman in her fifties, Margaret Murray of "the newspapering Murrays." Today, as she approaches her ninety-fifth birthday "Ma" Murray's fame across Canada rests on her reputation for salty editorializing and vivid denunciations of politicians and their policies. Reading her report of Branca's case in the 16 March 1939 issue, one realizes that along with her flights of descriptive prose and her disregard for most court conventions went solid competence in the mechanics of newspaper reporting. Single-handedly she exploited that case for between six and seven full columns of closely set type spread over three pages, not a dull line among them.

Her court report is filled with asides on mining lore, scraps of Bret Harte poetry and vignettes of all the personalities. The mine superintendent is "handsome Don Matheson." The accused George Gordi "has hair the colour of gold." The prosecutor is "a hundred dollar a day lawyer from Vancouver." A police witness is "one of the best revolver shots in the province." And defence counsel is "Angelo Branca, brilliant young Vancouver attorney, dark, flashing eyes, many impulsive gestures."

The description of the chief Crown witness, Jim San, head of Jim Bros., Chinese merchants in Lillooet, even includes a family biography:

Jim San is dark, spry, with a nose like a Jew. He is no heathen and is only peculiar in that he is wideawake and watchful for a good business deal in beans, spuds or gold . . . will sell you some groceries or maybe take in some laundry. . . .

The Jim brothers' women are always nicely dressed and are well liked by the white population. The children are smart and take keenly to the white man's learning. One little boy sings in the church choir and has a voice of great beauty. Mrs. Jim San is regarded by all the women as a very fine upstanding woman. She was born in Victoria, is well read, is a loyal Chinese but calls Canada her home.

All this in a court report, as is this delightful exchange:

Angelo Branca goes into action. He roars at Jim: "Where did this man come from?"

JIM: From Blidge Livah.

BRANCA: Where in Bridge River?

JIM: Maybe Blalorne. Maybe Pioneer. I don't know.

BRANCA: Have you ever seen gold that came from Bralorne or Pioneer?

JIM: I don't know where he come from. So long as he has gold.

BRANCA: How did you know this stuff was gold?

JIM: Gold is heavy.

BRANCA: This might be lead?

JIM: No. No lead. Lead not so heavy as gold.

BRANCA: From whom did you buy gold in February?

JIM: Me buy Peter Diablo (an Indian named Peter the Devil who can always produce a poke with a hundred dollars' worth of gold, which he hauls from secret diggings on the Fraser River), Fred Thomson, George Gordi.

BRANCA: Do you know the law about reporting purchases of gold?

JIM: Me buy all time gold before February, keep no record, make no report. Me make record now all time.

BRANCA: What was there about the accused that made you remember him?

JIM: I see man's face, I can't miss him.

BRANCA: What about his face?

JIM: Same face he got now.

Part way through her report "Ma" wrote:

One of the points in the case which has upset many hardrock miners is that they should throw George Gordi in the hoosegow. Gordi is a bachelor. A married highgrader is usually caught because his wife gets in the habit of telling, but a bachelor highgrader is said to be immune from detection because he can pound out gold at night without anyone looking over his shoulder or nagging him to come to bed or play cards. Thus there was amazement in camp when yellow-haired George was arrested.

"Ma" may have broken all journalistic rules against mixing comment with straight news, but Branca, reading the report, had to admit that nowhere in all her opinionated prose was there anything prejudicial to his client at his forthcoming jury trial.

A Williams Lake jury acquitted Gordi of the charge of illegally selling gold. He then pleaded guilty to illicit possession of gold and ᵥas jailed for six months.

Some of Branca's gold cases are still talked about in the Bridge River country. One of his clients, when visited by police, stoutly denied having any stolen gold. The police had a search warrant and for hours they searched his property without success. Finally they dug up his septic tank, and when they brought from the depths some tins containing high-grade gold he made the remark that is quoted in those parts to this day. "Now how in hell did that get there?"

Branca legends abound. One tells of his defending an alleged gold thief who, according to Mrs. Murray's newspaper, "had been caught with a table-full of loot, and the gold still under his fingernails." In addition to the incriminating evidence Branca faced a formidable prosecutor in Jack Nicholson.

The trial was at Quesnel, and picking a jury produced a curious situation. Practically all twelve men in the jury box were ranchers. It was a hot June day, and the windows of the courtroom were wide open. Just as Mr. Justice D.A. McDonald finished his address to the jury, from the street below came the sounds and smell of a cattle stampede. Whose cattle? Those ranchers needed to know quickly, and the quickest way to get out of there and find out was to return an instant verdict of not guilty.

Branca suspects his old friend "Ma" of inventing the version of the story that blames him for the timely arrival of the stampede.

The discomfited prosecutor bore no hard feelings. This was just before C.D. Howe called Nicholson to help Canada's war effort, first as a deputy controller of munitions supply, then as organizer of what became a giant synthetic rubber industry. Through the years, during which Nicholson has been, in turn, head of Polymer, federal cabinet minister, head of Brazilian Traction and B.C. lieutenant governor, the two old courtroom rivals have remained friends, and they both continue to practise law forty-odd years after the stampede.

A gruesome example of the greed that gold arouses is the case in which Branca prosecuted a woman for conspiring to steal jewellery from a patient who died in her private nursing home. He obtained his main evidence when the Assize Court assembled around the hospital bed of a nineteen-year-old girl who had been a maid at the nursing home. She told the court that her mistress removed the dead woman's gold wedding ring, then produced a brass ring and ordered her to place it on the ring finger of the corpse before the undertaker arrived.

The nursing home operator went to jail.

Of all the court cases involving gold in which Branca appeared, the most famous was the Hedley Amalgamated "salting" case of 1937. This affair caused losses to thousands of investors, it nearly wrecked the Vancouver Stock Exchange and it linked the provincial government with the scandal.

The Department of Mines had boasted that "salting"— tampering with ore to raise its apparent gold content— could never again be used to deceive the market. Then came an obvious and enormous deception, which led to fourteen months of public clamour before criminal charges were laid.

When the legendary forty-niners found pickings becoming slim in California and saw that gold mining there now required highly capitalized companies, they began looking for other fields. The discovery of gold in the Cariboo in 1859 caused a stampede northwards. Most gold seekers came by sea and up the Fraser River, but others came up the Columbia River and then via the Okanagan and Similkameen rivers, prospecting as they went. At the mouth of Hedley Creek, between Princeton and Keremeos, near where today's traveller on the Southern Trans-Provincial Highway crosses the creek, they found gold. The placers were soon exhausted and they pressed on northwards.

Years later, the Klondike finds sparked a new interest in gold mining all over British Columbia. In those days prospectors with companies to promote or claims to sell displayed their wares where opportunity offered. Samples of ore from Hedley on show at the New Westminster Fair of 1897 so impressed a visitor that he went to Hedley and bought four claims. One was the Nickel Plate claim. Before long the Nickel Plate was the biggest producing gold mine in Canada.

The Great Northern put in a railroad connecting Hedley with Princeton and the United States, and Hedley entered upon its great days, with seven prosperous hotels and a population of thousands. Several mines in addition to the Nickel Plate went into production. After a few years most of them closed, but Nickel Plate's Sunnyside Gloryhole shaft continued for years to have the most spectacular ore body of any Canadian mine. On a reducing scale Hedley carried on for the next twenty-five years, consistently making profits for the remaining producers and yielding more than $20 million in gold, until 1930, when production almost ceased.

In 1936 there was a flurry of excitement: newspapers announced that Nickel Plate's mill capacity was to be doubled, that Hedley Mascot had stepped up production and that new finds had been made. Promoters moved to float or revive companies having claims anywhere near Nickel Plate, and speculators crowded the Vancouver Stock Exchange to buy shares in these newcomers. A share issue by one new company was oversubscribed two and a half times before it could go on public offer.

Hedley Amalgamated, a company formed in 1934, shared in the excitement, partly because its claims on Stemwinder Mountain were about a kilometre from the fabled Gloryhole and even closer to the long-yielding Mascot. Moreover, sensational ore reports were rumoured.

On 13 February 1937, a *Province* headline said, "Hedley Revival the Bright Spot in Mining." Ten days later bigger headlines announced that trading in Hedley Amalgamated shares on the Vancouver Stock Exchange had been suspended. The stock had sold the previous day at from $1.10 to $1.20, but a landslide of orders on the morning of 23 February sent it down to $0.32 on the exchange when the suspension was applied, and to $0.20 on the curb market after the suspension.

The deputy minister of mines issued the statement, "So far as we know, everything is all right," though clearly it was not. Then the public learned that the minister of mines had formerly worked for Amalgamated. It was also disclosed that a government inspector had spent three days at the Hedley property just before the stock price began to rise. He had followed the prescribed practice of splitting drill cores, taking half of each core to Victoria and leaving the corresponding half at the mine. The half-cores that he took away, when assayed, showed a gold content equal to eighty-six dollars per ton of ore at a time when nine dollars per ton was profitable. The inspector reported this fabulously rich finding to the company president, but advised him not to disclose the news to the press.

A Vancouver assayer who was the company's consultant was suspicious of this report and drove to Hedley to test the matching half-cores. Finding their gold content almost nil, he immediately called a meeting of directors, at which it was decided that, rather than telephoning the bad news to the superintendent of brokers, the president would go by the night boat to Victoria to inform the Department of Mines. The following day, in the two hours between the department learning of the deception and the suspension of trading, 371 000 shares were traded on the Vancouver exchange and an untold number of others sold "over the counter."

Newspapers and politicians raised an outcry for a public inquiry. The *Province,* in a front-page manifesto, said, "Hedley Amalgamated has brought tragedy into many a Vancouver home. It has brought heart-burning to thousands of men and women." Mayor Telford predicted, "The Government will hush it up."

The government resisted demands for a public inquiry

but engaged a lawyer and a mining engineer to conduct an investigation in private. They discovered that a year before the fateful core sampling the Department of Mines, suspicious of claims in Amalgamated's promotional literature, had sent a different inspector named Richmond to the mine. He had reported, "I am unable to get samples of ore that would stand up with the assays that are being advertised." The department kept this report secret until the investigators disclosed it.

Again the press was censorious: "What rankles in the public mind is the burial of the Richmond report in the unsearchable archives of Victoria." Had the government published the inspector's findings, as was normal, the public would never have invested so enthusiastically in the stock.

The lawyer's efforts to determine whether there was stock exchange manipulation and the engineer's inquiries into events at the mine produced information that led to criminal charges against three men—the president of the company, the mine superintendent and the mine manager.

The president, Russell E. Barker, aged forty-nine, was a former box manufacturer turned stockbroker who owned a stockbroking company, had formed Hedley Amalgamated with a board that included three other stockbrokers, had sold the mining claims to the company and had awarded himself a large block of shares, with options to buy many more.

The mine superintendent, William Cox, aged fifty, was at times described as its consulting geologist, but the highest qualification the court was shown was a diploma from a German university which, it was alleged, merely confirmed that he had attended a series of lectures there.

The mine manager was an ex-policeman turned speculator, nephew of a mining man named MacKinnon who had been associated with Hedley in its great days. MacKinnon had once won first prize at the Vancouver Exhibition with a two-foot piece of ore containing gold worth, at pre-World War I values, $250; it had been taken from the very tunnel that Amalgamated was now exploring.

At the preliminary hearing Angelo Branca appeared for

the mine manager, whom he had known as a policeman. He cross-examined the Crown witnesses with such effect that, without calling his client, he was able to convince the judge that there was no case against him, and he was dismissed. The president and the superintendent were committed for trial.

When they appeared at the Vancouver Fall Assize of 1938, the superintendent, Cox, was now defended by Branca and the president by Leon Ladner, K.C. Appropriately, in the province's greatest gold scandal, one defence counsel was the son of a Klondike gold miner and the other was the son of a man who ran pack trains for the Cariboo gold miners in the late 1860s, before settling down with his brother to found the Fraser River community of Ladner that commemorates them.

Cox and Barker pleaded not guilty to: conspiring to defraud; conspiring to affect stock prices; conspiring to salt core samples. Dugald Donaghy, K.C., called more than thirty witnesses for the Crown. One told how, following the directors' meeting at which the assayer disclosed the worthlessness of the half-cores, those directors who were also stockbrokers considered it their duty to their clients as well as to themselves to unload their shares before the suspension of trading that would inevitably follow the arrival of their president in Victoria. Defence counsel had an almost hopeless case. Beyond assaulting the credibility of the prosecution witnesses there was little they could put before the jury. Branca tried to direct attention to the government's culpability, and he secured one illuminating reply in cross-examining the deputy minister of mines:

BRANCA: Isn't it your policy to protect the public?

THE WITNESS: You can't protect the public.

Mr. Justice McDonald nullified that effort by telling the jury:

You may say, "Why didn't the Mines Department notify the public about the early poor assays before letting them put money in the mine? Why did the Deputy Minister allow the sale of thousands of shares on the day of the crash when he could have stopped it at nine o'clock in the morning?" That has nothing to do with this case.

The jurors deliberated for five hours and found both men guilty of conspiring to defraud and to affect stock prices. Then, finding them not guilty of conspiring to salt the ore, the jury ignored the judge's instructions and added a rider "deploring the inactivity of the Department of Mines." The judge sentenced the two men to eighteen months.

Of the three prime questions surrounding the matter, only one had been answered: how the leak occurred that started the rush to sell. Who had salted the government's core samples, and how, was still a mystery. It was long, long afterwards that Angelo Branca learned the truth. The salting was done by a man who was not one of those jailed. How the innocent government inspector's samples came to show such high readings, when he swore there was no opportunity for them to have been tampered with, is easily explained. The salter, knowing the big stock swindle was doomed to failure if the inspector's samples reached Victoria in an unsalted state, provided himself with a snuffbox full of gold dust from the Kelowna Explorations mine down the road. He also found a means of getting into the inspector's locked car without detection or leaving signs of entry.

The inspector, after placing his half-cores in his car and locking it, went back into the mine office to complete his records, which took half an hour. He gave evidence that he could see his car from the office window. Be that as it may, the salter entered the car unobserved, dipped his thumb in the snuffbox and distributed his gold dust among the half-cores.

Part of the case against the conspirators was that they were promoting a mine which, according to the testimony of Crown experts, was commercially almost worthless. But later operations proved there was a valuable mine there all the time. It produced substantial quantities of gold for years afterwards.

Branca says: "Some of the directors of Amalgamated, who had put up money to get the company going, were most indignant about the scandal. They had nothing to do with the fraud, and they lost money. But it was their good names! They didn't want their reputations tarnished by being linked with a salting. They were solid citizens. They'd made their fortunes during Prohibition, rum-running."

Late one Sunday evening in July 1963, Angelo and Viola Branca were watching television. Angelo answered a ring at the front door and faced two masked men, one holding a gun and the other a tire iron. The man with the gun jabbed it into Branca's stomach and herded him and his wife to the kitchen. The second man opened a patio door and let in two more men, and they bound Angelo and Viola to chairs with adhesive tape.

One of them headed for the library where Angelo's gold coin collection was hidden. Another stood waving the gun at the captives. "He was so nervous," says Angelo, "that I was sure he was going to pull the trigger in sheer panic."

One intruder blundered into the bedroom of a visitor, a friend of one of their daughters, who screamed, "Get out of here." The men fled with the coins. By the time the girl released his wife, Angelo had freed himself. He ran to the telephone but found the wires had been cut. On the lawn and street the thieves, in their flight, had dropped 107 gold coins and two masks, but escaped with nearly 600 coins valued at $6500.

They underestimated the odds against them when they chose to rob Angelo Branca. The detective who received the first report of the robbery was an old friend; Branca was godfather to his son. A top criminal lawyer inevitably has defended some lawbreakers who remain grateful and the police have listening posts in the underworld. Branca's detective friend soon heard from an informer that a young man in downtown Vancouver was trying to find a buyer for "hot" gold.

Since undercover men are valuable only so long as they are anonymous, the police planned to catch the suspect without compromising the informer. Posing as the would-be buyer, the informer went in the suspect's truck to a secluded spot; the suspect left and returned with a sack. They headed back towards town. All the time they were shadowed by an unmarked police car which kept radio contact with a patrol car. The uniformed patrolmen stopped the truck for what they pretended was a routine highway check, and professed surprise when they opened a sack and found it full of gold coins. While this was going on the undercover man disappeared.

The truck driver was charged with possession of gold coins worth $6500 knowing them to have been stolen. He went to jail without learning who the pretended buyer really was. Nor did he disclose how he knew of the existence of the coin collection in the Branca home.

Branca solved the puzzle. Earlier he and his wife had hired a couple to occupy their home while they were in eastern Canada. The couple and their children were above suspicion, but the children had friends whom they entertained in the house, and an inquisitive visitor, investigating where he had no right to be, had seen the collection.

The coins were all recovered, but the robbery changed the Brancas' future. People who have had their homes broken into understand the sense of insecurity that the invasion creates. Viola, with that frightening memory, could no longer enjoy the home where they had been happy for so long. A house opposite that of friends, the Harold Bradshaws, came on the market and the Brancas left Vancouver for the North Shore and their fourth home in thirty-five years.

By the time the coin thief stood trial, the principal witness against him was a judge. Angelo Branca was appointed to the Supreme Court of British Columbia in October 1963, when he was sixty.

CHAPTER SEVENTEEN

Of all the messages of congratulation upon his appointment as a judge the one that stirred Branca most deeply was the letter describing him as "one worthy to take Denis Murphy's place, so long vacant, on the judicature." It touched him because Mr. Justice Murphy had been his ideal when Branca was a young man, and his idea of the perfect trial judge when he was experienced enough to make that assessment. The letter came from Gordon Wismer, as shrewd a man in a courtroom as he was in the back rooms of politics and the cabinet room of the legislature. Judge Murphy had retired twenty-two years before, yet Wismer still missed his strength and wisdom on the the bench.

What made Denis Murphy such a great judge? The question prompts Branca to enthusiasm.

"He had all the requisites, plus something else. His knowledge of the law was profound. He took the most meticulous notes. The value of that in his case was that writing anything fixed it in his memory, so that he could push away his bench book and review the evidence without a note. You knew if you got a good admission from a witness he would remember it. If your opponent misconstrued some evidence, you might miss it, but the judge wouldn't. He would be correcting him while you were still wondering.

"He was quiet, always respectful to counsel and witnesses, but fully in charge of his court. But he had more than all that. He had a feeling for the law, that innate

sense of it that makes a good judge into a great judge.
Chief Justice J.O. Wilson has it. Lawyers of my time talk
about B.C.'s three great judges—Murphy, Coady and
O'Halloran. Make it four, and I'll agree. You have to
include Jack Wilson."

Branca left the advocates' ranks with some regret. He
liked practice, in office or in court, and he knew that never
again would he share the comradeship in the barristers'
room at the end of the court day when counsel would
converge from perhaps a dozen courtrooms.

"One of the pleasures of being a courtroom lawyer," he
says, "is the banter when court's over and you're all getting out of your gowns. Everyone talking about their
cases, and boasting when they think they've done well,
and there's usually someone who cuts them down to size.

"I'd taken an appeal for a fellow convicted of passing a
counterfeit U.S. bill. By lucky timing an Appeal Court in
eastern Canada brought down a judgement which said
that for a conviction there had to be a certain element of
proof which the Crown had not proved in my case. So
Jack Taggart, for the Crown, told the court that because
of this new judgement the appeal must succeed. Down in
the barristers' room I was boasting that I'd won a case
without opening my mouth, and Jay Gould piped up, 'And
I suppose one of those judges—Jack Wilson, surely—
remarked that Mr. Branca had never been heard to better
advantage.'"

Becoming a Supreme Court judge meant a less drastic
change in lifestyle for Branca than for many new judges,
because right up to his appointment he was immersed in
much the same branches of law as would occupy him on
the bench. Some lawyers coming to the bench from specialized civil practices have to work hard to brush up their
knowledge of criminal and matrimonial law.

Branca also had an advantage in temperament. Elevation to the judiciary exacts from many a penalty of loneliness. The Honourable J.V. Clyne, who loves good company and good conversation, has spoken of the loneliness
of the high judiciary, "where judges talk only with
judges." Branca's gregarious friend from articling days,

Harold McInnes, never knew what loneliness meant until he became Mr. Justice McInnes. In his native Rossland, where his father was the leading merchant, he knew everyone. In his practice in Penticton, even when he was a busy Q.C. he loved to walk from his office to the coffee shop knowing that every third person on Main Street would want to pass the time of day with him. "Then," he said, "they made me a judge, and I moved to Vancouver too late in life and suddenly nobody ever talked to me any more except judges. Those first years were rough."

That may explain why this strong judge earned a reputation for being, off the bench, an unpredictable man: usually jovial and outreaching, he could be moody and irascible. This trait more than once put Branca, his oldest friend in Vancouver, in the role of peacemaker. One incident concerned a future chief justice of British Columbia.

Nathaniel Theodore Nemetz and Branca became Supreme Court judges on the same day, but they had other points of contact. Nemetz had briefly represented Michael the Archangel when Branca prosecuted him, and had defended the murderer Worobec when Branca asked for the death penalty.

If ever a new judge should have been assured of a cordial reception from a senior judge it was Mr. Justice Nemetz. His friendly nature warranted it, a gift which contributed to his professional reputation as a great conciliator. (For instance, the provincial government, concerned about labour unrest in the province, commissioned him to investigate and make recommendations for improving industrial relations. The Vancouver Club, which all this century had not admitted Jews, made him its first Jewish member.)

Judges often have to interview children of divorced couples before they can award custody—often suspicious and hostile adolescents caught up in an emotional turmoil between feuding parents. Few judges were as successful as Mr. Justice Nemetz at the art of winning their confidence and establishing a trust that brought out their pent-up feelings and helped the judge perceive their best interests. He is known as being "good with people."

Yet this friendly man, when he consulted as judges do with their senior brethren, met rebuffs from Mr. Justice McInnes. Branca observed his curtness and, from his long experience of Judge McInnes's ways, he advised Judge Nemetz that if ever the older man were uncivil to him again he should go over to the attack and "have it out" with him. A showdown took place. Thereafter Judges McInnes and Nemetz, so different in so many ways, were on the best of terms.

There, one has a cameo of Branca: in public a worker for interfaith co-operation; in private a Catholic peacemaker between a supporter of Protestant-Orange causes and the most distinguished member of Vancouver's Jewish community. Ten years later Mr. Justice Nemetz would describe Branca as "a man who defends the sanctity of the individual." He also called him "a justice of the old school of Murphy, Coady and O'Halloran."

Branca, unlike McInnes, was not coming to the Supreme Court from Penticton, and he never saw his judgeship as requiring him to sever all his friendships. A lord chief justice of England with a very English sense of humour said, "A judge must be at one and the same time a cold and remote figure, a stranger to the joys and sorrows of human life, but somehow also a man of the world, intimately understanding the emotions and preoccupations of mankind." The idea of Branca as a cold and remote figure, a stranger to joys and sorrows, is laughable. Remote he never was. Rather than talking mainly with his brother judges he came as close to keeping open house in his chambers as any judge I can recall. Certainly his visitors there represented the widest cross section of the public. Some court officials were scandalized at the ease with which people had access to him regardless of their status in the community. He never was a respecter of rank and position, and did not change on becoming a judge.

As presiding judge at Cranbrook Assize, he had completed a case and was leaving the courthouse when he saw a man, also leaving, whom he recognized as staying in the same motel, and picked him up. "You don't know me,

Judge," said the man. "But I know you. I used to listen to you at the Gold Bridge Hotel when you were on fishing trips in the Bridge River country. Well, I was foreman of your jury today, and I told those fellows, 'This guy always made a lot of sense when he talked with the boys in the bar up at the Gold Bridge. So you guys listen to what he tells you, and do as you're damn well told!' "

The lawyers practising in the Assize Court all knew Angelo Branca well enough to feel sure, when he left them for the bench, that he would not be a so-called "convicting judge." And anyway, juries return a high proportion of acquittal verdicts. Therein lies the point of a story from Mr. Justice Branca's first week as presiding judge of Assize.

The new judge, in equally new scarlet and black robes, heard his first case; the jury listened to his charge, then returned a verdict of guilty. The same thing happened in the second and third cases. Three cases, three convictions. The night the third case finished Crown Prosecutor George Murray, on his way out to the street, could not resist putting his head inside Judge Branca's chambers to say, "Goodnight, Judge *Jeffreys*," and then hurriedly leaving. The reference was to the most notorious "hanging judge" of all time who at the Bloody Assize of Winchester in 1685 sentenced 320 convicted persons to be hanged.

Branca's three were not hanging cases. The judge sent all three convicts to jail, but from there on his score as a convicting judge went into a decline. Of ten accused persons in his next Assize calendar he sent only one to jail.

Such figures mean little. The terms "hard line" and "lenient" applied to judges lose significance when it is remembered that it is jurors who convict, and that justice requires some uniformity in sentencing or the Court of Appeal will interfere. Uniformity of style, however, is not required, and here Branca was certainly not uniform.

At his investiture as a Supreme Court judge his chief had hailed his transition from gladiator to umpire. Reporting hard-fought cases in his court I often suspected the judge was finding it hard to resist the urge to leap down into the arena and make it a three-sided contest, the umpire thrusting away impartially at both gladiators. He was more ready to argue with lawyers than any other judge in recent years.

In nonjury trials he would make plain what he was thinking at various points of the trial. He let lawyers know when they had difficulties to overcome and were not convincing him. Some were put off their stride. The true courtroom fighters adjusted their cases accordingly. "Thank God Angelo's no Stoneface on the bench," said one of these. "I hate never knowing what the judge is thinking until I get his judgement."

Judge Branca communicated well with juries, addressing them in lay language and explaining in simple terms the questions they had to decide. His urge to streamline the long speeches incidental to jury trials made him take shortcuts not risked by most.

Judges' charges—the review of the evidence and the law before the jury retires to consider its verdict—are long in Canadian courts. Judges know that their three- or four-hour addresses tax the attention span of many jurors. But they cover perhaps three times as much ground as is required of a judge in England because of the accumulation, down the years, of Court of Appeal rulings upsetting convictions by reason of some omission in the trial judge's charge. (When Lord Goddard entertained the then Judge J.V. Clyne at the Old Bailey and asked him, "What did you think of my summing up to the jury?" he replied, "Brilliant. Lucid in the extreme. But if you stopped there and said no more to a British Columbia jury our Court of Appeal would certainly overturn you.")

To guard against providing grounds for appeal like "The learned trial judge erred in failing to instruct the jury . . ." our judges have in front of them typescripts from which they read time-tested legal formulae adapted to the case. The procedure makes the charge long but is designed to be appeal-proof.

Mr. Justice Branca was trying a man accused of murdering his wife. When the evidence and addresses were all in, he called a conference in his office and suggested to

Crown Prosecutor (later Provincial Court Judge) T.G.
Bowen-Colthurst, Q.C., that he drop the charge of capital
murder and proceed on alternative charges of noncapital
murder and manslaughter.

All his efforts to persuade the prosecutor failing, the
judge strode to the bench, pushed aside the typescript,
discarded the usual formalities and plunged in: "Gentlemen of the jury, I want to tell you something. If I were a
juryman here the first thing I would do is eliminate any
consideration of capital murder. I don't think this case
warrants a verdict of capital murder."

The prosecutor looked surprised. The judge continued:
"But you don't have to accept my advice. Do what you
want. By the same token, Mr. Rankin says you should
acquit this man. If I were a juryman I would find immediately that the evidence doesn't warrant an acquittal."

It was Harry Rankin's turn to look surprised. His lordship continued: "But I'm not sitting on the jury, so if that
doesn't sound good to you, don't accept it." He then
briefly explained the difference between the charges,
reminded the jurors that the evidence was fresh in their
minds and told them to do their best. It was the shortest
murder charge in my experience, if not in British Columbia legal history.

The jury soon came back with a manslaughter verdict,
and the judge sent the man to prison for two years. The
verdict was never appealed. Nor was any other overturned
on the ground of insufficient instruction by the trial judge
when Mr. Justice Branca was cutting through the under-
brush of directions normally required for the guidance of
juries.

Judge Branca was impatient with police witnesses
whom he considered overzealous for convictions. In a
murder case at Nelson he asked an RCMP officer whether
he was aware that it was his duty to give evidence both
favourable and unfavourable to the Crown. When the
officer said he was, Branca told him, "Then perhaps in
future you will put it into practice, instead of being just
aware of it."

His concern for the rights of the individual sometimes impelled him to publicize matters that as a trial judge he had no power to remedy.

While ruling that he had no authority to upset a Workers' Compensation Board decision denying payment to a waitress who claimed she had been injured at work, he criticized the board's handling of the case. He said that by refusing to let her confront her superior at the hearing and question him on his version the board gave her less than natural justice.

Newspapers published his forceful remarks, after which the board, though under no legal obligation to do so, reconsidered the woman's claim.

Another intervention in a matter where he knew he had no jurisdiction was on behalf of a prisoner in the B.C. Penitentiary. In 1958, when he was thirty-two, this man had pleaded guilty to gross indecency. It was his third similar conviction. He had no lawyer. After receiving the opinions of two psychiatrists, a lay magistrate committed him to permanent detention as a criminal sexual psychopath. This meant lifelong detention as distinct from a life sentence carrying parole.

For seven years, Judge Branca was told, the man had been protesting from prison that the proceedings which led to his committal were irregular. He had no money, he could not obtain a lawyer and he had been unable to secure an appeal hearing because essential documents were missing from the court files.

His mother's efforts had finally brought about an application to the Supreme Court for his release. Judge Branca concluded he had no jurisdiction to quash the detention order. All he could do was air the matter publicly and provide some ground upon which a review could be sought. From the bench he said that the magistrate seemed to have abdicated his duty and neglected his obligation to safeguard the interest of an undefended prisoner. "It is hardly conceivable," he added, "that a file in a matter of such paramount importance, where a man might suffer perpetual imprisonment, is not available for review by the Court."

A transcript of Branca's criticisms reached the minister of justice in Ottawa. Civil Liberties Association lawyers took up the matter. At the request of Chief Justice Davey of the Court of Appeal, the Attorney General's Department set up an investigation. What was called a "new" transcript was provided. Finally five judges of Appeal (rather than the usual number of three), with a lawyer now representing the prisoner, reviewed the whole proceedings.

The transcript and the report of the investigation, neither of which had been available to Judge Branca, did not support some of the man's complaints about irregular proceedings, and the court ruled against him by four votes to one. Mr. Justice Tom Norris, Branca's old trial adversary, would have released him.

There is no happy ending. The man was still in prison in 1980, when he was finally paroled. But he cannot complain that he did not have a full hearing.

Mr. Justice Branca sat in the Supreme Court of British Columbia from October 1963 to the end of 1965. Although he says he enjoyed being a trial judge, it was not the period of his greatest service to his province. That began in January 1966, when the federal minister of justice appointed him to the British Columbia Court of Appeal. "This appointment," Branca told the assembly when he was sworn in, "is the realization of an ambition that goes back to the day of my call to the bar."

It was a great day for Angelo Branca for another reason. Among those present—as she had been at his elevation to the Supreme Court—was his mother, happy but not at all overimpressed by the occasion.

Old friends say there is as much of Teresa as of Filippo in their son's make-up. She was no more awed than her son by rank or position. When the Jewish community honoured him with the Yeshiva award, his hosts gave a banquet, and the elder Mrs. Branca, at the head table, was delighted to be seated next to the Catholic Archbishop of Vancouver, the Most Reverend James Carney.

She had all the Catholic's reverence for the hierarchy.

Still, His Grace was young enough to be her youngest son, and she was the eternal Italian mamma at the supper table. Rabbi Marvin Heir duly pronounced the Hamotzi, "the blessing before the bread." Being in Hebrew, its significance escaped her. So when she saw guests, including the archbishop, reach for the cutlery, she turned to him and scolded, "Don't you *pray* before you eat?"

She was then ninety-two. Except for a time following her husband's death, when she lived with Angelo and Viola, she always insisted on maintaining her own establishment first in her old east side home and finally in a residence with people of her own generation in West Vancouver. She was ninety-five when she died.

CHAPTER EIGHTEEN

Two months before his sixty-third birthday, Branca left the courtrooms where trial judges work with witnesses and sometimes with juries and joined the judges of Appeal, who rarely see a witness or hear a word of evidence but wrestle with the printed word and the oral arguments of lawyers expounding on transcripts. When a case comes to them on appeal they receive the evidence in the form of a verbatim transcript of the trial, made up in an Appeal Book which includes copies of the exhibits and all the relevant documents. The judges listen to lawyers who direct them to those pages of the Appeal Book they rely on to win their arguments, and to those law books that support their cases.

Judges can peruse the Appeal Books in the privacy of their chambers before hearing the appeal, and lawyers are unwise to presume they have not done so. One lawyer appointed at public expense to conduct the appeal of a convicted man began by saying, "May it please your lordships, I have diligently searched the Appeal Book for evidence to support this appeal and am reluctantly compelled to advise your lordships that I have quite failed to find any . . ."

He was interrupted by a curt "What about page 367?" from Mr. Justice Branca. "And page 411? And page 417?" After some argument the court adjourned the case for two weeks so that counsel could explore his material further. Branca's intervention did not change the outcome. The man lost his appeal, but only after the evidence which cost him his liberty received the most thorough scrutiny.

Three judges sit to hear most cases, five in some instances, particularly capital and constitutional cases. They participate to the extent of asking counsel to amplify arguments and to meet any objections from the bench. They usually reserve judgement for study and consultation in private and sometimes devote fifty or sixty out-of-court hours to considering a single case. Their decision is usually unanimous, but a majority decision suffices.

Judges of Appeal provide reasons, often at considerable length, for every judgement. When the court is unanimous only one main judgement is usually written, but in many cases, and always when there is dissent, some or all of the judges write their reasons.

Those judgements deemed to create precedents or to be of intrinsic interest go into the printed volumes published periodically to make up case law. If a dissatisfied party appeals from a Court of Appeal judgement, the Appeal Book plus the judgements of that court and the grounds of appeal are compiled into a printed "Case on Appeal" so that a similar presentation may be argued before the nine judges of the Supreme Court of Canada in Ottawa.

Branca can never have included in his prayers the "Judges' Prayer" composed by Chief Justice Gordon Sloan, "Give me the grace, good Lord, to button my lip." Ebullient and irreverent, Mr. Justice Branca brought disputation into the dignified Court of Appeal. This court, more than any trial court, is a place where an individualist if he wishes can show his style unrestrained by concern for juries or witnesses. Few Appeal Court judges choose to. Heaven preserve the law from benches of individualists all adding to the multiplicity of judgements, but, as Chief Justice John Farris said, "Every Court of Appeal needs an Angelo Branca."

Branca argued more, showed his feelings more openly and used more colourful language. To friends from his bar days he was apt to be more forthright than friendly in disagreement. With Ernest Alexander, Q.C., experienced in the practice of the Court of Appeal and quite imperturbable, he would sometimes trade verbal punches in a way that reminded listeners of sparring partners in a boxing ring. "Some lawyers thought that on our bench he was prone to shoot from the hip," says a former colleague. "Then we would reserve judgement and he would go off to his chambers and spend untold hours on research before he wrote."

Court officials still talk of days when Judges Branca and Norris, sitting on either side of the presiding judge, thought the legal ramifications of some criminal appeal were not being explored as thoroughly as they could have been. So they would take opposite sides and, from the bench, argue the appeal more vigorously than the advocates at the counsel table.

When Dick Vogel, later deputy attorney general but then recently arrived in Vancouver from Creston, appeared for the first time in Court of Appeal, one of the judges was Angelo Branca. He had advanced only a few sentences into his argument when Mr. Justice Branca took it over. The judge had studied the Appeal Book. "I won a resounding victory, for which I got a great deal of credit to which I was not entitled," says Vogel.

Procrastination by the Department of Justice usually provoked a testy comment from Judge Branca, as when very junior counsel was sent by his seniors to ask for an adjournment because the Crown was not ready.

"Dammit," said the judge from the bench, "your department has lawyers, the Mounties, the navy, the army and the air force, and it still can't get its tackle in order."

"I'm new to the department," explained the young man.

"Fine," said the judge, good humour instantly restored as he gazed down on this most junior in the hierarchy of fifty-plus federal lawyers in Vancouver. "I'm sure things will change for the better now."

A *Sun* profile said of him, "During his period on the Appeal court bench Justice Branca was often the strong liberal voice. But his decisions also reflected a desire to uphold laws that helped maintain an orderly, conventional society." This may be inferred from some of his decisions.

Prince George city council refused to grant a business licence to a sexual aids boutique called the Garden of Eden. The owner took his case to the Court of Appeal, where Branca, too, would have refused the licence, saying, "I can readily understand that people of sensitive tastes living in Prince George would be quite shocked just to look at the catalogue, let alone realize that the many items described would be offered for sale locally. I am unable to agree that . . . moral considerations are irrelevant." The court overruled him two to one and directed the issuance of a licence on the ground that protection of public morality was an irrelevant and hence unreasonable ground upon which to base a decision under the licensing law.

He was in the majority and wrote the main judgement when the Court of Appeal, by two to one, decided in favour of the *Sun* and against the Gay Alliance Towards Equality. The newspaper's Classified department had rejected a paid advertisement which said, "Subs. to 'Gay Tide,' Gay lib. paper. $1.00 for six issues," followed by a Vancouver address. GATE alleged an infraction of the Human Rights Code and was upheld by a board of inquiry which found, "It was the personal bias of various individuals within the management of the advertising department which was the real reason motivating the refusal to publish, and not a genuine concern of the newspaper for any standard of public decency."

In his twelve pages of reasons which embodied the Appeal Court's majority judgement in favour of the *Sun* Branca wrote:

Many people in our society may well entertain a bias against homosexuals or homosexuality on moral or religious grounds. A bias motivated because of a belief that homosexuals engage in unnatural practices or that their sexual practices are immoral or against religion does not make it wrong in the sense that it is unreasonable. . . . If the bias was honestly entertained, then there was not an unreasonable bias.

Spokesmen for GATE later complained that Branca was prejudiced against homosexuals because of his religious beliefs. They took their appeal to the Supreme Court of Canada, which by a majority of six to three upheld the British Columbia court. In writing the majority judgement Mr. Justice Martland stated flatly, "A newspaper has the right to refuse to publish material which runs contrary to the view which it expresses," a statement of the law of Canada that newspapers saw as a victory in defence of a free press.

On the other side of the coin, two years earlier Judge Branca had voted to quash a conviction by a Vancouver Provincial Court, upheld in County Court, which had declared a stage performance of *The Beard* to be obscene.

If the Court of Appeal ever had a "Great Dissenter," he was Angelo Branca. His brother judges at one stage chaffed him so much about his being a permanent minority that he retaliated by announcing, when next presiding over a three-man bench, "The judgement of the Court is that of my two dissenting brothers."

His tendency to dissent showed itself in two areas. One was his demand for a high degree of proof to sustain a conviction ("I thought the guy was guilty but the evidence was not quite conclusive"). The other was a readiness to gamble on the chances of rehabilitation.

All judges accept the principle that in sentencing a lawbreaker the scales must be fairly balanced between rehabilitation, deterrent, and protection of the public, but Branca looked hard for special circumstances that might tilt the scales. If ever he thought some offender was delinquent because of denial of parental care and love in childhood, he was apt to cry, "Special circumstances." (This trait was apparent in his days at the bar. He probably never fought harder than he did at Quesnel to save a handicapped farm boy with a cleft palate who was charged with murdering his employer. "I was proud to get that poor bastard off," he says. "He couldn't stand seeing that farmer's wife brutally ill-treated by her husband. She was the only person in his whole life who had ever shown him affection.")

Since rehabilitation rather than leniency for compassion's sake was his objective, he accepted that courts may have to be cruel in order to be kind. There was no mistaking his sympathy for a youth of sixteen who asked for a reduction in a stiff sentence for theft. He had been on probation twice and in a government school five times.

"This boy was taken away from his family at the age of two and has been in several foster homes," said Judge Branca. "It is clear from the reports that none of them gave him the love, the sense of security or the discipline he needed." These words suggested his application for a reduced sentence was about to succeed. On the contrary, Branca wrote the court's judgement confirming the sentence, which meant that he would spend some years in a correctional institute, "in the hope that he might there receive proper discipline and be encouraged to take up a suitable trade and be enabled to adjust himself."

Judge Branca dissented when the court sent to prison a young man who had tried to extort $10 000 from the mother of his best friend. The trial court had put the young man on probation, but the Court of Appeal cancelled the probation order and substituted a one-year prison term. Branca dissented, saying, "The young man in my judgement showed great courage and determination in shaking off his habit of taking drugs. He has been off drugs for eight months. To send him to jail at this juncture to associate with experienced criminals might wreck this man's future life. I am not prepared to take that chance."

When the court increased from fourteen to twenty years the sentence imposed on Peter Ian Woods for attempting to murder three youths in Jericho Youth Hostel, the dissenting Judge Branca would have reduced the sentence. "If mercy and compassion are to be meaningful," he said, "the penalty should be of such a degree that it will not foreclose the rehabilitative potential of an offender, particularly a first offender."

Even when circumstances led him to confirm or extend jail terms, Branca could later have misgivings. A trial judge had sentenced Steve Ponak and Conrad Gunn each to fifteen years and a $10 000 fine for narcotics trafficking. The Crown asked the Court of Appeal to increase the sentence, alleging that these men were the wholesale source of capped heroin for the Vancouver market.

By a two to one majority the Court of Appeal increased the sentences to life imprisonment. Branca wrote the main judgement, in which he said, "These traffickers know that very few addicts are able to climb back to the sanity of non-addiction, and they know that their profits are reaped from an ever widening number of human wrecks. . . . They have played for big stakes in a very dangerous business. The penalty must be equally imposing."

Mr. Justice Taggart dissented only to the extent of saying the sentence should be increased to twenty-five years instead of life, leaving open the possibility of parole.

After Angelo Branca had retired from the bench and was back practising law he was at Matsqui Prison talking with the chaplain, Fr. Maurice Hanley, who nodded to a prisoner returning from an exercise run. "That fellow," said the chaplain, "is our star student in the university program. Now he's working on a master's degree. He's here for life." The convict was Conrad Gunn.

Branca worried over that information. He knew the judgement meant no parole, that any remission could only come from an unusual intervention by the cabinet. Finally, he wrote a report for consideration as possibly relevant in any remission proceedings in the future. "Jack Taggart was right," he says. "We should have allowed for parole."

Branca's proneness to dissent came partly from his zeal to remedy imperfections in a judicial process that can never be perfect. A question that confronted the Court of Appeal in 1974 was: should every person who pleads not guilty to committing a crime, and who has not funds to pay, be provided with a lawyer at public expense? Legal Aid paid for a lawyer only in those cases in which conviction was likely to result in imprisonment or loss of livelihood.

A young man and woman, both eighteen, newly out of

high school and unemployed, were charged with possession of marijuana. Under Legal Aid policy they were
refused free services of a lawyer. A date having been set
for their trial in Provincial Court, they unsuccessfully
asked the Supreme Court to prohibit the lower court from
trying them without their being legally represented. The
matter then went to Court of Appeal.

Five judges heard the matter argued in Appeal Court,
and the majority decided that an accused person lacking
funds does not have the right to have counsel assigned to
him in all cases. Branca would have prohibited the trial of
the young people unless they were provided with counsel,
and he adopted the reasons which the other dissentient,
Chief Justice Farris, summarized thus:

The issue to be determined is: can these two young people be
assured of a fair trial when they have to defend themselves
without the assistance of counsel? In my opinion, to ask the
question is to answer it, and that answer is an emphatic "No."
Simply stated, it is my opinion that:

1. An accused person is entitled to a fair trial.
2. He cannot be assured of a fair trial without the assistance of
   counsel.
3. If, owing to the lack of funds, he cannot obtain counsel, the
   State has an obligation to provide one.

That obligation did not pass into law because the chief
justice and Judge Branca were outvoted, but in practice it
is now in effect, because if it appears to a trial judge that
lack of a counsel fee might deprive an accused of a fair
trial, he has only to say so to secure the co-operation of
Legal Aid.

In many cases in which he was the dissentient judge,
Branca based his reservations on his suspicion of circumstantial evidence or his concern about conviction through
mistaken identity.

In 1972 he and two brother judges heard an appeal from
a conviction of murder. The story told them was that a
small-scale drug peddler walking at midnight in Vancouver's Chinatown was stabbed to death by an attacker who
cried, "Rip me off, would you?" A witness said the arm

that wielded the knife was tattooed with a heart and an arrow or lightning bolt.

A suspect was convicted of murder, and appealed on the ground of mistaken identity. Both his arms bore tattoo emblems but they depicted a knife, a snake and a rose. The Appeal Court, by two to one, upheld the jury's conclusion that he was the murderer. Judge Branca was not satisfied that the accused had been properly identified as the assailant, and dissented.

The man who died on the sidewalk in Chinatown was Russell Beaver. That was the name of the last partner-in-crime of Robert Hughes, of Branca's famous *Hughes* case.

A time-honoured court practice ceased after Judge Branca seized upon a sentence in an Appeal Book and wrote a protest that found a place in the law books.

The transcript of a trial, like many a transcript before it, showed that during the proceedings the judge said, "I would like to see counsel in my chambers." Before 1977 most judges would add, "with the reporter." Others called in only the lawyers, with the result that there was no record of what was said. Branca wrote:

It appears that during the course of the trial the learned trial judge called counsel into his chambers to discuss certain aspects, and that this was done in the absence of the accused. This is a practice which must be discouraged.

It is a cardinal principle of our jurisprudence that a trial, with or without a jury, is a public trial except in certain statutory cases; that the members of the jury, the accused and the public are entitled to see and hear the examination and cross-examination of every witness called to testify and all objections made by counsel; and to hear and see the rulings made by the trial judge. It is of great importance not only that justice should be done substantially but that it appear to be done, but it cannot appear to be done where the learned trial judge has many conversations with counsel in his chambers.

There may be exceptions, but, if so, the substance of the discussions in his chambers should be disclosed in open court and recorded.

One more little imperfection in the justice system was corrected.

Those who think of him as the perennial defender may be surprised that Branca stoutly opposes the proposals of the Canada Law Reform Commission to further restrict police when interrogating suspects. One proposal, that such questioning be in the presence of an independent official and statements obtained in any other way be inadmissible, he terms nonsense. He deplores any tendency to follow trends in the United States where, he believes, the police are hampered in protecting the public because of the restrictive rules on interrogation. Adequate safeguards against improper use of statements obtained from accused persons are, he says, already built into the Canadian system of justice.

While considering it the duty of the police to press their investigations to the limits permitted by Canadian rules, Branca sets himself so strongly against overstepping those rules that one can sense his anger in the cold print of his written judgements.

The Court of Appeal was told that the then deputy chief constable of Vancouver had issued a directive that juveniles suspected of indictable offences be fingerprinted and "mug shot" (photographed) as though they were adults. The only evidence against a thirteen-year-old boy charged with housebreaking was his fingerprints, and his lawyer asked the Court of Appeal to declare that evidence inadmissible.

Branca concurred with his brother judges that the evidence, though illegally obtained, was technically admissible, but he wrote a thirty-three-page judgement in which he said:

The fingerprint man said the child did not object. Who in his sane mind would expect a child of thirteen, in the custody of two police officers, who was not charged nor advised of his rights, to object? He probably had no idea of his rights. The thought of two police officers taking a child of thirteen to be fingerprinted reeks of injustice. The evidence was obtained in a manner so grossly unfair to the child and so unquestionably tainted as to bring the administration of justice into disrepute.

The directive that juveniles be fingerprinted and photographed was withdrawn.

One of Branca's judgements provided a precedent for courts to exclude evidence that has been obtained by using a false judicial process. A man sentenced to twelve years in jail for robbing a bank at Annacis Island appealed on the ground that statements he made to the police should have been ruled inadmissible at his trial. On his arrest he had been locked in with a cellmate whose offer he accepted to put him in touch with a bondsman who would stand bail for him. Later the bank robber went through a procedure which purported to be the signing of bail documents by the bondsman in front of a justice of the peace. In fact, the cellmate was a police undercover man, the false bondsman was an RCMP sergeant and the false J.P. was a Delta Municipal Police officer.

Having secured his release on the strength of the fake bail documents, the bogus bondsman asked for immediate payment of the money he said he had put up as bail security, hoping the prisoner would lead him to where the loot was cached. This the man refused to do, but in the course of his refusal he made statements that the supposed bondsman, in his true role as police sergeant, gave in evidence which led to conviction.

In the judgement of the three-man bench, which unanimously quashed the twelve-year sentence and ordered a new trial because of the trick used to obtain the evidence, Branca wrote:

How low on the scale of fairness and justice can tactics sink before a stop must be called? . . . It was the action of irresponsible policemen, totally bankrupt of all ideas of fair play, prepared to stoop to any tactics to discharge their duty as policemen and totally ignorant of all those civil rights which one living in our society is entitled to, including one's right to protection of the law.

Misuse and abuse of authority he regarded as perverting the law. All good judges revere the law but Branca more than most vented his feelings about it in his written judgements. This is perhaps why, at the age of seventy-four, he was singularly honoured with the Reverence for Law Award of the Fraternal Order of Eagles of North America. He was only the eleventh in thirty years to receive that award. The first was President Truman; another was United States Chief Justice Earl Warren.

For twelve years Branca discharged his duties in Court-room 309 with seriousness and sometimes with passion. In the chambers and the corridors, he was the incorrigible Angelo. His reverence for the law was matched by his irreverence towards the Supreme Court of Canada. Victoria lawyer Cecil Branson, on his way into Court of Appeal, was taken aback to hear from the judges' hall the unmistakable voice of Mr. Justice Branca greeting his chief justice and a brother judge: "Well, fellows, did you see that Ottawa shat all over us again?"

Some judges are downcast or feel personally affronted if the Supreme Court of Canada overturns their judgements, but not Branca. He remembers, in days before Canada became mistress in her own house, when appeals were still taken to the Privy Council in England, many decisions of the Supreme Court of Canada were there quashed and the judgements of courts like the British Columbia Court of Appeal restored.

"The Ottawa court, " he says, "is only right because it is final, not final because it is right."

His farewell ceremony in March 1978 on compulsory retirement at the age of seventy-five was far from sad. "Retirement," said Branca, "is just something which opens a door to another phase of one's life."

CHAPTER NINETEEN

There is no truth in the story circulated by lawyers that because the speeches at his Court of Appeal farewell ceremony went on forty minutes longer than planned, Angelo Branca's first two clients on his return to the practice of law were kept waiting.

But his farewell was on Friday and he resumed practice on the Monday at 8:30 in the Standard Building, where he had articled more than fifty years before. He had, however, gone up in the world, since the Braidwood-Nuttall offices (in which he became associate counsel) are on the top two floors of the building, which in his student days had been the chambers of the august Farris firm.

His return to practice might well have been deferred if predictions about the lieutenant-governorship had proven correct. In November 1972, Vancouver and Victoria newspapers had reported that the next lieutenant governor of British Columbia, to be appointed the next year, would be Angelo Branca.

The item caught the imagination of people not normally excited about such appointments. Catholics were gratified at the prospect of having the first Catholic lieutenant governor in their lifetimes. For the Italians it would be a "first." The Jewish community was pleased, regarding Branca as almost one of its own. Vancouver's East End thought it had come of age: another local boy—David Barrett—had newly become premier.

Three months later Prime Minister Trudeau telephoned Walter Owen, Q.C., and invited him to be the next lieutenant governor. What happened to the Branca prediction? No public explanation was ever given, but the facts up to a point are clear. At that time, whoever was Government House incumbent received a $35 000 salary and $18 000 expense allowance and out of this was required to provide everything, even the official car ("Cadillac or better").

Lawyers who leave lucrative practices and settle for the reduced income of a judge do so in the expectation of a judge's pension, but at that time Branca was five years away from age seventy-five. All his earnings from legal fees up to the age of sixty and a judge's salary for ten years had barely made him rich enough to afford the high personal cost of discharging the lieutenant governor's functions in the manner considered obligatory. ("No one gets rich being lieutenant governor," Walter Owen would say five years later.)

When Branca was approached he said he would take the post only if leaving the bench at seventy did not mean loss of his judge's pension at seventy-five "in case I'm not fit to resume work then." Political friends told him, "Ottawa will arrange that." Ottawa could not arrange it in the time available. Outgoing Lieutenant Governor Jack Nicholson was overdue and anxious to be relieved. Owen, knowing it was his last chance, was prepared to take the post without conditions, and was appointed.

Branca's friends drew consolation from the fact that the office would again become vacant in 1978. Then, retired and his pension secure, he would be available. Political "insiders" again told him the offer would be coming. In 1978 Brig. Henry Bell-Irving was appointed. Local politicians who took the trouble to inquire were told that British Columbia's strong man in the cabinet, Justice Minister Ron Basford, had had to advise Prime Minister Trudeau that protocol prohibited the offering of the lieutenant-governorship to anyone who had once declined it.

The Bell-Irvings have been in British Columbia even longer than the Brancas—at least a dozen years longer. No one would ever grudge Henry Bell-Irving the honour, least of all those who had read in the Canadian official war history of his part in the assault of Monte Fronte, that "brilliant, next to impossible feat" of the Seaforth Highlanders in the 1943 Sicilian campaign. One may regret that his nomination was not deferred one more term (he is ten years younger than Branca) so that an appointment could have been made that, for once, would make the non-British segments of the population feel part of the royal connection.

Columnist Allan Fotheringham had written concerning the predicted Branca appointment that "someone in Ottawa thought it was about time to get away from the W.A.S.P.-vice-regal syndrome." Of twenty-eight governors and lieutenant governors all but one have been of British stock in a province where half the population is now of non-British origin. The one non-British lieutenant governor came eighty years ago, and he was summarily imposed on the province over the protests of Victoria. In 1900 Lieutenant Governor Thomas McInnes (father of Magistrate "Billy" McInnes) had so antagonized the legislature that the members had walked out when he rose to present the Speech from the Throne. Laurier dismissed him, then learned that provincial politicians were fighting over which of two Anglo-Saxons should fill the vacancy. Laurier settled their nonsense by sending from Quebec his old friend the Seigneur Henri Gustave Joly de Lotbinière. The politicians protested, but Sir Henri so endeared himself to the people that before his five-year term ended they petitioned the prime minister to retain him.

If protocol lost British Columbia the novelty of a different breed of Queen's representative, whom should one blame? Trudeau, sliding down banisters at royal palaces and pirouetting behind the Queen's back, seems an unlikely slave to royal etiquette. He had already appointed a native Indian as Alberta's lieutenant governor and named a New Democrat to be Canada's first non-British, non-French governor general. Branca's age (he was just seventy-five when the Owens left Government House) was unlikely to have worried the prime minister. Trudeau appointed a retired judge five years older than Branca to the Royal Commission inquiring into the nation's health services, and was applauded for it.

Certainly he could not have doubted Branca's attachment to the monarchical system. In his public speaking, especially when addressing ethnic groups, Branca often stresses how much Canadian law owes to the British connection. At a meeting of the Ontario Italian Professional Men's Association in Toronto in 1976, he spoke of "that vital tie with the Mother Country through her Majesty the Queen. We have a degree of freedom unexcelled and rarely equalled in any other country. These liberties which we enjoy were fought for by our forefathers in England." This conviction comes, of course, from his studies of the development of law and his reverence for the rich English contribution to it. Much as he glories in the ancient culture of Italy, his favourite characters from history are the barons who gathered at Runnymede. Within hours of arriving in London during a trip to Europe, he was standing in that Thames-side meadow and, as he puts it, "telling Vi that we might well be standing on the very spot where Langton told the King in 1215, 'Sign this—or else.' " Anyone visiting his law office can hardly miss the reproduction of the Magna Carta that hangs in the Braidwood-Nuttall reception room.

Appointing a man so unlike the traditional stereotype of lieutenant governor as Angelo Branca would have brought a change of style to the viceregal role. And he would have had at his side a gracious chatelaine of Government House. Her warmth of personality complementing Angelo's energy, Viola Branca could well have been a greater success in Victoria than her husband.

Though ready to forgo the pleasures of practising law if invited to be lieutenant governor, Branca would not accept a lesser outlet for his energies. He was asked to run for election as mayor of Vancouver and went as far as listening to the suggestion over lunch with a Liberal would-be reformer who sought a change at city hall. "I was curious about the proposal," Branca says, "but there was never really a chance I could seriously consider it."

Friends who heard his name linked with the mayoralty were relieved to learn he was not interested. Given the minimal power conferred upon the mayor by the charter of the City of Vancouver, any attempt to keep his energies exercised in that field would have diminished both the man and the honourable estate of retired judge of Appeal.

At Vancouver Airport late one Sunday night in 1980 when planes were delayed by weather, a court official saw Angelo Branca in the crowded concourse and asked, "You meeting a plane, too?"

"No," answered Branca. "I'm going on one. I'm consultant on a case in Regina. God knows what time we'll get there."

He was unaccompanied and carrying his briefcase. By choosing to travel Sunday night he would have all Monday for his conference, and thought he would do a little preparation on the plane. The official, who had known Branca's work habits for thirty years, shook his head as he said, "Angelo never slows down." He was seventy-seven.

Branca was aggrieved when Fotheringham questioned the propriety of his "swift re-entry into the world of client-counsel fees" after retiring from the bench. The columnist wrote: "The public judgement of the correctness of officials in high places suddenly appearing in the market place will be affected by the swift surfacing of Angelo Branca. . . . The point that rather bothers the public is of people on high—whether of the bench, the cabinet or mandarin rank—who would seem to be cashing in on their prestige rather too soon."

"The law is my life," retorts Branca. "Would he take away my life when I am in the fullest enjoyment of it?" He says that if there is any inequity, it falls upon the retired judge who in most provinces of Canada is debarred forever from appearing in the superior courts and whose advocacy is limited to hearings of statutory bodies and the like. That apart, they are confined to consultancy. Chief Justice J.O. Wilson and Justices James Coady and Charles Tysoe, who all retired before Branca, became consultants with leading law firms and were able all the more to enjoy their retirement.

Consulting does not satisfy Branca. He misses the excitement of the courtroom, the stimulus of cross-examination. So what would he like for excitement? "They say retired judges should not appear as advocates in courts where their former associates may be presiding. Then why not just let us take examinations for discovery? No judges there, and we'd be able to cross-examine."

Some people make news all their lives. Neither retirement nor age lessens Branca's proneness to create headlines. In 1979 he took issue with the Canadian Broadcasting Corporation over a television feature called "Connections: The Second Series," a sequel to two programs on organized crime in Canada. Branca complained that the filmmakers had sought permission to interview him following his retirement, telling him that the CBC was interested in his life as a judge (they say they told him the subject would be "Ethics and the Judiciary"), and on that basis he consented to the interview; that in the half-hour interview there was a short reference to his previous social contacts with Joe Romano, a Vancouver stock market speculator who at the time of the interview was being investigated on securities and extortion charges, and that was the only portion of the interview televised, in a program about organized crime.

In a four-page letter to CBC president A.W. Johnson giving notice of intention to sue, Branca said that the alleged libel and slander lay in lifting out of context the short passage of dialogue and inserting it into a documentary film about organized crime. He asked for an apology and an assurance that it was never intended to suggest he had any connection with crime, organized or unorganized. Saying he was also protesting "in defence of good Italian people," he wrote, "I feel particularly bad about the pointed stigma that CBC has put upon the Italian populace of Canada."

He then honoured the old adage, "A lawyer who acts for himself has a fool for a client," and went outside his own office to consult one whose specialties include the law of libel.

The president of the CBC replied at some length. In his first letter he said:

The subject of the program series to which you refer was organized crime in Canada. Few would equate that very small group of criminals with the broad sweep of the Canadian population who are of Italian origin. The contribution of that community to Canadian life is, of course, celebrated by all. Indeed, a good many CBC programs have focussed exactly on that theme. . . .

I have called for a thorough examination of the circumstances surrounding your interview. I do not feel I can do more than to assure you that no imputations were intended, or indeed were made, concerning your own reputation. The program narration, I would submit, put it very clearly: "Joe Romano co-exists easily within the respected levels of B.C. society. His friends and business associates are from a wide spectrum of legitimate occupations."

From the assistant director of TV News and Current Affairs came a twenty-nine-page transcript of the interview and an extract from the film script, including narration, with a covering letter in which he said, "May I assure you that no imputation regarding your reputation was intended by the program."

Having received these letters and the transcripts, and in consultation with counsel, Branca decided not to proceed further in the matter.

Controversies of the day still provoke his lively interest. He disagrees with media complaints about judges speaking their minds. "Judges sometimes see things that shout out for comment," he says. "If a judge proves wrong he is open to criticism for being in error in what he says, but not for exercising his right to speak. Those people who criticized Provincial Court Judge Bewley don't know how much his provocative comments down the years helped to keep a sense of proportion in his court between prosecutor and offender. But whatever he said, the big thing is that judges not be intimidated into silence for fear of exceeding their jurisdiction."

For Branca's belief that judges' comments need not be restricted to law, he has what is, for him, the best of precedents. Judge Murphy, five years on the bench and invited to address the Canadian Club, told the assembly that Canada was sleeping when it should be preparing for war against Germany. The press was scandalized at such mischievous talk, but because it came from the revered Judge Murphy, a Victoria editor wrote more in sorrow than anger when he called it "a mental aberration which we cannot explain but must perforce excuse." One hundred days later World War I broke out.

No longer an active judge, Branca freely voices his views.

Had he still been a Bencher he would have voted against the majority that tried to restrain barrister and solicitor Don Jabour in his advertising. "I think those forms of advertising which inform the public about the services offered by a particular law firm are in the public interest," he says, "especially if they give the man in the street some idea of what that lawyer's services might cost. I respected Mr. Jabour's reasoning. If nothing else, the right to advertise should enable an energetic and ambitious young lawyer to make his mark more quickly than has been possible up to now against the competition of the big firms. Such a young lawyer may have something to offer the public that they may not necessarily find in a big office at the same cost."

Branca would again have voted on the losing side, had he still been a Bencher, in the 1981 controversy over changing the law to permit three nonlawyers, representing the public, to be appointed as Benchers. This proposal aroused such strong feelings that the most accomplished woman advocate in her province, Mary Southin, Q.C., resigned from the Benchers only months after holding the treasurership of the Law Society, its highest office. Having opposed the change, she resigned because a majority of the Benchers refused to consult the society's membership before asking the attorney general to permit lay Benchers. In a later referendum of the whole profession, out of 2040 lawyers voting, those favouring lay Benchers won by 56. Whether or not to make the change is for the provincial government to decide.

Branca's objection is not to lay observers as such. "At Benchers' meetings there should be nothing to hide," he says. He simply maintains that any professional body given self-governing powers by the legislature should accept its mandate to conduct itself to the satisfaction of the legislature without needing token representation from outside.

Noting that one argument in favour of permitting lay

Benchers is that the innovation would make good public relations, Branca says, "Our public relations start with the client. A complaint I hear increasingly is from people who receive legal bills higher than they had been led to expect. There may be reasons for the increase—the trial ran longer than expected; the case took an unforeseen turn; some disbursements were bigger than expected. The fact remains, the client pays the lawyer for his knowledge, and he expects that knowledge to include some idea in advance of how much a lawsuit might cost."

What if a lawyer has been compelled to spend more time or money on the case than could reasonably have been anticipated? "When you undertake to act in a lawsuit and accept your client's deposit you give him a figure of what the lawsuit will cost him, and that's it. Your judgement on that figure has to be good, but that's part of your legal skill. If, for whatever reason, you find you have underestimated, you take your loss. Your bill to your client should basically be what you told him. There are going to be times when you accomplish all he wants in less time than you expected, but he has accepted your estimate. Those cases make up for the others. All the public relations in the world won't undo the damage done to the legal profession by one bill several times larger than the client had been led to expect."

Though the fact may do little to mollify an aggrieved client, often the extra billing consists wholly of disbursements and does not benefit the lawyer one penny. Here again Branca points to the lawyer's responsibility to control costs. "In Court of Appeal," he says, "a case came before us in which appellant's solicitors had ordered an Appeal Book complete with all the evidence and all the documents. It ran to eleven volumes. The ground of appeal was a narrow legal point, and we were referred to only one volume, and to only a few pages of that. Someone was billed six or seven thousand dollars more than he need have been just for his Appeal Book. Yet our Court of Appeal Rules require that counsel 'shall endeavour to exclude from the appeal book all documents and notes of evidence not relevant to the subject matter of the appeal or necessary for its decision.' "

A mention of the word "constitution" brought from Branca a prompt explanation of his views on its repatriation. Was this "Branca shooting from the hip"? Or an encore of the "Branca JA dissenting" judgements that enliven the Canadian law books of the sixties and seventies? I would soon know, for he immediately said, "Let me put my thoughts on that on paper. I'd like to check my law."

His thoughts on paper were the same as those spoken. He is for repatriation, but not for unilateral repatriation, and for a Bill of Rights to be inscribed within the repatriated constitution, the interpretation of those rights to be left to the law courts of the land. He wrote:

Much has been said about the repatriation of our Canadian constitution unilaterally by the federal authorities. I think it cannot and should not be done that way. I believe so because of the peculiar way in which each province entered into Confederation, and the agreed terms of union, particularly when British Columbia entered in 1871. It seems to me that in justice and for other reasons it is a two-way consideration.

The Supreme Court of Canada is due to speak with finality on this matter. I withhold further expression on it.

Then how about our Bill of Rights? Should it or should it not be inscribed in our repatriated constitution? What do we mean by fundamental rights? The Bill of Rights passed under the late Honourable John Diefenbaker declared that in our country there has existed and there shall continue to exist, without discrimination by reason of race, national origin, colour, religion or sex, the right of every individual to life, to liberty, to security of the person and enjoyment of property, which rights were not to be impaired except by due process of law; the right of equality before the law and the right to the protection of the law; freedom of religion; freedom of speech; freedom of assembly and association and of the press.

The Diefenbaker Bill of Rights was a declaratory statute and immediately following the preamble it stated, 'it is hereby recognized and declared that in Canada there have existed. . . .' The fact that the act was purely a declaratory one has been stated in a number of cases decided in the Supreme Court of Canada, and with one or two exceptions the statute has not been of any effective use.

The preamble to the act was beautiful. It recited that Parliament affirmed that our Canadian nation is founded upon principles that acknowledge the supremacy of God; the dignity and worth of the human person; the position of the family in a society of free men and free institutions. There is no question about the nobility of that thought, or that people who read that preamble were highly impressed by it; and there is no question that that is the way we Canadian people want our nation to be regarded.

People who oppose the inscribing of our fundamental rights in our constitution object to it for various reasons but mainly

(a) that this has never been done in the history of the British Empire.
(b) that the rights involved are so imbedded in the common law and in the hearts of the British people that there never have been any changes in these fundamental rights, so there is no need at the present time to so inscribe them.
(c) that if these rights are inscribed in the constitution changes will be almost impossible and the interpretation of the rights declared will be in the hands of the law courts.

The answer, it seems to me, is that these liberties ought to be immutable. Who would want the right of free speech to be impaired beyond what it is now, fenced in as it is in our country by the laws of libel and slander? We have accepted those laws as a suitable limitation to the right of free speech. What may be an infringement of the right of free speech according to law, and hence to be restrained, must of necessity be left to the law courts.

Why do we want to leave in the hands of Parliament or legislative assemblies the power to curtail the right of free speech? Those fundamental freedoms were fought for and preserved for us by our forefathers and we wish to preserve those rights for our progeny. It is so with all of the remainder of our fundamental rights of freedom.

The other objection is that the changing of these laws would be in the hands of the law courts instead of Parliament and the legislatures. This, it seems to me, is a useless argument. The courts interpret the law. The interpretation judicially declared simply states what the law in its peculiar context says, and the people are thereafter bound by that interpretation. The law courts of this country have never made or enacted law. It is the interpretation of the laws passed by legislators that is the subject matter of court investigation, generally in the area of whether or not such laws are within or without the power of the legislating entity that passed them. That has ever been the function of our law courts. Why leave these decisions to legislatures? Why remove them from the arena in which they have always been?

"Bon vivant," a newspaper called Angelo Branca at the end of 1980. And, indeed, he went into 1981 living a good life: regular hours in his law practice but driving home most days before the peak of "rush hour"; serving on a few committees connected with Italian or church groups or good causes; more general reading than formerly; still "getting my hands into good soil" in his big hillside garden; and time for socializing. At seventy-eight he was still finding plenty of use for his tuxedo.

Promoter Murray Pezim, the most flamboyant figure in the Vancouver stock market, gave him a seventy-seventh birthday party to remember by making him the victim of a fund-raising "roast," with five American show business celebrities as chief torturers. Seven hundred and eight people paid $200 each to attend and many others were disappointed because all dinner places were sold.

Facing the guests and trying to find words to thank Pezim he looked appealingly round the room and asked, "What can I say to him?" "Twenty years," snapped one of the Las Vegas comedians.

The event raised $100 000 clear for Branca's favourite charity, the Camp Miriam children's summer resort.

He maintains his old interests, from boxing to fund raising. A client called him just before his seventy-eighth birthday to say he thought a Port Alberni boxer might prove to be Canada's best heavyweight in years. So Branca left his office in midafternoon to go to Nanaimo to see for himself.

If Branca gave up practising law he would write. He has assembled transcripts and notes on his *Hughes* case, having been told that its significance in legal history warrants a monograph. He wonders whether he should review his notes and his memory of the Sons of Freedom Doukhobor turbulence and help to put that episode into its proper context in Canadian history. With the Branca penchant for the unexpected, he is more likely to work on a wholly unrelated theme.

He leaves it to sociologists to write definitively about social changes in his lifetime, but says, "If Canadians realized how great have been the advances they'd be proud of the society they've made." In his field, he says that the administration of justice is better. Legal aid for people without means is widely available. Politics is hardly a factor any longer in the appointment of judges. The Appeal Court bench he left in 1978 had no judge who had ever fought an election for a political party. Of the thirty-one British Columbia Supreme Court judges in 1980, only four had ever run for political office: two as Liberals, one Conservative and one NDP. And—changed days!—there had not been a scandal in the policing of Vancouver for twenty-five years.

He notes a broadening of civil rights, and rejoices in the disappearance of the old-time discrimination against minorities in hiring practices, which used to mean, "You had to be a member of the St. George Society or the St. Andrew Society, or have a relative in the Lodge, if you wanted a white collar job with the City or as a policeman."

He would not be a true son of East Vancouver if he did not point out that a citizen is more likely to be "mugged" or raped in Vancouver's West End now than in the notorious Hogan's Alley he knew in his youth. And that the nightlife scenes of prostitution and juvenile delinquency in the city centre were unknown then. And the old-time madams would not tolerate drug users, a situation that he contrasts starkly with his experience as a judge, when it seemed every prostitute going through the courts was caught up in the narcotics traffic.

These problems he sees as soluble. By temperament he looks forward. His attitude to life at seventy-eight can be summed up in the word awaited by so many worried clients over so many years in his office at Hastings and Main: "Next?"

EPILOGUE

The farewell address spoken by Chief Justice John Farris when Angelo Branca retired from the Court of Appeal on St. Patrick's Day of 1978 was a tiny perfect gem.

Sounding more than ever like his father the senator, the chief justice said:

This is not a wake. While it is sad that Mr. Justice Branca will no longer sit with us on this bench, yet to everything there is a season and a time to every purpose. This is the time to speak of a life well lived in honouring God and serving man.

Judge Branca's devotion to his family, his church, his profession and his community is well known. That devotion has received its reward in children, grandchildren, appointment to high office, awards and honorary degrees.

But today it is as a judge that we honour him. Every Court of Appeal needs an Angelo Branca. The law reports are filled with his judgements. They constitute the evidence upon which history will judge the judge. But we who have lived with him, worked with him, played with him need not await the verdict of history. We know him to be great, and this for many reasons.

He is great because of his complete integrity. No judge ever sat who surpassed him in intellectual honesty.

He is great because of the quality of his mind and his capacity for work. And, perhaps most importantly, he is great because of the warmth of his heart.

The hardened criminal, the drug peddler, received short shrift from him, but the young offender, the first offender, the victim of a moment's passion or of unbearable pressure, received from him justice that reflected the truest Christian values.

In this Court gaiety is not suspected to be a sin. Judge Branca is living proof that serious things can be done with a sense of fun. Many's the time our judges' corridor has resounded with peals of laughter prompted by one of his quips, often earthy and pungent in nature.

This I believe to be important, for, with Laurence Sterne, I am firmly persuaded that every time a man smiles, and much more so when he laughs, it adds something to this fragment of life. In this old building which has seen so much of anguish and despair his happy nature has been an absolute delight.

We who work in the Court House—staff, lawyers and judges—know of his infinite kindness and his many offices of tender courtesy. It is because of these that he is a beloved man.

We wish him well as he returns to his profession where for so many years he was a leader and an ornament.

God speed, Angelo.

BIBLIOGRAPHY

Books that the author has read with interest and profit include:

Germano, Giovanni. *The Italians of Western Canada.* Florence: Giunti, 1979.

Kilian, Crawford. *Go Do Some Great Thing: The Black Pioneers of British Columbia.* Vancouver: Douglas & McIntyre, 1978.

Marlatt, Daphne, and Itter, Carole. *Opening Doors: Vancouver's East End.* Victoria: Aural History Program, Provincial Archives, 1979.

Morley, Alan. *Vancouver: Milltown to Metropolis.* Vancouver: Mitchell Press, 1961.

Ormsby, Margaret. *British Columbia: A History.* Toronto: Macmillan of Canada, 1958.

Spada, A.V. *The Italians in Canada.* Montreal: Riviera Printers, 1969.

Walker, Russell R. *Politicians of a Pioneering Province.* Vancouver: Mitchell Press, 1969.

Williams, David R. *". . . The Man for a New Country."* Sidney, B.C.: Gray's Publishing, 1977.

Woodcock, George, and Avakumovic, Ivan. *The Doukhobors.* Toronto: Oxford University Press, 1968.

INDEX